THE
FOREST CITY
KILLER

A SERIAL MURDERER,
A COLD-CASE SLEUTH,
AND A SEARCH FOR JUSTICE

VANESSA BROWN

Published by ECW Press
665 Gerrard Street East
Toronto, Ontario, Canada M4M 1Y2
416-694-3348 / info@ecwpress.com

Purchase the print edition and receive the eBook free. For details, go to ecwpress.com/eBook.

Get the eBook free!*
*proof of purchase required

Cover design: Michel Vrana
Front cover photo: The *London Free Press* Collection of Photographic Negatives, [1968-02-10], Archives and Special Collections, Western Libraries, Western University. Back cover photo: Courtesy of Elgin County Archives. *St. Thomas Times-Journal* Fonds
Author photo: Rob Nelson
Map illustration: Antony Hare

LIBRARY AND ARCHIVES CANADA CATALOGUING IN PUBLICATION

Title: Forest City Killer: a serial murderer, a cold-case sleuth, and a search for justice / Vanessa Brown.

Names: Brown, Vanessa, 1980- author.

Identifiers: Canadiana (print) 2019013111X
Canadiana (ebook) 20190131128

ISBN 978-1-77041-503-4 (softcover)
ISBN 978-1-77305-398-1 (PDF)
ISBN 978-1-77305-397-4 (ePUB)

Subjects: LCSH: Serial murder investigation—Ontario—London. | LCSH: Serial murders—Ontario—London. | LCSH: Cold cases (Criminal investigation)—Ontario—London.

Classification: LCC HV6535.C33 L65 2019
DDC 364.152/320971326—dc23

The publication of *The Forest City Killer* has been generously supported by the Canada Council for the Arts which last year invested $153 million to bring the arts to Canadians throughout the country and is funded in part by the Government of Canada. *Nous remercions le Conseil des arts du Canada de son soutien. L'an dernier, le Conseil a investi 153 millions de dollars pour mettre de l'art dans la vie des Canadiennes et des Canadiens de tout le pays. Ce livre est financé en partie par le gouvernement du Canada.* We acknowledge the support of the Ontario Arts Council (OAC), an agency of the Government of Ontario, which last year funded 1,737 individual artists and 1,095 organizations in 223 communities across Ontario for a total of $52.1 million. We also acknowledge the contribution of the Government of Ontario through the Ontario Book Publishing Tax Credit, and through Ontario Creates for the marketing of this book.

The Forest City Killer is supported by the London Arts Council through the City of London's Community Arts Investment Program.

MIX
Paper from responsible sources
FSC
www.fsc.org
FSC® C103567

PRINTED AND BOUND IN CANADA   PRINTING: MARQUIS   5 4 3 2

A NOTE ON THE TEXT

This is a true story. All of the information in this book came from reliable sources. Dialogue from the text is based on police reports and interviews. Reconstructions of events throughout are kept to a minimum and are intended to help structure the narrative of the case. You will be given the facts available to me, and it is up to you to draw your own conclusions. More than anything, this book is a call to action, intended to renew interest in these unsolved cases and to urge the Ontario Provincial Police to reinvestigate these crimes vigorously, using all DNA and other evidence in their possession.

CONTENTS

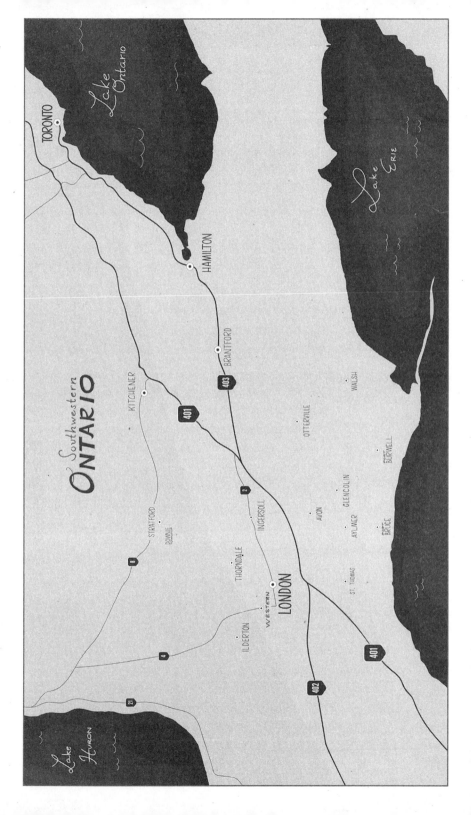

PROLOGUE

*"We are willows bending in the solitude of October rain,
reflecting distorted hues of destiny."*

— ANNE ENGLISH

OCTOBER 9, 1969. Dawdling around the back roads of Oxford County in a pickup truck, Ron Kiddie and Peter Kingma were on a duck-hunting excursion. They were two young guys, rifles in the back, gum in their mouths, listening to the radio and talking shit as they bounced along hills and uneven asphalt. It was unusually warm out, so they rolled down their windows to catch the breeze. The sun was low in the sky. With a little time left before dinner, they stopped to check for birds under the gleaming new concrete bridge over Big Otter Creek. It was shouldered by two hills and two curves — a great dark, low hiding place for waterfowl. Ron pulled over next to the narrow bridge. Walking across the short expanse, they each took a side, Ron on the north and Peter on the south, leaning over the guardrail as far as they could.

"Hey, Peter," called Ron. "Come see this."

Peter checked for traffic before crossing over. On this road, with the sharp turns and steep incline, they were hidden and trapped if a speeding automobile came over the hill.

"There's a body," said Ron, pointing down.

Peter looked. "Oh, that's just a dummy." To prove his point, he went and got his gun out of the truck to look down through the scope. As he squinted, he became very still and then slowly looked up at Ron. "There's a ring on her finger," he muttered.

Without hesitation, Ron skidded down the steep banks of the creek to find out what was going on. "I can see [pubic] hair," he shouted, as Peter followed. "And a vaccination mark on her arm!" On the edge of the water, he stumbled and accidentally stepped in the water. "Well, I'm wet now," he said, turning his head and looking back. "I better wade in and see before we call the police."

He felt the frigid water creeping up his legs as he pushed through the muck, the soft creekbed beneath his boots. He could see goosebumps on her flesh, her face floating just beneath the surface of the murky water. Her chin was tilted up, as if she were calling out for help. Her left arm and breast protruded from the shallow creek, naked white in the fading fall sunlight, and her right hand floated in a fist, her young finger decorated with a black Alaskan diamond ring.

In shock, Ron and Pete ran to the closest house, at the corner of Furnace and Cornell Road, only 100 metres away from the bridge, where the residents let Ron use the phone to call the Ontario Provincial Police (OPP), who agreed to meet with them twenty minutes later at nearby Otterville Fire Hall. Two officers followed them back to the creek, along with the farmer who lived in the house on the corner. He volunteered to get the officers some hip waders. Corporal Wild put them on and descended the treacherously steep riverbank.

It was about a quarter past six when Ron and Peter got back in their truck and drove away.

———

In a sleepy London, Ontario, neighbourhood, fifty-year-old OPP detective Dennis Alsop had just sat down to dinner. He was grabbing a quick bite to eat before heading out again to pick up his fifteen-year-old daughter Daphne, who would soon be finishing her ballet class.

The phone rang and he answered.

"They found her."

PART I

THE ENGLISH GIRL

CHAPTER ONE

MEET LONDON

"London, Ontario, my joy, my sorrow."

— ORLO MILLER

An introductory description of my hometown of London, Ontario — the Forest City — usually starts with population, geography, industry.

Almost 400,000.

Halfway between Detroit and Toronto in a valley surrounded by moraines, bisected by the Thames River, at whose forks the city was founded.

The dried-up industrial background and economic struggles of the average mid-sized North American city, a thriving medical science community, a burgeoning tech sector. There's a university here.

This is all the boring stuff.

I've lived in London, Ontario, my entire life. People say it's a small town wearing big-city clothes. There are two Londons, really. One of them is packed with aluminum siding, chain restaurants, and big box stores. The other one is where I live. It's full of art and music and eccentrics. It's a community where everyone is only one or two degrees of separation from everyone else. My partner and I live in a downtown-adjacent pocket of tiny century cottages, and we make our living with our used bookstore on Richmond Row. Our social sphere is the local arts scene and have spent the past twenty years cultivating our obsession with London's past. Sometimes we joke that London is the real site of the Black Lodge from *Twin Peaks*.

In all sincerity, London has many similarities to that twisted small town. It has a wild vibe about it down by the river, where addicts and homeless people have set up camps, but where you can also see posh yuppies jogging along beautifully kept paved pathways. In the east end are modest, sometimes shabby, bungalows with faded plastic toys on the lawn. There are seedy motels with heart-shaped bathtubs, flea markets, and pawnshops. We also offer enormous beautiful mansions, shaded by heritage oak trees lining boulevards with cobblestone sidewalks. The summers are hot. The humidity is oppressive and the mosquitoes are massive. In the winter, you'll find yourself trudging through knee-deep snow. We're at the bottom of an ice-age valley, so your allergies act up like crazy. In between brutalist and ugly glass skyscrapers, two cathedrals chime the hours downtown and have done so for the past century; one of these has Tiffany stained-glass windows.

Such deep contrasts mean you can experience a lot of different ways of life here. I've hung around the corner of Dundas and Richmond streets (known locally as "DNR," for all the drug addicts found there) wearing a dog collar and smoking clove cigarettes, partying with ten homeless kids in a one-bedroom apartment. I've also had dinner at the university president's manor on the northern hill of the city, overlooking wealthy Masonville. Some of the homes in Woodfield or Old North are over-the-top gorgeous, with detailed paint jobs on nineteenth-century wooden gingerbread trim, cherry wainscoting, pantries stocked with fancy jars, and living rooms you aren't allowed to sit in. At one time, London had more millionaires per capita than any other city in the country. It also has about as bad a drug problem as

Vancouver. Each aspect of the Forest City has its own lore, a cast of characters that is unforgettable, but perhaps only meaningful to someone who has spent a lifetime living here.

My irrational passion is hearing storytellers reveal the hidden layers of my hometown. While I grew up wanting to write novels, I've been heartily sidetracked by my irrepressible desire to hear old men (and women) tell tales. After spending eight years writing the history of a long-demolished hotel in downtown London, I focused on bookselling. Then I found out about the murders. Criminologist Michael Arntfield released *Murder City* in 2015, suggesting that London was the serial killer capital of Canada, if not the world. I devoured the book in a day or two, reviewed it for the *London Yodeller*, and then interviewed the author for the same publication. We carried the title in our shop, where I gladly talked about it with customers. I hopped online to see what other information I could uncover. This incredible list of unsolved murders that took place in the Forest City during the 1960s was a confluence of information that seemed expertly designed to grab me.

What really fascinated me was the idea that this massive cultural disruption could have happened in my hometown, that these killers had prowled the streets and taken victims with impunity, and no one talked about it. Even local history buffs like me didn't seem to know about it. It was hush-hush. Once I started to look for the evidence of this upheaval, it was everywhere and shockingly close at hand. The Big Three (as I call them in my head) were Russell "The Bedroom Strangler" Johnson, who climbed balconies up to thirteen stories to strangle single women while they slept; Gerald Thomas "Chambermaid Slayer" Archer, who hooked up with older female hotel and bar workers only to murder them in their homes; and Christian "Mad Slasher" Magee, who impulsively stabbed and raped women in the Strathroy area just outside of town. Most people in London, when prompted, knew about these psychopathic madmen. They remembered the news coverage. People even have personal connections with them. My sister-in-law's grandmother dated serial killer Russell Johnson during his murder spree. My mom's best friend woke up in the middle of the night with "Good Ol' Russ" standing over her. My ex-husband's aunt was the only survivor of murderer and rapist Christian "Mad Slasher" Magee, who left her for dead.

While these serial killers captured the imagination, the unsolved cases were even more intriguing to me. My parents had lived downstairs from murder victim Suzanne Miller when she disappeared in 1974, her car abandoned in the east end of the city, and her body found a month later. Customers at my bookstore eagerly opened up with very little prodding, sharing community rumours of who did what. A friend, unbeknownst to me, had been researching the murder of Frankie Jensen for decades. With all of these connections, how could a local history buff like me not have an inkling that this had taken place?

As I was growing up, my father, a federal fraud investigator, was a real educator when it came to the criminal life going on around us, despite the protestations of my mom. He told me about gangs and drug dealers and thieves, many who also committed the welfare and benefit frauds he put a stop to. We couldn't have Dad's name in the phone book because he testified against so many crooks, so our number was always listed under my mom's initials. I remember all the places he told me to avoid as a kid, only to realize now that they were the scenes of abductions or grisly murders. Perhaps because of its unique social geography, the degradation of mid-sized city economies, or the silo effect of the city's makeup, London seemed the perfect place for sex traffickers, drug dealers, and serial killers. They stopped here on their way through, as Ontario's superhighway 401 connects us easily with Detroit and Toronto. The Forest City was made a safe haven for the worst criminals by the covered eyes and ears of our citizens. Londoners can be remarkably incurious people.

Finding out about Jackie English was like wandering through Buffalo Bill's basement; there were all of these doors connecting rooms to one another, and behind each one was another appalling secret. Her abduction and murder were deceptively straightforward, but the circumstances around them were bizarre. Her story had the kind of twists and turns that even a veteran soap-opera scriptwriter couldn't make up. You think I'm exaggerating, sure. Every good storyteller begins a tale by saying, "You aren't going to believe this."

But really, you aren't.

After deciding to write a book on the subject, I reached out to Dennis Alsop Jr. He'd been in the news, having found boxes of files that belonged to his deceased father, a homicide investigator for the OPP. Detective Dennis Alsop Sr. and his partner, Detective Jim Topham, were the lead investigators on the 1969 murder of Jackie English. Dennis never gave up on the unsolved case; he continued to work on the files until his death in 2012.

I am a bookseller, but I don't just sell used books. I've been trained as an antiquarian bookseller. This means that I specialize in rare and antique paper materials, what people most commonly think of as first editions, signed copies, and old letters. I have a special relationship with stacks of old paper. It's my job to interpret them and find their value, not just from a monetary standpoint, but from a cultural one. The significant discoveries of lost manuscripts and letters have all involved one bookseller or another, and the 500-year-old tradition of our trade is all about recovering these materials and making sure they find the right home, usually in an archive or museum. It's our mission to salvage the scraps of paper people throw out.

So when Dennis Jr. walked into my bookstore holding two large file folders full of material, my heart beat extra fast. Anyone would be excited, but I was thrilled on a whole other level.

He was totally receptive to me, as, I learned later, he had been with everyone who got in touch with him. Dennis believes that he has a very special role to play in the transmission of his father's work to a new generation of people who might find answers. He's an imposing man, bald on top with messy grey hair around the back and sides. He's got age spots and expressive eyebrows. He has the kind of booming voice that would be great on the radio, and he absorbed many of his father's mannerisms, so that he gives the impression of having worked in law enforcement, which couldn't be further from the truth. I was grateful to discover that he's a born storyteller and needs only a bit of prompting to start laying out the history of his father and the Alsop family. He brought two files along with him to our first meeting — not that he'd let me open them that day. He dangled them in front of me, implying that he had to get to know me better first before showing me his secret stash. However, his choice of which files to bring along told me that I was on the right track.

When his father died, Dennis Jr. and his siblings helped their mother downsize and organize their father's possessions. That was when they uncovered three boxes of case files. Wanting to get to know his father better, and being curious like many of us would be, Dennis sat down and started reading. He read every word on every page in every file. The stories were incredible. Not only were there tales of derring-do from his dad's early years, but also detailed statements and information on cases that Dennis Jr. was pretty sure were still considered unsolved.

He hopped online and found a community of people on a website called Unsolved Canada. This website has been an incomparable resource for me. It's not Reddit, not Wikipedia. It's more than that. It's a place where victims' family members and concerned citizens gather online to try to solve these cases on their own. Although wack-jobs and troublemakers have poked their heads up from time to time, they are dismissed quickly when they reveal that they don't have a handle on the details or the deeper facts of the cases. The posters on Unsolved

Canada are people whose respect you have to earn, by gathering new information, posting unseen photos, or offering a credible, detailed new theory on an unsolved case. What I discovered was that users such as Have faith and chickapey and, particularly, rkay had posted hundreds of scanned newspaper articles, photographs, obituaries, and detailed reports. They had subscribed to Ancestry.com to get more information on suspects and paid to get high-resolution versions of photographs from university archives. They treated the online forum like a special group project in which only the really devoted "armchair sleuths" could take part, and they'd been doing it for years.

Reading their posts after his father died, Dennis Jr. understood that the family members of the murder victims had no idea what had gone on behind the scenes. They had scoured every avenue for information, dissected newspaper articles, and demanded interviews with OPP representatives, but they were still missing huge pieces of the puzzle. He had information that could help give them peace, or at least answer some of their questions. But what was the next step? Somehow, just calling people on the phone out of the blue seemed like a really bad idea.

Then he read an article by Jane Sims in the *London Free Press,* printed on October 3, 2012. Sims wrote about the annual walk held by Anne English, where she re-enacts her sister's final steps across the Wellington Road South overpass where she was abducted:

> Last year, English's sister, Anne English-Cremers, 59, of London decided to make that walk over the bridge herself in memory of a sister who never had a chance to reach adulthood. Halfway across the bridge, she had a sad epiphany. "That was the first time it clued in to me (that) she had no escape. There was nowhere for her to go when that car stopped but to get in. I just thought that would be horrible, what would you do short of jumping off the bridge?"

She's found new support in the past year from a group formed on the website unsolvedcanada.ca that is dedicated to digging into the case and looking for new information. English-Cremers said the group of five people has helped uncover some fresh leads. They call themselves the J.E. Crew . . . English-Cremers can't explain why people have now come forward to review the evidence. "It took 43 years to find a group of people who could stay with the story," she said. "I am so grateful."

The reporter's email address was at the bottom of the article, so Dennis Jr. sent her a message. Jane Sims passed his information along to Anne English, and the two were finally connected.

Anne remembered Detective Dennis Alsop Sr. fondly and shared her memories of him with his son. Over the years, she had gotten in touch with Detective Alsop to ask questions about the investigation and find out if there were any new developments. "The case always bothered him," she said. To Anne, he was an ally in the search for answers. "I felt good when he was there. And I remember Jim Topham, and I talked to [him] within the last ten years. He talked to me, but he wasn't helpful at all." Detective Topham has never opened up about the case. I talked to a source about tracking him down for an interview but was told that at his advanced age, it might be better to leave him alone.

Dennis Jr. had information for Anne, information that could change her life and the lives of other victims' family members. Suddenly, Dennis Jr. felt the purpose of his father's legacy, the weight of it on his shoulders. This had all happened for a reason.

"I want the OPP to simply say, this is who we think it is," Dennis says. "We can't do anything about it; it's not gonna happen. We can't prove it, but we know it. And they don't have to tell me. I think they have to talk to the families. I think we have done a terrible disservice to people. They think they own the case, but it's not their case. It's the family's case."

Dennis and his wife, Sandy — nicknamed Sam — are easy to become friends with. They are agreeable people, a pair of boomers living in the suburbs, where the trees are large and developed and the 1960s-era bungalows are neatly kept with green lawns and perennial flower beds. It's the kind of neighbourhood that has a lot of swimming pools. Their home has been beautifully renovated, and in the living room is a World War II motorcycle that Dennis restored. He likes to sit on the back deck and chat with his wife while he smokes his pipe, and their little white bichon frise, Sophie, runs around their feet. Dennis always smells like pipe smoke, and his thumb is eternally yellow from packing tobacco into the wooden bowl.

I'd been at their house many times, but for our special interview about his dad and his family's biography, we set up shop in their formal dining room. It's brightly lit and friendly, decorated with Indonesian artifacts, old keepsakes his mother brought over from Holland. While we talked, Sandy puttered around and offered me coffee. Dennis settled into his oak dining chair and told me all about the hero of our story.

CHAPTER TWO

MEET DETECTIVE ALSOP

"He thought we were angels compared to who he was dealing with."

— DENNIS ALSOP JR.

As a member of the Criminal Investigation Bureau of the Ontario Provincial Police, moustachioed detective Dennis Alsop Sr. handled a broad spectrum of offences, but his favourite criminals were thieves. He loved to reverse-engineer their grand designs. "Bank robbers and safe crackers . . . he loved those guys," recalls Dennis Jr. "He hated those guys, but he loved 'em because they were smart. They had a plan and they lived a very high life. They bought brand new cars. It was a cat-and-mouse game."

Conspiracy would catch his interest, and he could smell the whiff of lies when he took statements and interrogated suspects. Alsop had a good gut instinct, and it served him well. He was born to be a cop. His colleagues respected him. He worked hard and he earned everything he achieved through solid investigations and late nights.

He lived in a split-level suburban home at 283 Beachwood Avenue with his wife and four kids. The oldest was Doreen, followed by David, Dennis Jr., and Daphne. His wife was Emelia, and she was the anchor for a rough-and-tumble household of active people. She helped supplement Dennis's less-than-ideal detective's salary by working as a dental assistant, examining children's teeth in public schools, particularly in low-income neighbourhood schools. She made dinner for her family, kept house, and took care of her ailing mother-in-law. It was a challenging life, but one she handled with aplomb. In the end, she was happy, even though most of the time she did it alone.

Dennis Alsop had always wanted to be a detective. As a teenager, he cut out newspaper articles about thefts and murders and glued them in a scrapbook, where he deconstructed the facts and built a case file. The scrapbook belonged to a fictitious but prescient "Detective Dennis Alsop," years before he would ever go to the Ontario Police College and graduate in 1946. He liked the chase, the pursuit. It was what drew him to his wife, both in the circumstance of their meeting and her allure.

Emelia Haynes was the child of a Dutch colonel and lived in Indonesia before World War II. Her family was wealthy and owned a mansion with servants, and that lifestyle instilled in her a taste for quality and beauty that would stay with her always. In 1939, she decided to go to Holland for school. From the deck of the boat, she took a photograph of her farewell and captured the image of her mom and dad and two sisters waving goodbye to her. This photograph is haunting; shortly after, Emelia's family was captured by Japanese forces and held in an internment camp until the end of the war. Neither her parents nor her sisters ever told her about the horrors they saw. Emelia had been spared.

Dental school in Holland was obviously halted. Not knowing whether her family was dead or alive, she set aside her plans in order to help in the Resistance.

That was how she met Dennis, a sharp-looking Canadian codebreaker and Nazi hunter, seeking enemy collaborators. They both had rooms in the same boarding house. When he first saw her, she was wearing a wedding ring. Even though he thought she was married, he couldn't get her out of his head. The next time he saw her, the ring was gone, so he asked around about her. "Oh, she was never married," someone told him. "She just doesn't want to be bothered."

Emelia was not on the hunt for a husband and she wasn't easily distracted. Unlike so many of the girls around her, she couldn't be bought with a box of chocolates and a pair of nylons. Dennis only caught her attention when she saw him attending Catholic mass regularly of his own volition. This was very impressive to her. It showed a depth of character that she respected.

Their courtship was short but unique. In a barrage of bombs, the Germans hit the boarding house where Emelia and Dennis both lived. An upright piano barricaded the wall, saving their lives, but the instrument was blown to bits. Emelia was deeply saddened. She had played the piano all the time, and it was one of the few things that made her happy in that dismal, war-torn landscape. After the Allies took Germany, Dennis gathered his mates and piled in a truck to go into the newly conquered territory and find his girlfriend a piano to play. He couldn't give her much. He didn't have a penny, but he had ingenuity, courage, and grit. Emelia thought the world of him.

They forged a sixty-six-year marriage that was built on that foundation of respect. While Dennis spent increasingly more and more time hunting criminals, Emelia was proud of her partner and the work that he did. In the early years of forensic science, he was an identification officer, with specialized training in fingerprints. There were only a handful of officers in the province with his qualifications, and the force sincerely needed him. One summer, they rented a cottage and within an hour of their getting there, an OPP cruiser pulled up and took Dennis away. He missed the entire vacation.

Emelia Alsop knew that Dennis was a special kind of person. He was doing what he was born to do. He had a spirit that sought justice and he wanted to solve unsolvable puzzles. She supported him as he went to school and earned his stripes at the OPP. She stood by his side when he came home late at night and left early in the morning, working about eighty hours a week. The other dads dressed casually on the weekends, but Dennis was perpetually in a suit and tie ready to head out the door. A call could come at any minute, so you couldn't count on him to be around, but when he was there, well, according to Emelia, he was a wonderful father and loving husband. The pair were incredibly affectionate, and Detective Alsop equally adored his kids. They were the fruit of a successful life. They were happy.

"Me and my dad always got along," recalls Dennis Jr. "I had to go to school. I had to work hard, but that was more my mother. You know how some dads are pushy and they want their kids to excel in all the sports? My dad wasn't into sports. The only sport he played was golf and he got me involved in golf when I was ten years old. We'd golf two or three times a year."

They had legendary barbecues attended by officers who checked their firearms at the door. During those late summer nights, the kids would run in and out of the yard, their feet thumping up and down the stairs, while judges, cops, and their significant others leaned against kitchen counters and lounged on Emelia's mid-century modern furniture, cold bottles of Labatt's beer dangling from their fingers. Dennis spent most of his time outside at the grill, making his charcoal burgers. This was him in his element, smoking a Dutch cigar and drinking a rye and water, celebrating the end of a criminal's career. A party for a conviction was always the best kind of party.

He didn't discuss his cases at home. There were one or two situations he vented about, where he was frustrated with the higher-ups or couldn't get enough evidence on someone he knew had committed a crime. The only time his family heard him complain was when he couldn't find resolution to the justice he craved. There was no chatter about body bags or shootouts at Sunday-night supper, which was his favourite meal of the week because everyone was together. But when he took a phone call, little ears listened through closed doors. Once, when he got a call that a notorious local criminal mind was getting out of the psychiatric ward, he drove to sit in the hospital parking lot, just so the bad guy would see a squad car the minute he stepped out into the fresh air.

In Alsop's journals, co-workers he didn't get along with were omitted. He simply didn't include them, erasing them from the written history of his career. "He didn't think they were good enough to put in his diaries," says his son. He lived by the maxim that if you didn't have anything good to say, it was better to say nothing at all.

His beat was Middlesex County, the rural area around the city of London, and his focus was on robberies and murders, not missing persons. Still, on October 6, 1969, he made a note: "Missing girl in Treasure Island area." It was the first missing persons report he ever tracked in his notebook.

It wouldn't be the last.

Detective Alsop (far left) on the bridge over Big Otter Creek.

London Free Press Collection of Photographic Negatives, [1969-10-10], Archives and Special Collections, Western Libraries, Western University.

Detective Alsop pulled his car over to the side of the lonely rural road, a short distance from the bridge. There was already a team assembled, scattered like ants over the tarmac. He stepped out of the car in his black dress shoes and charcoal suit. Walking towards the scene, he nodded his acknowledgement to his colleagues. Corporal Wild stood along the rail, and Alsop came up alongside him to look down at the body in the water.

"Blunt-force trauma to the head," said Corporal Wild. "No sign of her clothes or a weapon. No blood. We've got the dogs coming out to search the woods."

"She hasn't been here long," said Alsop.

"Nope," said Wild.

Alsop looked down at Jackie floating in the water. Every time the flash went off, the water lit up, her white skin almost blinding, stretched out, her hair floating like seaweed. He imagined her smiling, so pretty, like her picture in the newspaper.

CHAPTER THREE

MEET JACKIE ENGLISH

"Dave bought me a ring, black Alaskan diamond."

— JACKIE ENGLISH, DIARY ENTRY, AUGUST 8, 1969

If she'd gone on vacation with her best friend, Vicky Larazavich, everything might have turned out differently.

Jackie and Vicky had been best friends since the English family lived at 55 Euclid Avenue. The Larazavich family was just up the street at 39 Euclid, and the two girls were inseparable. In between their grade nine classes at South Secondary School, the girls got it in their heads that Jackie could tag along on the Larazavich family vacation to the Maritimes that summer. Jackie was over the moon. But at the last minute, Vicky's parents made it clear that this was a vacation just for the family, and it wouldn't be appropriate for Jackie to come along. So she unpacked her suitcase and said goodbye to her best buddy, only to find herself stuck in London with no vacation and no plans for the summer break.

Instead, the summer of 1969 was when Jackie grew up. Her mom wasn't really paying attention. Her older sister, Anne, had moved away. It was just fifteen-year-old Jackie and her fourteen-year-old brother, Fred, and Fred really took care of himself. They all did. It wasn't entirely dysfunctional, but it wasn't perfect.

Jackie English at her grade eight graduation.

London Free Press Collection of Photographic Negatives, [1969-11-06], Archives and Special Collections, Western Libraries, Western University.

Jackie's mother had gotten Jackie a job at a restaurant called the Latin Quarter that spring, around April 17, her fifteenth birthday. It was a posh restaurant downtown at 132 Maple Street, owned by Johnny and Dorothy Downs.[1] Jackie worked as the salad girl in the kitchen. It was her first time making money outside of babysitting, and the first time she found herself with male peers, colleagues who were older than her. They watched her, an attractive and nubile young woman who seemed so innocent and unaware of how she distracted them.

But Jackie was aware of their attentions, and she wanted to dress in a way that expressed her new sense of womanhood. She was sexual; she was free. She was discovering for the first time what it meant to be a grown-up.

She and her sister loved clothes. They would try on outfits and look at fashion magazines. Anne liked monotones — black and white, pale pink and cream. Jackie was attracted to bright colours — yellows and purples and oranges. The contrast between them was head to toe. Like most women at the time, Anne wore her hair long and even ironed it straight on the ironing board. Jackie wore her brunette hair cut around the ears with kiss-curls moulded in place with bobby pins while she slept. The younger of the two, Jackie presented herself distinctively, like a colourful bird. She knew what people thought of her, and it was her greatest

---

1   This stretch of road is now Dufferin Avenue between Richmond and Talbot Streets.

strength — her brightness, her non-confrontational smile, the way she filled a seat at a party with just the kind of happiness people wanted to be around. Men wanted to be around her. They loved her. Jackie projected low-maintenance, fun female companionship. Her clothes needed to reflect that. And so, with her new job, she could make the money she needed to put together her first mature wardrobe. She would adorn herself in clothes that gave her feelings of sexiness and power.

Jackie had power. While she seemed easygoing, Jackie was stalwart when she said no. She wouldn't budge. There was no room for compromise, which frustrated her siblings; when Jackie had made up her mind, the conversation was over.

She was strong, but she was nervous. She was still worried and insecure. She was, after all, not yet sixteen, with a single mom who worked a lot, was emotionally cold, and certainly not a confidante. Jackie had more freedom than most, even in 1969. That freedom left her with a feeling of constant unease.

David Papple worked at the Latin Quarter as an apprentice chef. He was nineteen years old. He'd been eyeing Jackie since she started at the restaurant. They spent a lot of time joking around in the kitchen, and he was amazed at how comfortable she seemed in the ribald atmosphere of the restaurant staff. She could definitely hold her own.

He threw parties in his apartment, as did the other guys who worked at the Latin Quarter and lived in the Downs's building next door at 134 Maple Street, which had become a party house for the staff, who'd get off work at midnight and stay up until six in the morning. Walking up the stairs, you'd find a record spinning and a gaggle of young people lounging on second-hand furniture in a cloud of smoke. The girls took swigs of peach schnapps or sweet vermouth. The boys gulped cheap whisky, pretending it was good, pretending that they were real men as they put their arms around small female shoulders in delicate blouses. They weren't trying to be predators. They were only following their instincts to get closer to these shining creatures with perky breasts and big eyes, to smell them and do everything they could to get them to take their clothes off.

Greg Carter and Rob Mohring had a party at their apartment at the beginning of July. They were older than Jackie, and they offered her a beer. She'd never really had one before. After she finished it, she decided she liked it and had another. By the time David Papple got there after his shift, Jackie was drunk for the first time. She was drowsy and slurring her words. David took her to his place next door, where he watched her take off her clothes and tuck herself into his bed, oblivious to her surroundings. He told police he didn't have sex with her that night. He told them that he didn't want to hurt her.

When Greg Carter came to check on her, he walked in on Jackie and David naked in bed.

When she got home, she wrote in her diary in a code that her sister would later decipher. "July 12 . . . Went to Dave Papple's party. CYT JVSZC QMU KMVVEIJ EZTY LIJVYYA. QMU UTVEXXIJ. E HMCIJ TIMVU.[2] Mom asked if I was drunk. What an ass. Got home at 4 am."

Her mother had no idea. Neither did Anne — Jackie didn't tell Anne every little thing. She didn't tell Anne that Greg saw her naked with David, her new de facto boyfriend. She didn't talk to her sister about the rush of power and feelings of horror that swept over her with this change. Her sister, who was only sixteen years old herself and now living with her fiancé in Hamilton, had gone through the same thing the summer before and didn't think it was anything out of the ordinary.

Jackie started going over to Dave's every night, or at least

---

2   Code translates to: "GOT DRUNK WAS CARRIED INTO BEDROOM. WAS STRIPPED. I FAKED TEARS."

most nights. Fellow Downs family employee Paul St. Cyr[3] saw her coming and going. Sometimes they stopped to chat. He didn't say anything to her, but he had an idea of what was happening, and his gut told him that Jackie was in over her head.

Whether or not Jackie had a handle on the attention she was getting from men, she was getting plenty of it. Two weeks into their relationship, David went on a trip out west, with Paul St. Cyr. While he was gone, she confided to her diary that she kissed someone named "Lloyd," probably her married co-worker Lloyd Lackey. During their rendezvous, he warned her that her co-worker at the Latin Quarter, Greg Carter (who had seen her naked), was going to ask her to the drive-in. News of Jackie's newfound sexuality was making the rounds. She revelled in it by going shopping.

Three days later, she met up with David. He had brought her back a present from his trip: a black Alaskan diamond ring. She took note of it in her diary, and the following entry on August 9 contains a little ink star: "*Went over to Dave's."

One day in the summer of 1969, the English family went horseback riding, and during the excursion, Anne was thrown off a horse. She pinched a nerve in her back, which made it difficult for her to walk, and she ended up staying with her mother longer than expected. The family lived in an apartment at 133 Elmwood Avenue. It was a small place, and the tone of Anne's stay was such that she was there "as a guest." She and Doris were alone at home one afternoon, and Anne recalls that her mother was in a terrible mood. Anne couldn't deal with it, so she picked up the phone and dialed David Papple's number. Her sister was there.

"She's on a tear," Anne said. "You'd better come home."

"Okay," said Jackie.

---

3   Paul St. Cyr was not interviewed for this book due to his health issues.

As soon as Jackie came home, Doris "went to bed and stopped," as the sisters used to say. This left the two of them sitting there, doing nothing.

"I'm gonna take Rags for a walk," said Jackie. Rags was the family dog, a sweet-tempered collie.

"I'll come with you," said Anne. She wanted to get out of the house, even though she couldn't move very easily. She expected that her sister, who was always thoughtful and kind, would help her along and walk slowly so they could chat. Instead, she threw a stick for Rags and then chased after him, putting a large distance between them. Then she grabbed the stick and threw it again. There was no way for Anne to catch up.

Hobbling behind, Anne watched her sister duck into a phone booth and make a call. By the time she got there, Jackie was already off the phone.

"Okay, let's go home," she said.

Anne was aggravated. Her sister had put her through all of that just to make a private phone call. At first she figured she was calling David, but they had a phone in the apartment. Why did Jackie go to the payphone? They never discussed it, but Anne knew that Jackie had needed a special kind of privacy. She figured it wasn't David on the other end of that call.

Eager for more income, Jackie convinced her sister to help her get a job at the Metropolitan Store restaurant on Wellington Road South, waitressing at the lunch counter. Anne had worked at Banner Pharmacy there and knew the manager. The Metropolitan was part of a plaza called Treasure Island, also housing the Busy Bee grocery store. There has continued to be a grocery store in this location pretty much ever since. During my 1980s childhood, it was a Loblaws Superstore with a ball pit. Parents could leave their kids to play in the urine- and snot-coated colourful balls. It was great, and I loved it. It was a kind of childhood freedom you

The Metropolitan discount store and restaurant on Wellington Road South.
London Free Press Collection of Photographic Negatives, Archives and Special Collections, Western Libraries, Western University.

could never have today, for good reason, and I'm surprised we could have then, considering everything that had gone down in this city less than twenty years earlier.

The Metropolitan, a national chain of discount department stores, had its name in big red letters emblazoned across the front of the plaza. The location was the perfect spot to capitalize on the adjacent London Gardens stadium where there were concerts and hockey games almost every night. It was next to an exit off Highway 401, so truckers and travellers stopped in for quick meals, and Londoners came shopping for the bargain prices. Girls who worked there made good tips and got discounts on their purchases.

As if to celebrate, Jackie hopped on a Greyhound bus with her little brother Fred, for a week-long trip in the dog days of that summer, before her new job began. Despite their young ages, the two of them spontaneously went to Toronto on their own. It was a trick their older sister had shown them. They arrived at their aunt's house unannounced, shortly after midnight, startling her out of bed. This forced her to host them even if she didn't want to. The rest of the week was spent visiting family and going to the Canadian National Exhibition — known as the CNE or the Ex — Canada's largest fair, filled with games, an enormous midway, and the latest inventions. Everything was shiny and new. Jackie was a little kid again, going on rides with her brother, eating hot dogs, and having sleepovers with her cousins.

Her diary didn't mention Dave at all. She didn't call him; or at least, she didn't make note of it. Perhaps this was a chance to forget.

Her mother, Doris, picked them up and they stopped for dinner at Jackie's sister's house in Hamilton on the way home. Anne made "Beef, salad, baked potatoe [sic], peas, chocolate cake, bananas, fruit cocktail, coke."

"She wrote down every single thing I served for dinner," recalls Anne. "She detailed the menu. I remember . . . I was in the bathroom with her. I see her profile. I was sitting on the tub. She was whining, 'I'm so tired. I'm tired.'" Jackie washed her hair at Anne's house so she would be fresh and stylish when she returned to the affections of three competing men. If she talked about it to Anne, it was only in passing. The visit was otherwise forgettable, but it would be their last meal together.

After she got back to London, it was a whole week before Jackie saw David outside of work. Instead, she looked forward to her new gig. She couldn't wait to start her second job and line her pockets with more money. Visiting the Met store in anticipation on Thursday, August 28, with friends of the family, Mrs. McIntyre and her daughter, Jackie saw a beautiful coat. "My daughter wanted it," said Mrs. McIntyre, "but I just couldn't afford it at the time. Several days later I was sitting in [a different] restaurant having a cup of tea when Jackie walked in with the coat. She had bought it with her own money and she looked just like a doll."

With her new capital, Jackie told Fred that she was going to buy a motorcycle for her boyfriend, David Papple. As the summer came to an end, Jackie found herself transformed. She was a woman of her own means. Things could only get better.

She started her first shift at the Met on September 2. On September 15, the English family moved away from the apartments at 133 Elmwood Avenue in Wortley Village. They had lived there for less than a year, and while it was inexpensive, it was also cheap in a way that Doris didn't like. Their new place at 129 Kent Street, Apartment 5, was one of Latin Quarter owner Johnny Downs's properties, and even though it had shared bathrooms, was well kept and respectable. Paul St. Cyr drove the Downs's panel truck and helped them move furniture. Now Jackie was only a block away from David, and, as if by fate, her mother had to go to the hospital for surgery. For the next week, Jackie went essentially unsupervised. She spent as much time with David, or with anyone else for that matter, as she wanted. Their neighbour and friend Agnes Murray kept a close eye on fourteen-year-old Fred, but kept a looser eye on her.

Soon after the family moved to Kent Street, Jackie took a bigger step by moving into a separate basement room, Apartment 4, which was divided from the area shared by Doris and Fred. On October 1, she finally admitted to David that she had dropped out of school. She was thinking about going back, but to be honest, making money was really appealing. And going to high school seemed so . . . juvenile.

The summer had prepared her. Jackie was ready for her independence.

CHAPTER FOUR

MEET THE ENGLISH FAMILY

"We're not going away. We deserve some answers."

— ANNE ENGLISH

MARCH 23, 2016. My phone rang just a few minutes before I was scheduled to give a keynote address for the Architectural Conservancy of Ontario London Chapter. It was their annual general meeting, held at the historic Grosvenor Lodge on Western Road. The Lodge, a beautiful old mansion, has been restored and is used for weddings, conferences, and seminars. I'd just finished setting up the projector and screen so I could show pictures of Hotel London,[4] the demolished landmark about which I'd recently published a book. A crowd of architecture fanatics was quickly filling the room, but when I saw the call display on my phone, I turned to my partner, Jason, and showed him what it said.

Anne English. I had to take this call.

I scurried to the kitchen to get away from the noisy room. Jackie's sister said hello to me. She had a friendly, musical voice,

---

4   Hotel London stood on the southeast corner of Dundas and Wellington. It was torn down in 1972. My book about this hotel was published in 2015.

and, like Dennis Jr., she was totally receptive to my project. She sounded excited. We promised to talk again soon.

———

The first time I met Anne in person, she picked me up in front of Centennial Hall to drive me down to the annual Jackie's Walk. I immediately felt comfortable with her. With her casual nature, she is an amalgam of many Ontario ladies I know. She has big red hair and jewellery, and speaks in a sharp Souwesto accent. Her first focus was to make me feel welcome, and I couldn't have felt more so.

Jackie's Walk happens every year on October 4 at 10 p.m. We arrived around 9 or 9:30, where about ten or fifteen people met up at the McDonald's on Wellington Road South, right near the site of the Metropolitan Store where Jackie English worked. Dennis was there smoking his pipe, and Sandy was holding onto Sophie's leash. Others had brought their kids, who played tag on the grass. We sat at the outdoor tables in the freezing cold because there were so many smokers, and everyone wanted to know if Anne had any updates on her sister's case. I was nervous to meet them because I was very aware that I was the new kid on the block. They'd all been at this for ages, and I was an outsider.

Sitting in the McDonald's parking lot that night, I felt all my reservations come to an end. There were familiar faces from my community and even an old friend from high school. Carol Murray, whose mother, Agnes, identified Jackie's body, immediately started to chat with me. They all seemed excited to have a writer there. They wanted me to work on the project, and they couldn't wait to see what I would accomplish. The conversation was casual and contagious. As we started the walk, the chatting continued with the familiarity of old friends getting together for a reunion. But it was strange. It was eerie.

You couldn't escape it, no matter how much you smiled at the person walking next to you. The crackling of our feet over the gravel, the whoosh of cars on the highway below; it was all exactly what Jackie heard. The streetlights glowed in the fog, and the long grass swayed in uncut patches along the road. This was what Jackie saw and felt, the night breeze on her skin, before she got into a car and disappeared forever. That seems like a pat description as I write it, but there was this bizarre dichotomy between the everyday nature of our camaraderie and our other-worldly surroundings. Away from the strip mall, the air changed. There was an emptiness to the expanse. It was like a travelling funeral visitation, chatting about your kids and job with a cousin while there's a dead body at the other end of the room. The feeling was so utterly unique that it made me catch my breath.

At the crest of the overpass, we stood around in a circle on the sidewalk. Streetlights glowed in the fog like muddied torches. We were unable to contain our desire for answers. Some shared theories about what happened the night Jackie was taken. Others talked about going to the bridge over Big Otter Creek to commemorate the day Jackie's body was found. Maybe someone prayed. Voices got lost in the din of the highway. We all waited, deferring to Anne, until she finally made mention of heading back. Then we wandered to the fast food patio, talking for another hour or so until people offered each other rides and headed home.

———

Anne English is single, retired, and twice divorced. She lives in a modest but beautifully decorated one-bedroom apartment surrounded by walking paths and big trees. I like her style. We sat on cozy chairs in her living room, as we settled in for an interview.

For Anne, her sister's murder set off a chain of events that profoundly affected her life. It altered her relationships with her family and her perception of the world, in ways both negative and positive. The good things are ones she made out of the bad. Resiliently, she went on to marry and have kids. She's had a relatively normal existence. She's got good girlfriends, and she told me about her grandkids and the things they've destroyed. But they're just things, she said, laughing. She's led a life that doesn't allow for her to hold on to sentimental objects. After Jackie died, she learned quickly that you couldn't hold on to anything. Life took things from you. It's more important to be kind, to laugh, to value friendships, and avoid drama.

Her memories are muddled, as are the facts of the case. Anne isn't the type of person who clings to nostalgia, and after almost fifty years of trying to find peace about her sister, the information sometimes gets confused. She actively stops you from talking to her about other murders, because she doesn't want to somehow get mixed up with what she knows about her sister. Decades of frustration have gone by. While some of the sleuths working the case have larger issues in mind, like how law enforcement handles cold cases and civilian rights to information, Anne's purpose is not political. She simply wants someone to tell her what happened to her sister. This tragedy belongs to her and her brother, Fred, and for Anne, it seems like an injustice that they haven't been given all the facts, even if the OPP believes they have to hold back information to protect the integrity of their case. The question of who killed her sister has become the prime mover of her life's story, even though she has made a point of filling her life with joy and people and friendship.

While we were talking, a squirrel came to the window and Anne jumped up and went to the kitchen, where she got some peanut butter for her furry friend. That's when she shared with me that she's had lots of wild animal pets, including a mallard duck and a raccoon. She keeps pictures of them in her family photo album.

For someone whose life has been so strongly affected by tragedy, Anne is one of the most positive and vivacious people I've ever met. Her reaction to the destruction of youth and life was to embrace living and wring every drop of good out of it.

She's not someone to dwell on the past, generally. She's moved on. However, her dedication to solving the case forces her to focus when needed. The more I pushed her, the more she recalled. I didn't just want to know about the murder. I wanted to know who her sister was and about the path their lives took up until October 4, 1969.

When the English children were little, their mother, Doris, left her husband, Walter, and took off to London to put some distance between them. After that, the girls didn't see as much of their dad. He was a travelling insurance salesman, living in hotels, but he sometimes stayed with his children and his estranged wife. She would iron his shirts and make him dinner — the niceties of marriage with none of the intimacy.

Anne remembers going with him on trips to Toronto and visiting the racetrack. "He gave me two dollars for every race I was allowed to bet. Did other people take their kids to the races?" she wondered aloud.

"I just loved time with my dad. It was just cool to be with him. I remember in grade six, my girlfriends would come over to the house. My friends always thought he was gorgeous. I just saw him as my dad. He was a lot older than my mom, thirteen years older. Obviously he was very attractive at fifty-two, when my girlfriends were over. But according to my mom, he was a gambler. They never had anything because he gambled everything. She told me a story, and I don't know if it's true. She said he went to Las Vegas once and lost everything, and she had to go down and pick him up." It was Doris's role to be the stable parent in her kids' lives, and while hanging out with their dad was a treat, day-to-day fun was had with Mom. At least, when they were little.

"We would play — Jackie, her, and me — we had a little folding cart for kids with Mother Goose on it. I remember her having tea with us. We'd be Mrs. John and Mrs. Brown and Mrs. English."

But something happened to Doris, and the children would never know what it was. All of a sudden, their mother became cold and distant, no longer the affectionate maternal force in their lives. She had become a stranger.

"In grade six, my dad sent me out with money to get my mom a birthday present. I got on the bus and went to the Eaton's Centre [in downtown London], and I got her a white pleated skirt and a navy blue shell — a mock turtleneck. I remember she was in a mood, and I remember thinking, *This will make everything go back to normal.* Nothing ever went back to normal. I don't know what happened, but her entire personality changed forever. I think she ended up taking them back; the clothes didn't make her happy. Something happened in her life."

After the change in Doris, life altered greatly for her children. They moved all the time, attending a long list of London schools and living in all kinds of apartments. Anne remembers that it was as if their mother was on a mission to live in the dumpiest place she could find. She didn't put much stock in things or the idea of home. Doris was a single mother, but she made decent money and could have afforded to live better than she did. Instead, she moved from one low-rent building to another, taking her kids with her.

While going to Aberdeen, a low-income school, Jackie and Anne became avid fans of the London Public Library's Bookmobile, the first of its kind in the province. It was a remodelled bus filled with bookshelves and stacks of titles for people to borrow. It had a regular route around the city. When it pulled into the Aberdeen parking lot, the girls were ready, waiting to max out the borrowing limit. "We took all the time we were given to make our choices," explains Anne. This gift of reading and natural intelligence meant that all of the English children grew into articulate and knowledgeable adults. Fred seems to me to be particularly brilliant.

What may have seemed an unconventional upbringing to some was normal to Jackie, Anne, and Fred. They learned the value of hard work, and all of them knew they had to contribute to the household. Anne and Jackie each paid $15 a week to the family for room and board, as would Fred when he was old enough. Doris worked at the Latin Quarter and got Jackie her job there. Anne worked at Banner Pharmacy in the Metropolitan Store at Treasure Island. That was where she met Ralph Duby, who later became her husband, and it was Anne's advice that later led Jackie to get a job there as a waitress.

Perhaps it was while Jackie was working at the Metropolitan that the killer first saw her, the bright and beautiful fifteen-year-old who exuded a keen attitude and was light on her toes. Maybe she poured him a cup of coffee and smiled at him. Maybe she reminded him of another girl at another counter in another town, one he had met years before — one who had become his first victim.

CHAPTER FIVE

THE DISAPPEARANCE OF
JACKIE ENGLISH

"There is a sex maniac on the loose in London."

— FRED GOSNELL, CITY COUNCILLOR

OCTOBER 4, 1969. Jackie woke up late that Saturday in her apartment on Kent Street. After breakfast, she put on a pretty dress, the one with a bold black-and-white checkered skirt. She arranged her hair with her signature kiss-curls at her cheekbones. Slipping on her brown leather penny loafers, she went around the block to David's place at noon. Inside his apartment, she casually lounged and listened to records with him, flirted, perhaps necked. She asked him to go with her to visit her mom in the hospital; Doris had been admitted for surgery.⁵ They got on the bus and went to St. Joseph's Hospital around 2 p.m. Up in the shared ward room, Jackie sat down to chat with her mom, who lay in a hospital bed. The big old windows bathed the room with light. Doris later remembered thinking that her daughter was out of sorts. She said that Jackie didn't want to go to work at the Metropolitan that night, but she encouraged Jackie to go anyway. Doris said

---

5   No one remembers what the surgery was for exactly, but it may have been gall bladder surgery.

Jackie had a responsibility to show up and follow through on her commitments. Otherwise, their visit was uneventful. Jackie said goodbye to her mom one last time, took David's hand, walked down the hallway, and stepped onto the elevator.

Later on, David didn't recall any of the conversation between Jackie and Doris; Jackie didn't seem upset to him. It's possible that Doris's memory changed after Jackie's disappearance, as she tried to make sense of what had happened to her daughter.

Outside it was a beautiful sunny day, very warm for October. The busy downtown corridor of Richmond Row was littered with shoppers and pedestrians. Walking among them was the young couple, holding hands and making each other laugh. The air, the empty afternoon, let them fall into lazy happiness. They listened to more records in his apartment, and David Papple would later tell police they had sex — awkward youthful sex with no protection. Afterwards, wrapped in his arms, Jackie talked to him about getting married. She had told a friend that she secretly hoped he would give her an engagement ring for Christmas.

He had to work at 4:30 p.m., but Jackie promised she would be awake when he finished his shift. He should come over to her place and get her. They went to the back parking lot where she kissed him goodbye.

After David left for the Latin Quarter restaurant kitchen, Jackie ran into Paul St. Cyr. Paul worked for Johnny Downs, doing handyman work and odd jobs at Downs's various properties. That day, he was washing Johnny's station wagon. Paul was happy that Jackie stopped to talk to him. They'd spent a lot of time together since she started working at the Latin Quarter, but for the past week, Jackie hadn't been as friendly, and he wanted to know why.

"What is the matter, Jackie?" he asked her. "You are not the same. You never smile anymore. You are pale. What is the matter? Are you in love?"

"Yes," she said. "I'm in love with Dave."

"Are you going to get married?"

"When he makes up his mind," she replied, hopefully.

Paul asked Jackie if she wanted a ride to work. She turned him down, saying she had a ride, but a neighbour saw her leave in a cab a few minutes later. Perhaps she just didn't want to get a ride from Paul. She knew he didn't approve of her relationship with David, and maybe she didn't want to hear any more about it.

It was a busy night at the Metropolitan. The Leighton Ford Crusade, a religious event, was winding up at the London Gardens Arena next door, bringing extra crowds. Saturday nights were busy anyway, as folks blew off steam by going shopping after a long workweek. Later, customers and employees would be asked to find significance in what they saw and heard. Mrs. Margaret Magee, a friend of the English family, was there with her sister and their kids. She saw Jackie around 8 p.m., but said that they didn't speak.

Linda Hurst was working with Jackie in the restaurant. She told Alsop that Jackie wasn't herself at all that night, and she hardly spoke to the other waitresses or smiled at the customers. They were busy, running off their feet. In between all the hustle and bustle, Linda got the impression that young Jackie English had something on her mind. Of course, this could also have been an interpretation of events made in hindsight. People often reach for ways to make narrative sense out of tragedy.

When the restaurant closed at 10 p.m., the staff wrapped things up for the night. The tables were wiped, the chairs stacked. Most of them would drive home or catch a lift with a friend, leaving in droves. Headlights stretched across the white exterior of the building as cars pulled up and pulled away, leaving the parking lot empty very quickly.

The overpass where Jackie English was abducted.
Courtesy of the Elgin County Archives. *St. Thomas Journal-Times* Fonds.

Taking the bus was a real hassle. You see, the Metropolitan was about as far on the edge of town as you could get. It was abandoned, dark, and isolated at night. The lonely bus stop was on the other side of the highway, across the overpass extension of Wellington Road, and even when you got to the intersection of Wellington and Exeter Roads, the sparse route serviced the stop twice an hour at best. Missing the bus meant standing around in the cold for a long time. If you decided to try to make it across the highway in time, walking in the yellow glow of streetlights, your footsteps would echo across the expanse of the asphalt parking lot and then disappear into silence as you stepped on the roadside grass. On the overpass, the din of cars whipping by on the 401 would make it necessary to shout even to a walking companion right next to you. It was windy, with no trees to break up the gusts of cold October air. Taking the bus was uncomfortable, something to be avoided, but that night, it appeared to be Jackie's only option.

Alsop recorded multiple eyewitness accounts of the last sightings of Jackie as she left work that night. Consistent information was that she wore her uniform, white with orange stripes down the front, and carried her black-and-white checkered dress over her arm. She had on her new grey coat, pantyhose, and brown penny loafers. Her purse was beige camel with a shoulder strap.

Metropolitan employee Alice Faye Cox, age seventeen, sat in her sister's car around 10:15 or 10:20 p.m.

I saw Jackie come out the front door and walk across the parking lot towards Wellington Road. Just before she walked away, she looked both ways on the parking lot. She stood there for a minute. There were not many cars on the lot at that time. I did not have time to change my uniform when I left work; so Jackie would not have either, for she followed us out. She had a coat on, like a jacket, and she was carrying her street clothes over her arm.

Colleague Theresa Anne Daniels, age seventeen, said that Jackie seemed jittery that day.

I was sitting in a car waiting for Linda and Debbie to come out, to give them a ride home. At least fifteen minutes afterwards, Jackie came out and just stood there. She looked around as if she was looking for someone. I thought she was meeting someone or I would have offered her a ride. She didn't look worried. She looked as if she was ready to smile.

Jackie stood there for about half a minute, then walked towards Wellington Road. When I saw her outside, she was wearing her uniform and had her grey coloured coat opened. She had a dark navy blue or black skirt over her arm. This skirt had big white checks in it. We waited for about another five minutes. Then Linda and Debbie came out. We then drove straight across the parking lot to the stop sign, then went straight. I did not notice any car stop on Wellington Road nor did I see anybody walking on the parking lot, or Wellington Road. When we left the parking lot, we were about the last car to leave. I would say there were two other cars if there were any.

Martin Van Boekel, age thirty-five, worked at the Busy Bee Food Market in Treasure Island, adjacent to the Metropolitan Store, and knew Jackie.

> I started to walk from the store west, towards the gas bar, near Wellington [Road]. I was at the first light standard on the parking lot when I recognized Jackie English walking kitty corner across the parking lot. I kept walking ahead of her and when I reached . . . the bottom of the overpass, she was more on the side of me, about 150 feet away. The lights on the overpass were on.
>
> Just before Jackie got on the overpass and beside a large green sign, a car came up beside her going, about twenty to twenty-five miles per hour. Jackie was still walking when the car came up beside her. The car stopped and a back door on the right side opened. I didn't hear any words at all. As soon as the car stopped, Jackie went to the car and got in. I would not say the car had been there more than half a minute. It seemed as if she knew them in the car. I thought that there were more than one person in the car. The car was not stopped long enough for any conversation to take place. The car appeared to be a dark colour car, possibly a dark blue or black. I would only be guessing to say what kind of car but that car had only two tail lights, small ones, one on each side; square-shaped.

This description of the car stuck with authorities and was published in the press.

Thomas Lawrence Nagle offered yet another account. He said he was driving on the Wellington Road overpass at about 10:25 p.m.

I was driving south on Wellington Road to pick up my girlfriend at Food City . . . As I started down the south side of the [Highway] 401 overpass, I noticed a car facing north. It was stopped off the east side of the roadway on the grass . . .

The driver, a male person, was seated behind the wheel. Another male person was seated in the front seat in the middle. A third male person was standing beside the passenger's side of the car, with the right front door open. I am not sure if it [was] a two or four door car.

The one outside was leaning against the car speaking with a young girl. The girl was standing . . . towards the back of the car, away from the male person. I looked in my rear view mirror and saw him, the man outside, take a step towards the girl and she stepped back about one-half a step . . . the two inside the car seemed to be facing each other and were talking. I heard no yelling or conversation because my car windows were up.

The car is definitely a 1966 Ford Falcon, light to medium blue, one piece wheel discs, parking lights on when I saw it. The driver had dark hair, age eighteen to twenty-two years. The passenger in the car I cannot describe, except he was about the same age. The man outside was about a head taller than the girl. The girl was a head taller than the car. The girl had dark hair and a light coloured coat on.

I picked up my girlfriend at Food City and returned past this location at 10:40 p.m. and the blue car was gone and no one was walking on Wellington Road.

Police later searched all registered 1966 Ford Falcons and found nothing.

There was also an anonymous witness who called the London Police on October 15, almost a week after Jackie's body was found. He said that around 10:25 that night, he was driving northbound on Wellington Road when he observed a light blue Ford product car make a U-turn in front of him and head south on Wellington Road. He described the occupants as one male driver and one female.

That was it.

Jackie English was gone.

CHAPTER SIX

JACKIE ENGLISH IS MISSING

"I'm personally getting damned concerned."

— POLICE CHIEF FINLAY CARROLL

David Papple finished his shift at the Latin Quarter around one o'clock in the morning. He went over to Jackie's apartment, but there was no answer when he knocked on the door. He figured something must have happened and she was staying at family friend and co-worker Agnes Murray's apartment in the same Kent Street building for the night. Their plans were off. He wasn't upset, as he assumed he would see her the next day at work.

Work started at the Latin Quarter at 11 a.m. on Sunday, October 5. Just before Papple left for work, Agnes Murray showed up at his apartment. A short, sprightly woman with a Scottish accent, she was tough as nails and didn't take any shit. The English kids always listened to her reasonable instructions, and that's why Aggie was shocked when she discovered that Jackie hadn't come home and hadn't called. She had hoped to find Jackie at David's house or the restaurant, where she'd get a stern talking-to. Instead, Jackie was nowhere to be found. Aggie and David promised to stay in touch and let each other know if Jackie called or showed up for her shift later that day.

David Papple talked to the restaurant hostess Margaret Dunlop. He told her about how Jackie hadn't come home the night before. It wasn't like her to not even call. Margaret agreed, and she decided to find out what was going on with the sweet fifteen-year-old girl who she later told police was always cheerful, bubbly, and terribly responsible for her age. Paul St. Cyr told his co-workers not to worry, Jackie would show up. She was probably just off at a friend's place.

On the phone, hostess Margaret Dunlop and Agnes Murray agreed that something was wrong. They dreaded scaring Jackie's mom, Doris, who was still recuperating in the hospital.

The Latin Quarter restaurant was host to members of the London Police as regular customers. One of these was Officer Ron Haldane. He called that afternoon to make a dinner reservation, and Margaret decided it was time to do something. She told him that Jackie hadn't been home all night. When he came in to eat, after 5 p.m., he promised Margaret he would call a detective and get an investigation started.

Paul St. Cyr was put on Jackie's salad position in the kitchen for the night. Co-worker Lloyd Lackey, whom Jackie had written about in her diary, unpleasantly slurred, "We have our frog tonight for the salad lady."[6]

The restaurant staff was in a tizzy. As late became later, David started to panic. The couple had planned to get photos taken that evening by the restaurant's cook, John Oliver, who was also an amateur photographer. They'd been looking forward to it. Why would Jackie not show up? Something must be wrong.

Lloyd Lackey was distraught. He asserted that when he saw Jackie, he was going to give her a piece of his mind for putting them through this.

---

6   "Frog" is a ethnic slur for a French person.

Aggie finally called the police and reported Jackie missing the night of October 5. "If [Jackie] was going to be late coming home, she would phone and ask if she could stay an extra half hour. She was usually on time, and if she wasn't, she'd let me know," she said. She had been entrusted by Doris English to take care of the children, and now she felt sick with fear.

When David got off work, he went straight to Aggie's house and found the police there.

As soon as Doris found out that her daughter was missing, she signed herself out of the hospital.

Anne, who had been taking care of her ailing father, went to London as soon as she found out her sister was missing. "I was living in Hamilton and my dad came to visit me. My dad stayed with me, and he got sick. I didn't have a driver's licence, but I drove him down to the hospital in his car. I honestly thought it was my cooking that had affected him, because he was in the bathroom and he was sick, sick, sick for a couple days. He was diagnosed with cancer."

Her fiancé, Ralph, was away working when she found out about her little sister. "I didn't have a telephone. The police came to my door and told me I had to telephone London. [I] assumed something was wrong with my mom, and that's when they told me Jackie was missing."

Before she went to London, she stopped to see her father, who was still undergoing treatment in the hospital. "I had to wait for visiting hours, so I went to the hospital and talked to the doctor. She said, 'Don't tell your dad.'

"It's funny how you can relive certain days. My dad was in bed and I had been staying with him twelve hours a day at the hospital, and I said, 'I've got to leave. I've got to go home to London,' and I couldn't tell him why. I almost did, but the doctor came in. I can still see the puzzlement on his face."

The three remaining members of the English family, along with David Papple and anyone else who wanted to volunteer, began to search for Jackie in earnest. Following a tip that a purse had been found behind the Dorchester Apartments on Richmond Street North, Doris and her crew scoured the area for three days. Even after the purse was discovered and determined not to be Jackie's, Doris continued to hunt for her child in that area, stuck in a desperate mental loop.

They searched every day. David found himself unable to sleep and unable to work. Police said that the missing girl's bank account was untouched, although there was extra money in it that no one could account for. Anne does not recall how much.

They had no leads. All they could do was congregate at Aggie's house, hit the streets to look for Jackie, or pray.

Little Carol Murray told the newspaper that she prayed for Jackie every morning in her grade three class at St. Peter's Separate School. She loved her babysitter Jackie. Aggie Murray's stalwart personality shielded Doris, as she did everything she could to help the English family that week. The English family spent most of their time in Aggie's living room, where she made sure they ate and were taken care of — and protected from nosy reporters.

Doris was convinced that something had been bothering her daughter before she disappeared. She could not accept the idea that her child had taken a ride from a stranger. "Something had been bothering her all week and I don't know what it was. She seemed to be terrified about going to work. She just wouldn't have left, and that's not because I am her mother. Ask anyone who knows her. Jackie came to see me in the hospital Saturday afternoon, and I knew something was wrong, but I couldn't tell what it was. She didn't want to go to work and that's not like her.

"There's no way Jackie would have left on her own. I know something has happened."

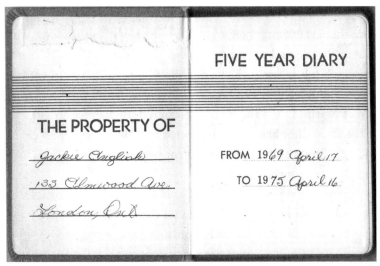

FIVE YEAR DIARY

THE PROPERTY OF

Jackie English

133 Elmwood Ave.

London Ont

FROM 19 *69 April 17*

TO 19 *75 April 16*

Jackie English received this diary for her birthday on April 17, 1969.
Courtesy of Anne English.

OCTOBER 8, 1969. Doris discovered her daughter's diary and turned to it for answers. Most of it was unsurprising, the chronicles of a teenager and her day-to-day life. She had made notes about the weather, dinners with friends, and her shopping excursions. However, there were some passages written in a kind of code, all capital letters. Maybe there would be a clue there. Anne figured out the secret code inside, and what was hidden upset David. "This was the first time that I knew Lloyd was seeing Jackie," he told Detective Alsop. "When I read about the French kissing, I was hoping that maybe Jackie was exaggerating a bit."

The encoded elements of Jackie's diary did not reveal anything that helped the case. It seemed like the innocent record of a teenage girl's reckless adventures. There were only two items in the diary that have never been figured out.

The first is the picture of an unidentified young man, sitting on outdoor stone steps, smiling for the camera. On the back of the photograph is written the name Ricardo Frohpo.

The second is an entry in the phone numbers section included at the back of the diary:

Vicky Larazavich — 39 Euclid Ave. 433-0582
Jim Gurmin — 74 Bruce Street 439-0706
Mr. & Mrs. L. Papple — 226 Highbury Ave. 451-2896
Dave Papple — 134 Maple St. 434-8607
Greg Carter — 134 Maple St. 434-1686
Linda Stokes — 46 Bruce Street 433-4297
Mary Letanche — 47 Euclid Ave. 433-2515
LLL 401 KE 439-7180
132 Maple St. Latin Quarter Rest. 433-1795
Anne Duby 387 Concession Road Hamilton Ontario

What does "*LLL 401 KE*" mean? Whose phone number was 439-7180?

You can, believe it or not, do a reverse phone number search for the year 1969. The phone number belonged to Peter and Heather Knoepfli of 112 Arbour Glen Crescent, Apartment 1109. The previous year, the number belonged to an "F. Knaepfli" at the same address, which was probably just a spelling error.

I managed to track down Heather Knoepfli. She told me that in 1968, she and Peter moved to London for a short time while he worked for Silverwoods Dairy as a long-range planner in senior management. That was when they lived at Arbour Glen Crescent briefly before moving to a townhouse near Springbank Park. They lived in London for only eighteen months. She did not remember Jackie English or the murder case. She said there was no reason for either of them to have spent time with a fifteen-year-old girl, as they had no children then and didn't require a babysitter. They did not volunteer at youth programs or go to a church where they would have met her. It was a complete surprise to Heather that her phone number from 1969 was found in the diary of a murder victim. Peter graduated from Western

University's business school in London in 1963 before moving to Toronto where he met his wife.

At this point in time, there is no connection between the Knoepflis and Jackie English. The letters and numbers — LLL 401 KE — are likewise a mystery.

Every day, Doris left the house to look for her daughter. Her legs ached. She wasn't hungry, she couldn't sleep. Every person who had an idea or a lead, no matter how cockamamie, had her ear. She recruited anyone who would help her and relied on the hangers-on who swarmed Aggie's living room. There were friends from the Met and the Latin Quarter, kids who had gone to school with Jackie, people who just wanted to be part of the drama, pastors and rabbis and psychics.

In the end, none of it mattered. She looked to Detective Dennis Alsop with the one question that he would never be able to answer.

CHAPTER SEVEN

JACKIE ENGLISH IS DEAD

"Jacqueline was the victim of a vicious beating."

— OPP CHIEF INSPECTOR JAMES MCBRIDE

OCTOBER 9, 1969. While Dennis Alsop sped in his cruiser up Highway 401 to Big Otter Creek, supporters of the English family congregated in Aggie's apartment. It wasn't a big place, and all week it had been cluttered with people.

Agnes Murray got wind that the police were coming with terrible news. Worried that sixteen-year-old Anne would insist on going to identify her sister — which she correctly assumed she would want to do — she asked Anne's best friend Judy Topping to find an excuse and take her out for a while. When they returned, Aggie had already left to do the horrible task for her.

———

Agnes drove east on Highway 401 for an hour in the dark, to Tillsonburg. She pulled into the parking lot outside the large brown-brick modern hospital. Lights glowed from the windows. She walked up the ramp and into the emergency entrance, stopping at the nurse's station to get directions to the morgue.

An attendant came to get her, and they got into the elevator.

In the basement, her steps echoed in the hallway as she walked towards the doors of the morgue. As she approached, the pathologist came out of the exam room. He looked over the edge of his glasses at Agnes Murray.

"She *wasn't* a virgin," he snarked.

Normally quick with a comeback, Agnes was stunned. She silently followed him into the room, lit from the ceiling by fluorescent lights. On a metal exam table was a body. She stood a few feet away as the pathologist pulled back the sheet, revealing Jackie's face. Her features were swollen, pale, and bluish, distorted by lying in Big Otter Creek for three or four days. There were bruises on her head and blood matted in her hair. It didn't look like her at all.

"That's not her," said Aggie. She was sure it wasn't Jackie. It couldn't be. It didn't even look like her. "That's not Jackie."

"I'm quite sure it's her," said the pathologist skeptically.

"There's a birthmark," said Aggie. "On her thigh."

The pathologist sighed. He pulled back the sheet, revealing Jackie's leg. There, on her thigh, clear as day, was the distinctive birthmark.

The scene at Big Otter Creek where Jackie English was found.

Agnes sat in the car, her hands gripping the steering wheel, tears streaming down her face. She couldn't drive like this. She had to get herself together. She had to be strong for Doris and the kids.

———

"There were just so many people," Anne recalls.

Doris sat still on the couch. People offered her water, tea, something to eat. She didn't want anything. The trip to Tillsonburg Hospital and back would take at least an hour, probably a bit longer. Waiting for confirmation of her daughter's death, Doris went numb inside. Then she heard the door open. In a moment, Aggie stood in front of her.

"Just tell me yes or no," said Doris. Tears ran down her stony face.

"Yes," said Aggie.

"I don't want anybody to talk to me," said Doris.

She went into Agnes Murray's bedroom and shut the door.

"Then it seemed like everybody left and the apartment was empty," remembers Anne. Everything was quiet. There was no sound of wailing or choking sobs. No screams of grief. Anne sat next to her fiancé, Ralph, and they had no idea what to do. After a while, she decided to check on Doris, who was still alone in Aggie's bedroom.

"Mom?"

Doris lay on the bed with her back to Anne, seemingly asleep.

"Mom?"

Anne tried to wake her up, but Doris didn't move.

She noticed a pill bottle on the nightstand. It was empty. She picked it up and looked at the label, which read "Agnes Murray." It had been filled just a few days before. Anne stood there, the pill bottle in her hand, and took a look at her mom lying there peacefully. Then she turned and walked calmly back into the living room where Ralph was waiting for her.

"Mom took all of Aggie's pills," she said. "She's dying."

Ralph immediately picked up the phone to call for help.

"Wait!" Anne cried. "Stop." She stood there quiet for a moment, thinking. "No. Let her. If that's what she wants, that's fine."

They sat back down on the couch, the minutes ticking by. Anne knew that Ralph didn't agree with her, and if she left him alone, he would make that phone call. He wanted to get help, but she stared at him, the glare of her eyes holding him back from making his move. They were in a deadlock. They sat there for what felt like almost an hour.

Then there was the sound of the door opening. Anne turned to see her fourteen-year-old brother Fred peek around the door frame.

"Where's Mom?" he asked.

Anne looked at Ralph. "Do what you have to do," she told him.

———

Aggie told the press, "The one who is the most heartbroken is Freddie. He's been trying to be so brave for his mother. He told her yesterday he had to go out, [but he] went downstairs to their apartment and had a good cry."

Anne couldn't shake the feeling that she had seen it coming. In January 1968, she'd been walking with her friend Judy Topping through Old South. The English family lived at 55 Euclid Avenue at the time. There was an ice storm, and the two girls were huddled in their winter coats, heading to one or the others' house or maybe to the store. At that time of year, in the middle of January, it got dark early. By dinner time, it felt like the middle of the night. "It was dark, nothing moving." There were long shadows, and the heavy snow amplified every sound. It was easy for them to scare each other with the story of the girl who had been abducted from their neighbourhood and murdered just the week before. Anne and Judy thought the killer could be lurking anywhere, and they delighted in the thrill of danger. In the glow of the streetlights, their words made clouds of fog over their heads as they discussed the dreadful details of the recent killing.

"Jackie was the next victim," Anne remembers.[7]

For the next fifty years, Anne and Judy stayed friends. Jackie's death "kind of stunted me. Everything changed, so the friends I had before Jackie were cemented and we would be friends for a long time after."

It's an interesting turn of phrase. Anne refers to her life in two ways: things happened to her either "before Jackie" or "after Jackie." She doesn't say "death," or "murder." What happened to her and her family was so much more complex than a single, violent act. It was everything that came after it and the way it filtered everything that came before.

Memory plays tricks on her. "I lost the whole year before Jackie."

After her suicide attempt, Doris was committed by her brother Jack to the London Psychiatric Hospital,[8] where she would stay for a year. The children found themselves with no parents — at least, none in any capacity to be of help.

Anne visited her mother at the psychiatric hospital, which proved to be a frightening experience. She remembers a hospital Halloween party that took place only weeks after Jackie's body was discovered. Doris was already receiving electric shock therapy and was very angry about her treatment. She was heavily medicated. At the party, Doris had a pair of knitting needles, even though Anne said that her mother never knitted anything in her life. She remembers watching her mother jab the needles at other

---

7   There are actually several other suspected victims of the Forest City Killer during this period.

8   The London Psychiatric Hospital was called the Ontario Hospital at the time.

patients in a threatening, frightening way. Doris told Anne that her hospital roommate, a young girl, had tied a noose in their shared room to hang herself. She had asked Doris to kick the stool out from under her, and Doris obliged.

Doris would beg her daughter to let her come home, but Uncle Jack assured Anne that her mother needed to be in there, no matter what kind of a fuss she made, even though it was a horrible place to mourn the loss of her daughter.

———

With Jackie's story topping the news, law enforcement found itself plagued by time-wasters, false tips, and empty leads. London was a small city, and many people could claim a connection to Jackie English. This made them feel like they were somehow part of the tragic excitement. The gossip and chatter led to useless information that Alsop nevertheless had to follow up on and document. If he wasn't answering the phone, he was typing. The clacking of the keys echoed against the walls as it grew dark outside, pitch black. Eventually, he would fall asleep at his desk and wake up to the buzz of the office outside his door. He'd go to his locker to get a fresh shirt, throw his suit jacket back on, and start a new day.

CHAPTER EIGHT

THE FUNERAL OF JACKIE ENGLISH

"What does it take to wake a city up? Does everyone shut their eyes to those who don't belong to them?"

— DORIS ENGLISH

OCTOBER 14, 1969. Jackie English's remains were placed in a white casket in the Needham Memorial Chapel, a converted Victorian mansion with big trees on the front lawn. The parking lot was packed with cars and undercover officers writing down each licence plate.

About eighty people attended the service. They sat in neat rows facing the front of the room, where the closed casket was laid out with flowers. Next to it was a photograph of Jackie, the only one anyone has seen since the OPP confiscated all other contemporary photos of her.[9] In this one, her grade eight graduation photo, she smiles.

Siblings Fred and Anne sat in the front row, their parents painfully absent. Anne could think only about her little brother. He sat beside her wearing the jacket that Jackie had bought him for his grade eight graduation — when his mother couldn't afford

---

9   These photographs have never been returned to friends and family, despite numerous requests.

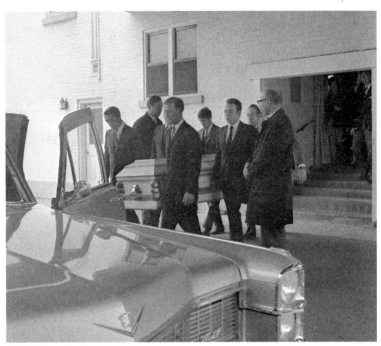

Pallbearers carry Jackie English to her final resting place at Mount Pleasant Cemetery.

London Free Press Collection of Photographic Negatives, [1969-10-14], Archives and Special Collections, Western Libraries, Western University.

it, his big sister had ponied up the cash. But he had grown a lot since graduation, and his pants were too short, revealing white socks. "Fred's a real introvert," Anne recalls. "He has no use for most people. If he likes you, that's a real bonus. He's very bright, exceptionally bright, but he's very reclusive. He doesn't have the time or the energy for most people . . . but Jackie was his best buddy. He was just sitting there. I kept looking at him. I was concerned about him. He was there, but he wasn't."

Jackie was buried at London's Mount Pleasant Cemetery. It is one of the oldest graveyards in the city, with huge trees and green grass as far as you can see. The markers there list names of the first pioneers who settled the area and victims of the many tragedies of the past. London, Ontario, had survived a cholera epidemic in

1832; a great fire in 1845; and the disastrous sinking of the river boat *Victoria* in 1881, which left hundreds of bodies to drift onto the banks of the Thames River. These events were memorialized on old stones surrounding the family, as Jackie's white coffin was carefully lowered into the ground, now the marker of another dark time in the Forest City.

Standing nearby was Detective Alsop, brow furrowed and hands stuffed in the pockets of his suit. His mind was elsewhere, combing through the events of the past two weeks, the past three years, the past ten years.

"He had files and files and files on every deviant in the city," says his son. "All of a sudden, instead of working with bank robbers and safe crackers, which he kind of grudgingly respected, he was working with strange people that he couldn't comprehend."

For Alsop, watching Anne and Fred stand helplessly by their sister's graveside, there could be no stronger motivation to solve this puzzle. Something inside him had reached a boiling point. He had to find Jackie's killer.

During the reception, young Fred sheepishly approached his Aunt Jo from Toronto. It was at her house where he had his best memories of his time with Jackie: sleepovers with his cousins, hot dogs, subway rides, running around at the midway of the CNE. Aunt Jo's was exciting and different, but also a home where there was a mother to take care of him. Instinctively, he knew what he had to do. He asked if he could come and live with her in Toronto.

She said she would have to chat with her husband about it.

A week later, Aunt Jo called. She said she and her husband had discussed it and decided that Fred could come. It was too late, and Fred's trust in her had been broken. That small interaction set the tone for the way he would relate to the world for the rest of his life.

"Nah," he said.

Life became a blur of survival. Fred went to school and came home to sit alone in his room. "If he wanted to stay in his bed all day, then I knew where he was and it was okay," Anne says of his depression. She was looking for work. She needed to support herself and her little brother. She went back to her old employer, Banner Pharmacy in the Metropolitan Store. Every night after her shift, she drove over that same overpass where her sister was last seen. I asked Anne if that bothered her, and she said she hadn't even thought of the connection until I asked her almost fifty years later.

Johnny Downs gave young Fred a job as dishwasher at the Latin Quarter, in the same kitchen where his sister had worked, so he could save up money to buy her a tombstone.

PART II

THE MYSTERY MURDERS

CHAPTER NINE

THE MURDER OF JACQUELINE DUNLEAVY

"It bugs you. You keep wondering why and who did it.
Just because it's unsolved doesn't mean they go away."

— SERGEANT GARRIT WEETERING

JANUARY 9, 1968. It was a Tuesday night, and the city was covered in snow.

Nineteen-year-old Wayne Hebblethwaite slowly backed his car out of the driveway of his foster home on 6 Lyndhurst Drive in Old South, London. The sky was clear and crisp. Pretty brick houses with verandahs and gingerbread trim were covered in long shadows. His breath hung in the air. As the car rolled, the snow crunched, but he couldn't hear it. Wayne was deaf and mute. This new car, which he'd gotten only a week before, was specially equipped to allow him to drive. No more city bus for Wayne. Even though it was a school night, his foster parents, Lloyd and Margaret Green, told him it was okay to go out and show off his wheels to some old friends.

Wayne had met his two friends Jim George[10] and Dave Noiles while he was staying at May Court House, a residence

---

10 Crawford James "Jim" George.

on Woodward Avenue that worked with Family Services and the Children's Aid Society. Jim still lived there, and Dave lived nearby in the neighbourhood. Both boys were a lot younger than Wayne, but maybe that was what made them so easy to be around. They didn't judge him. They looked up to him. Tonight, he couldn't wait to show off his new car, and his fourteen-year-old compadres were the perfect audience.

Wayne never expected to drive, much less own a vehicle. His birth parents had abandoned him when he was six because they couldn't handle his disability, but the Greens had a daughter who was also hearing impaired. They knew what they were doing. They worked with him on sign language, taught him how to manage daily tasks on his own, and made him feel like part of a family — for the first time in his life. Now he had a sister and parents who really cared about him. He felt like a good example to his friends, especially Jim. After graduating from the Ontario School for the Deaf in Belleville, Wayne lived at May Court with Jim for only a year before the Greens took Wayne in. He wanted to show his old housemate that hard work did pay off, even for people like them.

He pulled up the long driveway to May Court and saw Jim and David waiting for him on the steps. New wheels, no parents, real freedom. They cruised up Oxford Street to a place where they knew they could hang out without interference from anyone.

The old buildings of the Children and Parent Resource Institute, known as "CPRI" today, and formerly the Children's Psychiatric Research Institute, are set back from the corner of Sanatorium Road and Oxford Street West, sharing an expanse of green space with Matthews Hall Private School, previously known as the Katherine Harley School for the Retrainable Retarded. Across Oxford Street is the London Hunt Club, a country club and golf course for the city's elite. Jim and Wayne were both familiar with the grounds of CPRI, since wards of the Children's Aid Society went to there for counselling and testing. From CPRI to behind the Katherine Harley School, there was a winding road that led to a back laneway — today interrupted by fencing — hidden from passing cars, neighbours, and cops, where kids could congregate to park their cars, get physical, and enjoy contraband activities. Wayne knew the way.

One of the boys would later tell police that they pulled into the parking lot to turn around, on their way to go tobogganing — suspiciously without toboggans. Maybe they were off to smoke a joint or drink — the bonding rituals of teenage boys. Whatever it was, they wanted to keep it a secret from authorities.

Their headlights fell on a form lying in the snow.

The three boys clambered out of the car, their feet trampling the footprints the killer had left. They crept forward and saw her eyes, open and motionless, staring up at the starry winter sky from a badly beaten, bloodied face.

———

They sped away down slippery roads.

In that confusing moment, David Noiles recalled the time he found Mrs. Forrestal, a lady who lived on his paper route. It was an early September morning, the sun just coming up and the streets empty. Summer was on its way out. He was riding his bike when he saw her there, lying on the ground next to her house, stiff and cold. She'd fallen off her porch. He'd never forget her crumpled still body, the way she didn't move when he called out to her, when he touched her. That January night, he hadn't yet had his first kiss, but he'd seen enough dead bodies for a lifetime.

Wayne was focused. He panned the streets looking for an open shop, somewhere that had a phone that his friends could use. He turned towards the Oakridge Acres Plaza at Oxford Street and Hyde Park Road. All the storefronts were dark, but there was a police cruiser sitting in the parking lot.

The officer in the car was Constable David Smith. He'd pulled over to fill out some paperwork on a hit and run he'd been dealing with in that end of town. The culprit's husband was a lawyer, so the case had turned into a real pain in the ass. It was quiet. The parking lot was completely empty. He was surprised when a car pulled up next to him and two young boys got out. They were all wound up, and talked over each other as they told him they had found a dead body up the road.

Dead bodies were nothing new for Smith. As a police officer, he had attended many scenes of car collisions and fatal confrontations. His job was to call it in and stay with the body. As he told me, one of the first things he had to do was write his name on the hand of the corpse. It was then his duty to watch the scene and be the primary touchstone for chain of evidence. It might take all day, as investigators came and processed the scene. Meanwhile, officers like Smith had to stand guard, and even accompany the body to the morgue.

As such, Smith's first thought was to preserve whatever scene he was going to. He told the boys to stop their car some distance

Police analyze the scene where Jacqueline Dunleavy was found.

London Free Press Collection of Photographic Negatives, [1968-01-09], Archives and Special Collections, Western Libraries, Western University.

away, and then he drove closer to the Katherine Harley School. He got out, flashlight in hand, and stepped closer.

In the darkness, every sound was amplified. It felt like hallowed ground, coming closer to this still form laid out with her arm above her head, just like Jackie English would be found in Big Otter Creek. Her blouse was torn open, revealing her small, youthful breasts. There were bruises and blood all over her head. Her skirt, yanked up, left her genitals exposed to the elements. He could see a scarf tied around her neck so tightly that her skin bulged out around it. Most disturbing was the puff of plastic sticking out between her lips, a travel pack of pink facial tissue cruelly jammed in her mouth.

While Smith knew she was dead just from looking at her, he followed procedure and bent down to check her pulse, her eyes staring past him.

Then he wrote his name on her hand.

To the surrounding homes, the scene glowed like a late-night sporting event under huge spotlights. The cherry lights on top of

Wayne Hebblethwaite, David Noiles, and Jim George sit in a police car waiting to be questioned.

London Free Press Collection of Photographic Negatives, [1968-01-09], Archives and Special Collections, Western Libraries, Western University.

cruisers spun without sirens. Officers struggled to get close enough to take photographs and collect samples without trampling pre-existing footprints and tire tracks and making it impossible to find out who did this — what kind of maniac would do this? They put cardboard boxes upside down over evidence, as it quickly disintegrated in the snowfall.

A sympathetic detective sent the three boys to the station so they could stay warm while they waited to be interviewed.

Officer Smith watched as another investigator leaned down and closed the girl's eyes. It was too disconcerting to work with her looking past everyone like that, her strawberry-blonde hair crisp with ice. Then he pulled the horrifying plastic bag out of her mouth, agape and slack. Smith knew that was the wrong move, handling evidence from the crime scene that way, but he didn't say anything.

The left side of her head was pounded, bruised, as if the killer started hitting her in the passenger seat of the car that brought her there. There were scratches along her vulva and breasts. She had also scratched her attacker, leaving drips of his blood on her skin and under her nails, later determined to be Type O. Despite her efforts, he dragged her unconscious body to this spot, then discarded her backpack nearby, the artifacts of teen life spilling out. Her snow boots, underwear, and stockings were tossed aside. Her coat was stripped away and laid out next to her, covered in splattered stains of semen and vomit.[11]

At 10:30 p.m., Detective Herb Jeffrey told reporters, "All we know right now is that we have the body of a dead girl. We don't even know who she is at this point."

Ambulance attendants lifted her onto a stretcher to transport her to the morgue at St. Joseph's Hospital. As they moved her, someone found her wallet, where there was a student ID card from Westminster High School. Her name was Jacqueline Dunleavy. That

---

11 It is unknown if the vomit belonged to the killer or Jacqueline.

was when they realized that she was the daughter of their colleague Constable John O. Dunleavy. Everyone knew John. He was chairman of the bargaining unit for the London Police Association.

Constable Smith had known Jacqueline personally. She baby-sat for him and his wife on several occasions. According to him, "she was just a kid." Even though he knew her, she had been beaten so badly that even as he wrote his name on her cold flesh, he didn't recognize her.

He got in his cruiser and followed the ambulance to the hospital.

When Jacqueline didn't show up after work, her parents knew something was wrong. While she'd been a wild teenager lately, routine and accountability were still driving forces in the family of five. Jacqueline adhered to her schedule. Her Tuesday and Thursday after-school shifts at the Stanley Variety convenience store downtown were part of a clockwork existence and ended at 6 p.m. Dinner was kept warm in the oven. Homework would be done before bedtime.

But the door didn't open and Jacqueline didn't come home.

Constable John Dunleavy and his wife, Emily, started to make phone calls to find out where she was — friends, family, the bus service. Of course, he called the station. Worried by the cold weather, John jumped in his car and began to comb the neighbour-hood in search of his daughter. He was still hunting for her as the police descended upon the Katherine Harley School parking lot, but he didn't drive by the crime scene. When the doorbell rang later that night, he found Superintendent of Detectives Herb Jeffrey on his doorstep, accompanied by Detective Sergeant Harold McBride.

A few minutes later, John Dunleavy was in a police cruiser, on the way to St. Joseph's Hospital to identify his daughter's body in the morgue. There, Constable Smith watched as John broke down in uncontrollable tears as he saw what had been done to his beautiful little girl.

At the police station on King Street, Wayne Hebblethwaite found himself in a bare room, alone. When he first got there, he tried to ask the officers if he could call his parents. The Greens would be worried. Not only that, they would be disappointed that they let him go out on a school night only to have him not show up for curfew. The police said no, and they asked him why he didn't have ownership papers for the car. It must be stolen, they assumed. He tried to explain he had just got the car. It was his first car, and the paperwork was coming in the mail. But they didn't understand. Instead, they just left him there, behind a locked door. He was scared. There was nothing to do but sit there and brood, imagine the worst, picture his life in a jail cell, or picture what had happened to leave this girl bloodied in the snow. His fear expanded to fill the empty space as he sat there, a policeman checking on him once in a while to make sure he didn't need anything. They watched him go to the bathroom. They gave him a cup of coffee.

At midnight, again he asked to call his parents. Again, they said no.

Finally, an officer came into the room. He gave him paper and a pen and instructed him to write down everything that had happened, from the beginning to the end.

It wasn't until around five o'clock in the morning that Wayne was released. He got in his car and drove home, the streets still dark. When he pulled into his driveway, he felt like a different person, shivering with adrenalin and exhaustion. He found the Greens panicked, desperate for his return. They met him with joyful hugs, and then they got down to the business of finding out what had happened.

The Greens weren't alone in their worry for their child. No one had notified any of the boys' caregivers that they were being held at the police station, even though the three teens were never suspects. Especially egregious was the fact that the Children's

Aid Society called to report Jim missing, and the police didn't tell them that he was right there at the station.

Wayne ate some breakfast. He tried to calm down. Eventually, he managed to go to sleep and woke up that evening, when his foster parents explained to him what had really taken place, that he wasn't in trouble, and that it had all been a mistake.

Mrs. Green told the newspaper that the police "apologized and accepted the blame . . . the girl's death is a terrible thing, but we can't let emotions interfere with what's right." She'd spoken with Superintendent Jeffrey, and he told her that it was a "slip-up — but that doesn't help my sleepless night when it's their duty to let us know." She was adamant that if they had known, her husband would have gone to the police station to help Wayne communicate. The young man didn't know what was happening. He was terrified and confused. It was Wayne's idea to go right to the police after they found the body, and she asserted that he should have been treated like a hero, not a criminal. The paperwork for Wayne's car arrived in the mail the next day. "Things we take for granted in everyday living are a real problem for a deaf person who is just not accepted in a hearing world," said Mrs. Green.

Russell Noiles, David's father, said they didn't know what had happened to their son until the police brought him home at 4:30 in the morning. "They should have told us," he said, although he had not reported his son missing. David told his dad that he had asked to call home, but the police wouldn't let him. "All I know is, I didn't get no phone call," said Russell.

Police officials explained that the boys were taken back to the station to keep them out of the cold. They were separated and denied outside communication as they waited to be questioned. As the police chief would say, there was too much "heat" to worry about it. Later, this judgement call would be questioned heavily by the press, with the mayor demanding an investigation.

In the newspaper, there seemed to be more information about the boys' detention than the actual murder. Story after story appeared over the next week. Chief Finlay Carroll said, "If they want an investigation, it is all right with me . . . it was a mistake and we admit it. We have apologized. At no time were those boys suspects. The reason they were held was simply because the investigating officers did not get around to questioning them until early Wednesday morning . . . I am not critical of the officers involved and you certainly can't indict the whole department because of an error. It was one of those things — they happen . . . The boys were helping the police. [The boys] are not mad at us."

During a special meeting about the detention of Hebblethwaite, Noiles, and George, former policeman and city council member Fred Gosnell said, "With all the violence, break-ins, and murders going on, I think it shows this police department needs beefing up. They haven't got enough men on the police department to do a good job and if the department is not beefed up, this situation will get much worse."

Law enforcement had been far too busy at the crime scene to worry about the three teenagers who found the body. Instead, they were focused on the fact that this girl was the daughter of one of their own.

———

It was the second violent death the Dunleavy family had experienced in the past five years. In September 1963, their relative Caroline Weldman fell victim to a violent death.[12] Caroline lived downtown at 248A Dundas Street, above the shops near Wellington. She had been found in her apartment, strangled with her housecoat sash. Eventually, two men were charged in her strangling: Peter Raymond Robichaud, twenty-three, and Frederick Earl Austin,

———

12 Caroline Weldman was the mother of Jacqueline Dunleavy's aunt, Shirley Dunleavy. Shirley Dunleavy was married to Gerry Dunleavy, John Dunleavy's brother.

seventeen. In January 1964, they were charged with non-capital murder, but the charges were dropped when they were committed to the Ontario Hospital for Criminally Insane in Penetanguishene, Ontario. Years later, Robichaud's daughter, Charlene Robichaud-Termeer, would advocate in an online petition to extend the stays of the criminally insane in Penetanguishene.

The morning after her death, next to nighttime shots of the illuminated crime scene and a map showing where her body was found, where she worked, and where she lived, young Jacqueline Dunleavy's face graced the cover of the *London Free Press*.

At her high school, Westminster, the flag was flown at half-mast. Jacqueline was in grade ten, and her principal, William Traut, offered the banal statement to the newspaper that she was an average student who didn't participate in extracurricular activities because of her part-time job and because she was a bus student. He did not close the school for the day or organize a memorial service. The only action taken by the student body was to send the student council to the funeral, as determined at an early morning emergency meeting. There was no mention of Jacqueline's death in the yearbook. Instead, the yearbook was dedicated to a retiring teacher.

Jacqueline's funeral was held on Friday, January 12, at 1:30 p.m. During the service, plainclothes police officers checked the licence plates of the cars in the parking lot. Her father's colleagues served as pallbearers in police uniform. Walking from the hearse to the gravesite, her family followed behind her coffin, Jacqueline's mother, Emily, leaning on her sister for support.

The graveside service in Woodland Cemetery was conducted by the family's minister, Reverend "Benny" Eckhart of the Church of Christ Disciples and unofficial police chaplain. In the eulogy, he described Jacqueline as a girl who believed everyone was good and everything was beautiful. He said that coming from

The Dunleavy family mourn the death of Jacqueline.

London Free Press Collection of Photographic Negatives, [1968-01-12], Archives and Special Collections, Western Libraries, Western University.

a religious family, she knew the scriptures and received praise from her Sunday school teachers. According to Pastor Benny, Jacqueline Dunleavy was an innocent girl devoured by a monster.

One man called the police and reported seeing Jacqueline Dunleavy on the night she died, getting into a white Chrysler station wagon that had pulled over and was blocking traffic.

Tread marks taken from Jacqueline Dunleavy's snowy crime scene were shown to four different mechanics, considered experts. They all said that this car must have had terrible alignment. It also had four totally different kinds of tires. The police swept the city for a white Chrysler with four different tires but found nothing. While the white Chrysler was considered a credible lead and was still listed in a report from the OPP in 1974, the idea that Jacqueline was picked up and where she was picked up from were only presumptions. Another eyewitness said Jacqueline was seen standing at the bus stop on Beaconsfield

Avenue, one block south of the Stanley Variety, where she would have been waiting for the 5 Springbank bus to pick her up. There were two routes for the 5, an A and B route. One of them actually stopped at the Children's Psychiatric Research Institute, but none of the bus drivers recalled seeing her.

A police official said, "We will crack this case. I just feel it. It is one of those things." Detective Herb Jeffrey said, "We feel the victim knew the person who picked her up." When asked about the type of person who would commit such a disgusting, violent act, Jeffrey ruled out an abnormal mind. He said, "Perverts destroy. This was more like the work of a healthy male." The implication was that a man had been overcome with lust and arousal, that this kind of behaviour — kidnap, murder, and sexual assault — was just a natural offshoot of a healthy man's desires.

Sitting at his desk at OPP headquarters, Detective Alsop picked up the phone to the London Police station. Jacqueline Dunleavy's murder was not in his jurisdiction, but he wanted to read the files. It reminded him of a case he'd investigated a couple of years earlier in the nearby small town of Aylmer. He had no idea how many similar cases would soon be piled up on his desk.

CHAPTER TEN

THE MURDERS OF FRANKIE JENSEN, SCOTT LEISHMAN, AND HELGA BEER

"OK, time to do right by poor Helga."

— RKAY

Serial killer expert Dr. Mike Aamodt, who runs the Serial Killer Database at Radford University, has said that a "common misconception is that serial killers are consistent in their crimes. That is, they always use the same method to kill, and kill the same type of victim. Although this is often the case, there are many examples of serial killers who use multiple methods, kill both men and women, and have victims of varied races and ages. Thus, trying to link unsolved murders by only looking for commonalities or discarding a victim because he or she doesn't fit the pattern of other murders might result in an ineffective investigation.[13]" Serial killers like Dennis Rader and Canada's notorious Clifford Olson have demonstrated that victimology is not always consistent; there are killers who break out of patterns in gender, age, and other characteristics when choosing their prey.

---

13 McCale, Christina. "Serial Murder — Separating Fact from Fiction: An Interview with Dr. Michael Aamodt." Justice Clearing House. March 20, 2018.

I haven't met many amateur sleuths examining the unsolved London murders who consider that the same perpetrator may have killed both the male and female victims in the area. Traditionally, these would be seen as two different sets of cases. I respectfully disagree with that assumption. It's my belief that the geography of the abduction and body disposal sites, as well as eyewitness accounts of suspects seen close to where the victims disappeared, mean it is very possible that whoever killed Jackie English and Jacqueline Dunleavy also killed Frankie Jensen and other boys like him.

FEBRUARY 9, 1968. Nine-year-old Frankie Jensen was rushing to get out the door. Up the block, a crowd of kids was slowly making their way to his house, 382 Hazel Avenue, and he was supposed to join them. Ever since Jacqueline Dunleavy had been murdered exactly one month earlier, parents had asked their kids to stick together, even in broad daylight at 8:30 in the morning, on the way to Westdale Public School. They were coming now. The gaggle of kids laughed and goofed around, crunching their way through the snow. Frankie's mother, Krista Jensen, struggled to help him get his coat done up. His zipper was broken, and by the time she found a solution to keep her son warm, the safety of the group of school children had already passed them by. Krista gave her son a kiss and watched as the sweet blond boy pulled on his handmade toque and ran out the door as fast as his little legs could carry him.

After walking up Hyde Park Road, Frankie took the commonly used shortcut to Westdale Public School: through the woods, across the creek, and through another field. It was a stretch of unmonitored pathway, through trees and brush that many of his classmates would have been too scared to take by themselves. As he stepped off the road, he heard the bell ring and looked up. He could see his friends ahead and waved to a few classmates, but was still far away. They all went inside the building. There were no teachers on the yard, no other late students. Frankie was all alone, the wind blowing snow against his plump red cheeks, when he disappeared forever.

The Jensen family owned Jensen's Guild House, a home furnishing business, at 193 King Street. According to newspaper articles, Krista was there when she got the call that her youngest son had not come home from school that day, and she immediately told her husband. They left the shop to go home and call everyone in the neighbourhood. Frank Sr. gathered friends and family armed with winter coats and flashlights, to go out into the snow and search for the nine-year-old. The police suggested that perhaps Frankie had run away and would return soon, but officers nevertheless came to help. They coordinated volunteers to look for a child who was lost or had run away, not one who had been abducted. The spectre of Jackie Dunleavy's death hung in the air as they swept his route to school, calling his name into the freezing shadows. Eventually, they had to admit that it was too cold and dark to search any longer. They'd resume the hunt tomorrow. Of course, there was no trace of him. His lunchbox, his unique hat, his coat — none of it could be found.

Someone reported seeing Frankie in a hardware store downtown on Waterloo Street. He'd been accompanied by a man, and they were buying batteries for a radio. Did someone bribe Frankie to get into a car? Other sightings — including one at Treasure Island, where Jackie English would later work — were reported, investigated, and proved to go nowhere.

Stories in the newspaper asked, had he run away to avoid bullies in class? Was his teacher negligent in reporting him absent?

In the weeks after Jacqueline Dunleavy's death, kids from Frankie's school, Westdale, had gone to their principal, Mr. Pickles, with disturbing reports of men hanging around the field out back, where they cut through to get to the school. An eyewitness got a good look at one of them, as the youngster hid off the path to jump out and scare his friends. Crouching in the brush, he heard a sound behind him and turned to see a man he would describe as pale skinned with dark hair and eyebrows. He was crouched, so it was impossible to guess his height, but it was easy to see what he was wearing.

A green jacket.

In those few weeks between murders, children playing outside found stashes of pornographic magazines discarded in the trees. Some were mainstream smut, like *Playboy*. Others were hardcore, underground publications, printed on poor quality paper, portraying more subversive sexual acts, things even the most worldly grade eight boys hadn't heard about. There were men who opened their coats to show children their genitals or who chased them across the field. The children told their teachers and principal about it, but they didn't do anything. At nearby Oak Park Public School, administrators acted with more precaution. They sent home a letter, warning parents about the "Candy Man," who'd been seen hanging around the school grounds trying to entice children into his white van.

Some people thought these sightings were of wandering patients from CPRI or the "retarded" kids from the Katherine Harley School.

The existence of creeps in the field near Westdale meant that parents diligently enforced the walking group of students. Each morning, it would start a ways away from the school and slowly get bigger as it got closer to Westdale. Frankie's house was the last house on the route. When he was late coming out of the house that day, one of his friends stayed back, waiting for Frankie. Eventually, his friends had gone so far ahead that the boy decided to leave, presuming that maybe Frankie was staying home sick. After all, Frankie had left school early the previous day for illness, which let his friends and his teachers excuse his absence at school that morning.

At lunchtime, this same boy who had waited for Frankie went home for lunch. On his way back to school, not yet knowing that Frankie was missing, he saw a light-coloured cream or beige car parked at the side of the road. He would have had to walk right past it. However, with the sightings of strangers in the neighbourhood, and the recent murder of Jacqueline Dunleavy, the little boy was wary. He was scared enough that he went far out of his way, off the sidewalk and away from the road, in knee-deep snow, just so he could keep his distance from the parked car.

Hundreds of Londoners went out looking for Frankie, despite frigid temperatures. There were at least 500 volunteers, and authorities had to start turning them away because it was impossible to organize everyone. There were hundreds of leads and even more hysteria. News spread across the province. A psychic from the Toronto area even called police with the name of a suspect.

While the Jensen family desperately searched for their missing son, they received anonymous phone calls about his disappearance. One such call had asked for a ransom, but the police assured them that these were crank calls.[14]

MARCH 21, 1968. Thorndale, Ontario, is a small town just a short drive outside of London. My partner, Jason, grew up there, and even in the 1980s, there were only 500 residents. In the 1960s, it was even smaller, a tight-knit community with one main road along which was the bank, the hardware store, and the funeral parlour. Children rode their bikes up and down King Street,

---

14 It is unknown if the Dunleavy family received harassing phone calls after Jacqueline's murder, but many other families of victims did.

promising to be home for dinner, after which they promptly disappeared again to play until bedtime. Neighbours casually walked into each other's kitchens through unlocked doors. Everyone felt safe.

It was March Break, and the kids in Thorndale were all out of school. This included Scott McGregor Leishman, a sixteen-year-old who lived on Valleyview Road, just one mile from where Frankie Jensen's body would later be found. After spending the day with friends, possibly fishing, he was seen getting into a white compact car occupied by one man between 4 and 4:30 p.m. Scott was wearing a black jacket and blue jeans. It was the last anyone ever saw of him.

APRIL 7, 1968. The Bunny Bundle Canoe Race was held in the Thames River, just north of Thorndale. More than one hundred canoes registered for the race, each one containing two paddlers. More than 200 paddlers made their way south along the river, passing by the back acreage of Frank O'Shaughnessy's farm. Standing along the shore with his family to watch the race, Frank saw something in the water, halfway across the river, next to a small island that divided the current in two for a short distance. He couldn't make out what it was; maybe it was a loaf of bread or the body of a dead animal. As none of the canoers passing so closely to it took note, he put it out of his mind.

APRIL 12, 1968. Joseph Bruckbauer and Ken Mullin were enjoying a beautiful sunny Good Friday, canoeing on the northern branch of the Thames River. They were heading from St. Mary's to Fanshawe Lake, and they found themselves on the outskirts of Thorndale. As they approached the small island off the shore of O'Shaughnessy's farm, they saw something, but initially passed it by. Their curiosity got the better of them, and they turned around to investigate. Now they saw two pale naked legs floating in the water. It was Frankie Jensen. His body, caught in some discarded wire fencing, had been

Frank O'Shaughnessy points to the spot where Frankie Jensen's body was found.

London Free Press Collection of Photographic Negatives, [1968-04-13], Archives and Special Collections, Western Libraries, Western University.

in the stream since he disappeared on that blustery February day. He was clothed only in his plaid button-up and undershirt. His high green boots with yellow laces were missing — which were unlikely to have fallen off on their own — along with the rest of his clothes and personal effects. In addition to other bruises on his head, he'd been killed by blunt-force trauma caused by a hammer or tool strike to the skull. Most significantly, there was pink tissue stuffed in his mouth, just like Jacqueline Dunleavy's.

Police divers checked the river all the way up to the bridge on Plover Mills Road, from which they thought the killer may have disposed of the little boy's body. They were looking for any additional evidence, or Frankie's missing belongings, including his red lunch pail. They found many of his things along the banks of the river, while other effects may have gone with the killer as trophies.

Frankie's older brother Carston had told the London Free Press that his brother had been terrified of the river. His worst fear was drowning.

Divers search for clues in the Frankie Jensen murder.

London Free Press Collection of Photographic Negatives, [1968-04-15], Archives and Special Collections, Western Libraries, Western University.

The day they found Frankie, his parents were in a canoe with friend L.T. Anderson, searching for Frankie in a pond near their house. They had just finished for the day when a police cruiser pulled up. A London detective walked over and asked to speak to Mr. Jensen privately. Frank followed him to sit in the police cruiser, and Krista got into Anderson's car to stay warm while waiting for Frank. Anderson turned on the engine to warm up the vehicle and turned on the radio.

That was when she heard the news. The announcer said police had found a body believed to be that of Frankie Jensen.

APRIL 15, 1968. London Police told the newspaper that they didn't think the killings of Frankie Jensen and Jacqueline Dunleavy were connected, even though Jacqueline's body had been found so close to where Frankie had been abducted. It did not seem to occur to them that the killer may have spotted Frankie when revisiting the scene of the last murder, a pattern of behaviour exhibited by killers such as Ted Bundy. Returning to the scene of the abduction, the body disposal site, or inserting themselves into the investigation — like the letter-writing Zodiac killer — gives serial murderers a chance to revisit the fantasy they fulfilled through sexual homicide, and the arousal that went with it. They might call the victim's family after the killing to get the same kind of thrill. It's for this reason police officers would write down the licence plate numbers at the funerals of each victim in the London killings, because of the old maxim that criminals can't resist returning to the scene of the crime. For Jacqueline Dunleavy's killer, revisiting those feelings of lust and power may have unfortunately coincided with the sighting of a young boy, unsupervised and vulnerable.

Likewise, Scott Leishman had been picked up very close to where Frankie Jensen's body was found. Both locations were also within a mile of Canadian National Railway (CNR) tracks. Similarly, Jacqueline Dunleavy had been picked up on a route that led under a railway bridge, where she might have stood at a bus stop overlooked by a raised railway track.

In the grocery stores of the Forest City sat stacks of pink tissues and toilet paper. No one in London wanted to buy it anymore.

MAY 15, 1968. Scott Leishman's body was also found in water. However, he was found in the harbour of Port Burwell. At first, his corpse was unidentified. He had been beaten about the head, and while the killer may have thought he was dead, Scott entered the water alive and respirated while likely unconscious. He may have entered the water in the same place where Jackie English would later be found at Big Otter Creek, but the rushing current that time of year took him all the way to the harbour. His wrist-watch was missing, possibly taken as a trophy. His body had been undressed and then redressed by his killer, who messily cinched his pants by his belt but left his zipper undone.

Port Burwell was also the end point of an old CNR railway track, and the site of a bridge that had been repaired by CNR employees that spring.

There is very little information available about Scott Leishman. Perhaps the newspaper was encouraged to report on other things in order to quell the growing terror in the Forest City. It would be easier if no one clued in that there might be a connection between the terrible killings that had happened in such quick succession. In the end, Scott's mother, Elizabeth Leishman, was left with no answers. She died in 2017. Her husband, Gord, was haunted by the loss of his son and took his own life in 1978.

AUGUST 5, 1968. Thirty-one-year-old blonde Helga Beer had been divorced for a while, and was enjoying her freedom. She had a job as a wig stylist, and with her cheerful smile and care-free spirit, she had become much loved by the clientele and her co-workers. She lived with her mother and brother in an apartment at 1231 Richmond North, near the gates of Western University and very near where Doris English would later hunt for her missing daughter. The extra spending money that came with single life and independence allowed her to go out on the town, walking under neon signs up and down the main drag of the Forest City, stopping in at bars, and meeting up with friends. Her time was her own. No one could stop her from meeting new people and getting the most out of life. That's what Helga wanted: to live.

Helga Beer.

London Free Press Collection of Photographic Negatives, [1961-08-30], Archives and Special Collections, Western Libraries, Western University.

Helga was one of two women who worked at the Elizabeth Arden salon, the dedicated wig boutique in Simpson's Department Store. In 1968, hairpieces were commonly worn to achieve the enormous hairdos that were in vogue at the time. To sell the product, the stylists had to wear these elaborate styles themselves, along with accompanying makeup and fancy clothes. They were dressed to the nines every single day, like beautiful birds, and would have stuck out from the crowd walking along London's busy downtown streets.

It was a Monday night, not the best night to find a good party to be sure, especially in the sleepy Forest City, but Helga had still managed to find someone to have fun with. She took him

ABOVE: The scene where Helga Beer was found.

London Free Press Collection of Photographic Negatives, [1968-08-06], Archives and Special Collections, Western Libraries, Western University.

LEFT: Parking attendant Edward Anderson.

London Free Press Collection of Photographic Negatives, [1968-08-06], Archives and Special Collections, Western Libraries, Western University.

to her friend's apartment at her old building, 186 King Street, then called the Kingsley Building but previously known as the Jack Tar Building when it was erected. This building still stands, home to the local HIV/AIDS clinic and many unsuccessful pubs. You can still rent apartments there, too, for a very affordable price. In 1968, it was a nicer apartment building filled with young jet-setters and wannabes, conveniently located one block from the railway station. This is where Helga was last seen, shortly after midnight, when she exited her friend's place with a tall man, about five-foot-ten, with dark hair and thick eyebrows. He was in his late twenties to mid-thirties.

AUGUST 6, 1968. Around 6:20 the next morning, seventy-six-year-old parking attendant Edward Anderson noticed a car had been left in a downtown lot overnight, at the end of Carling Street, where the Bell building and Federal government building meet today. Now there's a large orange public sculpture there in a landscaped courtyard. In 1968, the attendant crossed the parking lot to Helga's 1963 blue Volkswagen Beetle to see if there was someone sleeping inside. When he saw her almost nude body in the back seat, at first he thought she was a mannequin. She was naked from the waist down, her dark green shorts and brown loafers removed, scattered in the front seat. She'd been badly beaten around the head and strangled. Horrified, the attendant called the police. The station was only a block south, at 14 King Street.

When they arrived, officers found the windows rolled up tightly, unusual in the heat of the summer. The sealed windows may have helped muffle her screams and had certainly contained the smells of sex and blood inside the car. Once they identified her, they learned that Helga was a divorcée and unattached, a frequenter of the local nightlife scene, so they didn't assume she'd been raped. They assumed she'd had sex willingly, and was murdered afterward. Indeed, there was semen on her underwear and shorts, which were discarded in the front seat, leading them to think she'd redressed herself after intercourse and subsequently had her clothes removed a second time. She still wore her bra and bright green sleeveless blouse. However, if it was a sexual homicide, her state of undress may have been purposeful, creating a tableau that would have left her looking very much like other victims of the Forest City Killer — naked from the waist down, raped, strangled, lying on their backs. Helga was also in a Volkswagen Beetle, a vehicle that would show up again in the story of the Forest City Killer. While it belonged to Helga, the car had likely been driven by the perpetrator; Helga wasn't very good at backing up in a parking spot, and so she always avoided it. The car was found in an empty parking lot with plenty of spaces to pull in nose first, yet her car was backed into a spot under the shade of a tree. A fantasy.

But Helga was kind of a slut, wasn't she? Divorced. Single. A working woman. Not a mother. They even heard she was bisexual. As a result, the *London Free Press* didn't report very much on her death. They didn't even get the story right. When they reported the news of her murder, they printed a picture of the wrong woman next to the story. The story appeared first in the evening edition, around the same time that Helga's mother and brother returned from the beach to find out she was dead, but printed a retraction and the correct image the next morning, not before traumatizing the victim's family.

The police didn't try too hard to find Helga's killer, either. It was just the natural result, some would say, of an immoral lifestyle. The deadly blows to her head, which would have produced a lot of blood, had happened outside of the vehicle. The actual crime scene would never be discovered.

There was plenty of DNA evidence at the body disposal site, but over the years, storage techniques that didn't anticipate the use of DNA to solve cases allowed the specimens to deteriorate. Today, they are unusable.

OCTOBER 20, 1969. After Jackie English's body was discovered, London's City Council decided to offer a reward for information leading to an arrest in her murder. This reward began with the sum of $10,000. On the same day, the Chamber of Commerce got together and decided to join in, adding funds. By November 3, the reward had grown exponentially. Unlike many other crime-related rewards, this one did not come out of the police budget. Council voted to create a permanent fund in the city budget. The final amount that would be turned over in exchange for information leading to an arrest in Jackie's murder ended up at $50,000 — equivalent to about $300,000 today.

As Councillor Fred Gosnell told the press, "I propose that this reward not only be offered for the English murder, but for information on any of the murders we have had in the city over the past few years. We have had too many killings in this area. I have had calls from many persons and they are frightened. This is in no way to be considered against the work of our policemen, but some people will talk for enough money. We are paying top salaried policemen to work around the clock on this case, and if a reward of this amount will be of assistance, then it will be money well spent."

The $50,000 would be given to anyone who gave information leading to an arrest for murders including that of Jackie English, Jacqueline Dunleavy, and Frankie Jensen.

This award was never collected.

CHAPTER ELEVEN

THE DISAPPEARANCE OF LYNDA WHITE AND THE MURDER OF BRUCE STAPYLTON

"This case has wrung us dry."

— DETECTIVE SERGEANT LLOYD BRYSON

Lynda White was a pretty blonde freshman at the University of Western Ontario. She moved from her hometown of Burlington — a two-hour drive away — to go to school in London, as did two of her high-school chums. They opted to share a little house in the Blackfriars neighbourhood at 34 Argyle Street, which was close enough to get to classes but also walking distance from downtown night clubs and bars.

Her roommates had watched Lynda develop over the past few years, from a shy girl with dark brown hair to a more outgoing blonde. She had bleached her hair during senior year at Nelson High School, where she became a cheerleader and had dated one of the school's star athletes, Gary Daniels. Lynda was the teenage dream. Her family was close and loving. They had money. She had everything a girl could ask for. Going to university in London was her launching point, finally stretching her legs and transforming from that perfect teen girl to the perfect young woman.

Her reputation as an all-star followed her, since there were a lot of Burlington kids at Western. One of them, Pamela Freeman, went to the homecoming football game with Lynda that year. They enjoyed campus activities, sports, and flirting with football players.

NOVEMBER 13, 1968. Lynda and Pamela left the fluorescent-lit classroom where they'd been writing a French mid-term at the Huron College campus of Western University.

"Thank goodness that's over," said Lynda. "Let's go celebrate. You want to grab a drink at the Ceeps?"[15]

"No," said Pam. "I'm tired. I'm going to head home."

Lynda said goodbye to Pam and turned towards the main campus. It was about 8 p.m., and the wind had finally died down. With the clouds out of the way, Lynda could look up and see a sky full of glittering stars. The university campus was on the outskirts of the city, practically the countryside. It was a full display of the heavens, a night begging for adventure. She pulled her coat tight around her. Even without the wind, it was still just below zero and her breath glowed in the air. Her long blonde hair fell down her back and waved back and forth as she crossed Western Road to the student centre.

Her friend Jim[16] was sitting inside. She sat down to visit for a while, hoping she might find someone else to go out with. They visited, but Lynda got tired of waiting for Jim and his friend to give her a lift. She took off, hoping to find fun and friendship closer to home. Jim said he saw her get into a blue Volkswagen. He assumed she was hitching a ride, and so the story was later established in the press that Lynda disappeared after hitchhiking.

This was the narrative of Lynda's disappearance until criminologist Michael Arntfield re-examined the case. He found a new witness who said he knew Lynda and had driven her in the blue

---

15 The "Ceeps" is the Canadian Pacific Railway (CPR) hotel bar in downtown London. It is a frequent and somewhat legendary watering hole for Western students.

16 Jim's last name is unknown.

Volkswagen. Perhaps he had not come forward in 1968 out of fear. The driver of the Volkswagen was a fellow student. He and his roommate, who had given Lynda rides regularly, dropped her off at her usual spot near Saunby Street, close to the intersection of Wharncliffe and Oxford. He assumed Lynda lived where he had let her out, but that wasn't where Lynda lived. It was actually closer to the house of her tutor, whom she visited at least once a week. If she was heading to her tutor's house, she never made it, or perhaps her tutor was not home.

It is my belief that she would have then walked up to Gunn Street along the west bank of the river. From there, she may have headed south to cross Oxford Street via a small dark tunnel. Her house was only a block away, but she never made it. Instead, she disappeared somewhere near the bramble and woods surrounding the abandoned Saunby Mill on the riverbank that she walked so near to — today the site of a private school and some new townhouses. At the time, there was the ramshackle old industrial building, not torn down until the 1980s. Stretching overhead, passing trains would rattle by on the dark railway bridge.

Friends of Lynda White gather at her home at 34 Argyle Street.

When Lynda didn't come home before they went to bed, her roommates assumed she had gone out to a bar after her exam. But the next morning, when they discovered that Lynda hadn't come home at all, they were worried. So roommate Ann Hall called Lynda's brother, John, in Burlington, and he got in the car and came to London right away to look for his sister. His parents soon followed. They did not call the police immediately, as they knew law enforcement would not take notice of a missing person who hadn't been gone for at least forty-eight hours.

NOVEMBER 15, 1968. With Lynda missing for two days, civilian search parties combed the Western campus and surrounding areas: the river, the neighbourhood near her home, alleyways, and backyards. Lynda's father, Jack, a mining engineer, walked down by the Thames River, hoping to find some sign of his daughter. His children saw him walking along, pushing branches into the mud on the banks, tears rolling down his face, hoping to find some sign of her.

Someone told John that his sister had been spotted at the train station. He hurried to get there just as the train was boarding for the journey east towards Toronto. He frantically questioned fellow passengers and staff, until someone said they had seen a young woman with long blonde hair matching Lynda's description. She had just gotten on the train. In a flash, John jumped on the passenger car without a ticket. He walked from one end of the train to the other, opening car doors, walking the aisles, and looking at each person's face. Lynda wasn't there, and as the train pulled out of the station, he leapt from the locomotive to land precariously next to the tracks.

Lynda's friends and family went back to the house to take another look in her room. This time, they found something new. Her clothes were messily and mysteriously tucked under her bed. She was a tidy girl, and it was unlike her. Pamela Freeman confirmed that it was the same outfit Lynda had worn to the exam on November 13, the last time she saw her. Did they miss these clothes the first time they had searched Lynda's room? How did the clothes get there? They had all been out searching — no one had seen anyone come into the house. And yet . . . Ann and her roommate were sure those clothes had not been there before.

Officially terrified, John finally reported his sister's disappearance to police. They assured him that she had probably just taken off for a few days to blow off some steam after exams. The police assumed the bunched-up clothes indicated that Lynda had come home, gotten changed, and headed out for a night of drinking. You could only imagine the trouble a girl like that had gotten herself into. She was probably somewhere, just fine, recovering from the stress of exams, smoking some reefer in the back of a minibus.

Rumours abounded. Some people thought Lynda had been kidnapped because of her good looks and forced into sex trafficking. Other people swore they saw her out of town, at music festivals and with hippies, even though anyone who knew Lynda could tell you "she wasn't a flower child" as lawyer Bill Dunlop, a childhood friend of Lynda's, told the *Hamilton Spectator* in 1998. "She was more the prom queen type. She was wholesome and well-rounded, not a hippie."

Three years later, a construction worker was digging the foundation for a new animal hospital on Fairview Street in Burlington when he found Lynda White's wallet. It contained her driver's licence, social insurance card, birth certificate, and high-school boyfriend's photo. The area was now a landfill, but underneath used to be an old lover's lane that had been used in 1968 by many young couples. Police excavated the site, only to be told that Lynda had thrown the wallet out before she moved to London and had gotten a replacement. The lead turned out to be a red herring. Soil tests confirmed that the wallet had probably been carried in with landfill from other sites in the Burlington area. However, you still have to wonder why anyone would throw out an entire wallet, complete with old identification.

JUNE 7, 1969. When eleven-year-old Bruce Stapylton headed out at 10 a.m. on Saturday, his stepdad was not worried. Of course, he didn't have much time to be. A single dad, Mike worked at the Plaza Hardware store and had a lot of kids to take care of. He'd been married twice, but each of his wives had died, leaving him to care for both his biological children and stepchildren. Much to Mike's relief, young Bruce was self-sufficient, an outdoors kid who loved camping and who often disappeared with his gear to spend a night under the stars. He was known to leave his home at 455 Piccadilly, walk past the school he attended — St. George — and camp in the woods behind St. Peter's Seminary, at the end of the Old North subdivision in a place called William's Creek.

Some kids he knew told police that they saw him by Carruthers Field at Pall Mall Street and Colborne Street around 4:30 p.m. that day. This put Bruce, like other victims of Forest City Killer, near train tracks the last time anyone saw him alive.

SEPTEMBER 23, 1969. Bruce Stapylton's remains were found about four miles north of his home at the southwest corner of Adelaide Street and Sunningdale Road, on property owned by the Pocock family. There's a gas station there now, and his body lay approximately where the gas pumps are today. This area is currently populated with new subdivisions in the growing north end of the Forest City. If you follow the road east, it ends at Fanshawe Dam, where another possible victim of the Forest City Killer would later be found. If you jog one concession north, you'll hit Medway

Road, which takes you directly into Thorndale, where Frankie Jensen was found and from where Scott Leishman was taken.

As with Scott Leishman, it's hard to find information about Bruce. The newspaper did not report on his disappearance or any search for him, although large searches apparently did take place but were only mentioned in reports much later, when his body was found. The press also reported, incorrectly, that there did not seem to be signs of foul play. This directly contradicts information released later that Bruce was killed by blunt-force trauma to the head with an object that may have been a brick. His body was skeletal, and there were remains of clothing found near the body, but he had been torn apart by animals. He was decapitated, possibly by the elements and scavengers. One of his shoes was missing.

Considering the bizarre nature of this media "mis-coverage" compared to the other city killings, is it possible that the newspaper was pressured by city police to downplay the boy's abduction? Perhaps they did not want to contribute to more panic among Londoners.

Bruce's murder may not be connected to the Forest City Killer. There is another viable suspect, convicted pedophile Robert Hall, who lived near the Stapyltons. His backyard connected to a field where kids played. He also used camping trips, Bruce's favourite activity, to lure some of his victims to sexually assault. Like the prime Forest City Killer suspects, he also owned interesting cars, including an Amphicar that worked on land and turned into a boat in the water, which caught the attention of potential prey. Additionally, Robert Hall is not known to have murdered anyone, but in 2010 and 2011, he was convicted of abusing the boys in his neighbourhood.

There are also strong cases for two other suspects in the murders of Frankie Jensen, Scott Leishman, and Bruce Stapylton.

These three killings have traditionally been grouped together over the years by sleuths and professionals alike, as they were all young boys and in theory were attractive to a different predator than the killer of young women in the city. As you know, I disagree with this theory. However, the generally accepted main suspects for these murders are referred to in Michael Arntfield's book *Murder City*, where he theorizes that the two suspects knew each other, and one taught the other as a kind of demented mentor.

The first he calls "The Neighbour." This is certainly the man that Detective Alsop believed committed the murder of Frankie Jensen, as illustrated by his notes. This individual avoided interrogation by self-commitment to psychiatric institutions and by jumping from jurisdiction to jurisdiction to continue his predatory efforts. There are several unsolved Toronto murders that could be linked to him, also involving young boys. Arntfield leaves him unnamed out of respect for the Jensen family and their wishes. I know his name, but out of the same respect, I'll leave it out here.

The other suspect is Robert Bridgewater, also known as Robert Henderson. He is currently incarcerated for the 1989 murder of Jason Franklin, who was also found in the waters of Big Otter Creek.

Arntfield goes into further depth about these suspects in his book. I have not done so here, as I'm focusing on the killer of Jackie English, the Forest City Killer, and I don't believe either of these men murdered her. Bridgewater, I understand, was indisposed during the time of her death, and the Neighbour had a specific predilection for young boys. As far as I can discover, their DNA has not been tested against that found at the crime scenes of the three boys.[17] I've included Bridgewater and the

---

17 However, Michael Arntfield and I are in agreement that the Neighbour's name should be revealed, his grave exhumed, and his DNA tested against that found at the scenes of these crimes, as well as those in the Toronto area.

Neighbour here to acknowledge them as viable suspects in the murders of Frankie, Scott, and Bruce; however, it is my personal theory that these boys were victims of the Forest City Killer. The proximity of the date of Bruce's murder to that of Jackie English's and the location of his body's disposal being so close to Thorndale, a significant location for the Forest City Killer, makes his case impossible to ignore in connection to the other deaths, especially as this killer had possibly hunted in a spree of three murders just the year before. It wouldn't be implausible for him to hunt in a spree again, killing young Bruce before he went on to kill Jackie English, and then terrorizing a third woman we have yet to discuss.

If you take away the issue of victimology — the idea that all of the victims must have common traits — many pieces of the puzzle fit together in regards to the modus operandi evident in these crimes to tell us that all of these killings were committed by the same person or persons. All of the deaths involved blunt-force trauma and/or strangulation. All of them involved a vehicle and transporting the victim from one location to another. All of them took place outside. All of them were sexual in nature. In the cases of Dunleavy, Jensen, and Leishman, the locations of abduction and body disposal connect together directly on the map, demonstrating a relationship between body disposal sites and abduction sites. Other locations connect later on in theme if not direct correlation: proximity to railway tracks, historic graveyards, and the body of water that forms Big Otter Creek, and the Thames River. The victims' personal effects were taken as trophies or spread out as they were discarded. For Dunleavy and Jensen, there is the obvious connection of the pink tissue stuffed in their throats, which Arntfield considers a copycat move. I would disagree. I think it's the same person, or pair of criminals, picking children and young adults off the streets, re-enacting a sick fantasy again and again with variations, experiments, and alterations of behaviour based on convenience.

OCTOBER 1, 1969. Just three days before Jackie English was abducted and almost one year after Lynda White's disappearance, the *London Free Press* ran an article entitled "The Two Faces of Lynda White." The article showed side-by-side photographs of Lynda, one with her blonde hair and one with short brown hair before she had bleached it. In the photo where she appears as a brunette, she looks very much like Jackie English. If the Forest City Killer was tracking his murders through the press, he would have seen this article.

Police asserted that they had done everything they could to find Lynda White, and that she'd probably taken off. They compared her to a girl who had run away with her boyfriend in 1965 and remained unfound, who they said, "is probably married and raising a family by now."

Any excuse was used to explain Lynda's absence except for abduction and murder. Law enforcement officials interviewed even referred to "white slavery." They put forward rumours that Lynda had complained about school, and that she was probably still alive.

Her parents hired two private investigators to track her down.

After Jackie English's body was discovered the fall of 1969, City Council found itself launched into debates about hitchhiking. There was already a law that said hitchhikers had to stay on the shoulder of the road, so they wouldn't impede traffic, but should hitching rides be banned altogether within city limits?

"I don't think banning hitchhiking is going to stop people from going out and raping people and murdering people," observed university student Gary Cwitco.

This debate would permeate governing bodies throughout North America in the 1970s, as predators used hitchhiking culture to capture their prey. Today, hitchhiking is seen as a

highly dangerous activity, the result of successful public awareness campaigns to stop people from thumbing rides. However,
in 1969, it was pretty normal to catch a lift from a stranger to get
to where you were going. The idea that hitching was dangerous
seemed new to Londoners, including Joe Halford, the manager
of the Metropolitan Store, who was confronted with questions
about the safety of his staff following Jackie English's murder.
Didn't he make sure these women had a ride home? How could
he just send a youngster out into the night like that? Halford
dismissed responsibility, throwing the target on the back of the
London Transit Commission. The closest bus stop, he pointed
out, was one kilometre away, at the corner of Wellington Road
and Exeter Road, on the other side of the overpass. Even after the
trek, service was so sparse that it meant long waits in the dark.
The problem was with the bus system, not with him.

OCTOBER 10, 1969. The General Manager of the London Transit
Commission, C.K. Morningstar, said he didn't think there was a
connection between poor bus service and hitchhiking and went
so far as to suggest that people would keep thumbing rides even
if the bus service was stellar.

This point of view was suspect, considering that just the year
before, Morningstar had altered a bus route precisely because
there *was* a correlation between poor bus service and taking rides
from strangers. Community outcry led to the extension of the 2
Dundas route up Wharncliffe Road to Western Road, towards
the university, where the public believed that Lynda White had
hitched a ride before she went missing. It is currently one of the
most popular routes in the city, and the university students who
ride it with prepaid passes have no idea that its existence was
predicated on a murder.

CHAPTER TWELVE

WELCOME TO STANLEY VARIETY

*"Not one member of the London police force is
qualified to carry out a homicide investigation."*

— GORDON WALKER, CITY ALDERMAN

JANUARY 10, 1968. Joe Clarke said that as soon as two police detectives walked into Stanley Variety, his store where Jacqueline Dunleavy had worked, he knew she was dead. He'd heard reports on the radio earlier, he explained, saying that a young woman had been murdered.

A small, smarmy sort of fellow, Joe said to reporters that Jacqueline "was an extremely pleasant girl, well mannered, and not the type to get into trouble. When she was leaving last night, I asked her when she would be back. She said, 'You have me marked down for Thursday night,' and that's the last words she said to me. It was so busy when she left here, I didn't notice whether or not she got on a bus. I paid her last Saturday and she and a friend walked out of here happy as can be."

Joe Clarke lived above the store, as did other single men who rented from him. At the time of Jacqueline Dunleavy's death, Clarke and his tenant were both without a car. Just weeks after the murder, Stanley Variety was put up for sale. Joe left town in the middle of the night and was never seen again. A family

Joe Clarke stands in front of Stanley Variety.

London Free Press Collection of Photographic Negatives, [1968-01-10], Archives and Special Collections, Western Libraries, Western University.

remember reportedly visited him at the psychiatric ward in St. Thomas, but his residency there is not confirmed.

It's surprising that Constable Dunleavy let his daughter work for Joe, if he knew what was going on at the store. Somehow, the rumour mill on the police force about the goings-on at Stanley Variety didn't reach him, or he chose to ignore the stories. The shop was a hotbed for the local black market, filled with oddball stolen items that were sold to Joe for cheap resale by many of the city's most marginal characters.

There were other things happening at Stanley Variety, too. I was chatting with a customer at my bookstore — a parole officer — about Hotel London when he started to tell me a story about a memorable night he had at the West End bar, which was located in the old hotel. He and a friend met a show-off who boasted that he knew of a place where they could see smut films. The three young fellows, in hopes of seeing some bare boobs, walked across downtown until they got to the Stanley Variety store.

They knocked on the back door that led to the basement. Joe Clarke answered the knock, but he wouldn't let them inside. He didn't know them, my customer recalled, and they didn't know the password. Each week there was a different password to get in.

He told me this story while having no idea that I was working on this book, so I had to keep my jaw from dropping. He was the second person to tell me about the existence of this smut theatre, after galaxygirl, a regular poster on the Unsolved Canada forum. She is considered a credible source by many amateur sleuths who work to solve these cases.

The entrance to the Stanley Variety porn clubhouse in the basement was around the side at the back. You can still see the door today, boarded up, where Joe's clientele would descend into darkness and indulge in a bright screen depicting all kinds of debauchery. Because the entrance was outside, Jacqueline wouldn't have been involved in these activities directly. The perverts would have only seen her when buying cigarettes at the counter inside, where she had been working since late 1967. She charmed the regulars, many of them sexual deviants and criminals. She quickly became well liked on her regular Tuesday and Thursday shifts from 3:30 to 6 p.m.

Most of what we know about Stanley Variety is based on oral history and stories passed down over the past fifty years. Chatter on Unsolved Canada tells us that Joe Clarke was homosexual. He started hiring young women like Jacqueline because people grew suspicious of him hiring teenage boys. One of the first two female employees he had hired posted in the Unsolved Canada forum that she and her sister were once offered a ride by one of the shop regulars. She sat in the passenger seat, her sister in the back, as the man pulled out his penis and masturbated. Silent, she didn't know what to say and agonizingly waited until the ride was over and he let them out of the car. There is no record of Jacqueline Dunleavy experiencing anything like this before the night of her death, but she had only worked there for a few months before she disappeared. Still, the story paints a picture of what it was like around this little shop filled with stolen goods and sexual predators.

According to Michael Arntfield's book *Murder City*, one of the regulars at Stanley Variety was Robert Masters. He was twenty years old at the time of Jacqueline Dunleavy's murder. However, at the age of only thirteen he had murdered Sylvia Fink, a seven-year-old girl from his neighbourhood.

NOVEMBER 13, 1961. Sylvia Fink lived with her family on Princess Avenue just east of Adelaide Street. Their home was in what is now called Old East Village or "EOA," at the time a working-class neighbourhood that falls just east of Adelaide. Now a trendy neighbourhood, it was once known as one of London's rougher areas. Around 4:15 p.m., Sylvia's mother sent her with seven cents to go get a newspaper. On the way to the store, Sylvia stopped and asked a friend to join her on the errand, but the little girl refused. Sylvia had been looking for a playmate, which may have made her vulnerable to what happened next. The storekeeper saw her at 4:20 p.m. and told her that the evening edition of the newspaper had not yet been delivered. Sylvia asked him to save one for her and left.

She never came home.

At 5 p.m., Sylvia's worried mother went to the variety store, only to discover that her child had been and gone and was nowhere to be found.

The neighbours got together immediately and started looking for her. At 8 p.m., three men found her in the third-floor attic of an abandoned grocery store at Princess Avenue and Adelaide Street, only five doors down from where she lived. It was an isolated spot where kids liked to play. The children had even improvised play equipment out of the junk and wires hanging around. Hidden among the debris, behind two storm windows, they found Sylvia, with the coins her mother had given her scattered at her feet.

The little girl had been strangled by the belt from her own coat. Then, she had been positioned prostrate on the floor, face down, in the alcove. Robert Masters had secured the belt around a telephone cord above her and gazed at her corpse, dangling by her neck, as he masturbated. Afterwards, he hid her body, her shoes placed neatly beside her. There were bruises on her body, but she was fully clothed. Perhaps she had been nude and he redressed her.

A few days later, thirteen-year-old Robert Masters confessed to his parents and minister that he had killed little Sylvia Fink. Awaiting trial, he was sent to the London Psychiatric Hospital for assessment and treatment.[18] Masters was found guilty of manslaughter in January 1962. He had confessed to detectives and a minister, in the presence of his parents, and the case was otherwise built on circumstantial evidence. Judge Fox, who presided, wasn't sure that Masters had intended to kill little Sylvia. He called it "something less than murder."

The newspaper reported that throughout the court hearings, Masters had maintained a belligerent air of persecution.

"Don't you think you need help?" asked Judge Fox.

Still the tough guy, Masters nevertheless began to cry. "No."

"I disagree," said Judge Fox. "You think everyone is against you. No one in this court is against you."

"You want to make a bet?" retorted Masters.

"Everyone in this court," said Fox, "and I think I'm safe in saying Mr. and Mrs. Fink, wants to help you. But I'm satisfied I would not be helping you if I let you return to your home."

Masters spent four and a half years in rehabilitation at the Ontario Training School in Bowmanville. After his release in 1966, he returned to London, Ontario, where he married Patricia

---

18 His lawyer was William R. Poole, a famed litigator in the Forest City, whose wife was art critic Nancy Poole.

Masters and took a job as a hospital orderly. Even after rehabilitation and marriage, he couldn't resist his deviant urges.

———————

DECEMBER 13, 1969. He was sentenced to two years in a reformatory after attacking a woman on August 17 and another on September 3. His lawyer defended him by virtue of his mental illness. A psychological report ordered by police and reported on in the newspaper stated that Masters had "a very serious personality disturbance with a very dangerous future potential . . . we are going to see much more intense, violent activity from him." The report also said that he had a pathological infatuation with violence, meaning that hurting women turned him on. The Bowmanville school had not been able to help him.

The judge made some enlightening statements in reply to the defence:

> You're going to have to wait some little time . . . because at the present time the correctional institutions in the province of Ontario have no avenue open for the treatment of this man. The only psychiatric treatment they give is to pedophiles and there is no psychiatric treatment open to this person in penitentiary. It is simply a question of incarcerating this man for a period of time in the hope that in the meantime something may become available to him . . . All I'm doing is putting this man away. He's potentially dangerous.

———————

Even though Jacqueline Dunleavy, Frankie Jensen, Scott Leishman, Helga Beer, and Bruce Stapylton had already been murdered by the Forest City Killer, it wasn't until Jackie English died that there seemed to be a public outcry for a reckoning. An editorial in the *London Free Press* read:

> [English's] murder tells police that they may be dealing with one or more sex killers in London and Western Ontario . . . a girl on Oxford Street, another in a Carling Street parking lot, young boys in two incidents, a girl in Aylmer . . . the list is long.
>
> A few such murders could have been isolated incidents; now there are far too many to continue that assumption . . .
>
> The warning which will sound loudest to the community over this death . . . and make no mistake, there will be more such tragedies.
>
> There have been far too many sex-oriented deaths in London.

Jackie English's death had lit a spark. While Londoners didn't like to talk about unpleasant things, even people outside of the city had begun to pay attention to the rash of murders taking place. News of London's escalating sexual homicides became an international story, covered in the *Detroit News* on Sunday, October 26, 1969, by Joseph E. Wolff. He listed even more crimes from the Forest City, at the time unsolved, which created a frighteningly long list of the dead, in a place "where fears mount with the discovery of each new victim."

> There are similarities in some of the murders, but not enough for investigators to commit themselves publicly to the theory of one killer. But the fact that there have been so many murders in so short a time has alarmed this peaceful community and stirred its residents to take precaution . . .

The mystery murders began on the snowy evening of Jan. 9, 1968, when the body of Jacqueline Dunleavy, 16-year-old daughter of a London policeman, was found . . . One month later to the day, nine-year-old Frankie Jensen left his home at 8:10 a.m. for Westdale Public School where he was in the fourth grade. His partially nude body was found April 12, 1968 . . . Scott Leishman, 16, of nearby Thorndale, disappeared on March 21, 1968. His body was recovered two months later . . . On Aug. 6, 1968, the strangled and partially nude body of Mrs. Helga Beer, a London hairdresser, was found in her car . . .

Miss White's disappearance [on Nov. 13, 1968] was the next mystery for London police . . . On Feb. 3, 1969, Mrs. Jane Wooley, 62,[19] was found nude and beaten to death in her London apartment . . . Patricia Ann Bovin,[20] 22, a mother of two, was found in her apartment, a short distance from Mrs. Wooley's home, last April 24 . . . The body of Bruce Stapylton, 11, was found in a wooded lot on the outskirts of London on Sept. 23 . . .

Miss English, the latest victim, was last seen on Oct. 4 . . .

To the *London Free Press*, London Police Chief Finlay Carroll finally admitted: "There seems to be a pattern in some of the deaths. I now almost have to come to the conclusion that there could be a connection between some of them."

---

19 Jane Wooley was murdered by Gerald Thomas Archer.

20 Patricia Ann Bovin's murder, still officially unsolved, correlates with the murder of Victoria Mayo, to which a man named Sandor Fulep confessed. Fulep's DNA was posthumously matched with evidence from the Mayo crime scene.

CHAPTER THIRTEEN

DETECTIVE ALSOP INVESTIGATES

"We are fighting something that is evil."

— WILLIAM HAGARTY, CITY ALDERMAN

The Alsop family attended St. John the Divine on Baseline Road, a boxy brick house of worship. The four Alsop kids squirmed in their church clothes, standing up and sitting down and crossing their chests as the service progressed. They rose in a tidy line to take Communion and followed along with the liturgy. When the priest gave the final blessing, they couldn't wait to get out of there, go home, and enjoy the last hours of their weekend. Dennis Jr. remembers those mornings.

"We went to Mass every Sunday. That was a must. They were very religious people, my father more so than my mother, but they always went to church.

"In 1969, when all these things were happening, I can still remember at church, Mass is over and Father's still sitting there praying. He takes ten minutes, and we all want to get out of there. We want to go get breakfast, let's get going. And he's sitting there. I thought, 'I don't know what the man's been up to, but he must be a bad sinner.'

"But he wasn't praying for himself. This was his way of coping."

OCTOBER 10, 1969. After the discovery of Jackie's body in Big Otter Creek, her remains were first taken to the hospital in Tillsonburg, where they were examined by the aforementioned pathologist. In the 1960s, most coroners had not been trained in forensic examination, and this one was no exception. The distinction is important. Only a forensic pathologist understands specific elements of a post-mortem examination that can lead to an arrest. Types of evidence that are vital to solving a murder case can be irreparably destroyed or mangled by the wrong kind of exam, and these significant findings often make or break a conviction. There is no way to know how the Tillsonburg pathologist's initial assessment of Jackie's body changed the way Alsop's investigation played out. The OPP wisely sought out another examination in Toronto at the Forensic Centre; however, the opportunity to have a first, untainted look at the body had already passed.

Her cause of death was determined to be a blow to both the top and the back of her head. These blows would have caused a huge amount of bleeding. Police told Walter English that whatever hit his daughter was an edged instrument shaped like a "J" — perhaps a crowbar or tire iron.

Even though she had been missing for almost a week, in photos of the crime scene,[21] Jackie's body appears to have been dead for less than a day and not in the water for very long. It was as though she had been killed and carefully placed in the creek, posed, just a few hours before she was discovered there. Her body had no signs of captivity: ligature marks, bruising, or signs of starvation or dehydration. While there was speculation that she'd been tossed over the side of the bridge, post-mortem bruising didn't indicate strongly a fall from that height, and her supine pose was not one that likely happened accidentally. If you stand on the bridge and look down, you'll see that it's a big drop over shallow water, one

---

21 Photographs of the crime scene are not included in this book out of respect for the victim's family.

that would surely break your leg if you jumped. Anyone jumping off, or being thrown from above, would land in a jumbled heap.

So, if she had not been in the water for longer than forty-eight hours, when was she killed and where? What had happened in those five days?

I cannot access the coroner's report, and despite multiple requests, her family has been unable to gain access to it; thus, I can only go by the information at hand. Beyond the possibility that the cool, flowing waters of Big Otter Creek and lying on her back in a shaded position beneath the bridge slowed the rate of decomposition, Agnes Murray's account of not recognizing Jackie because of distortion in her face confirms what my sources tell me, which is that she had been in the water for a few days. Therefore, her head, which had been submerged while her torso floated, may have betrayed marks from a beating that were not visible in the photographs. The Tillsonburg pathologist's reports to the media that there were no other wounds or marks on Jackie's body vastly differ from the OPP officers' reports that Jackie had been the "victim of a vicious beating."

The pathologist's personal observation to Agnes Murray about Jackie's apparently absent virginity contrasted with his statements to the press that there was no immediate sign of sexual penetration. Inside her vagina was semen, correlated with Type-O blood. This was the same type as that of Jackie' boyfriend, David Papple. Semen can live in the body for up to five days after intercourse, so it is feasible that the semen belonged to Papple. He told police (at the time) that he'd had sex with Jackie on the afternoon of October 4, the day she disappeared, so they assumed the fluids had come from him.

None of her personal effects were found nearby except for her earrings, which floated in the water close to her. There was no blood found around her body, none on the sides of the creekbed, none in the bed of the forest surrounding the area. They knew she had been killed somewhere else and then brought to the disposal site. With the London Police force's regionally famous dog, Arab,[22] officials tried to find some evidence of a crime scene. They didn't find anything — not a scrap of clothing, not a weapon, not a drop of blood.

Since finding Jackie, most of the men hadn't slept for days, including Detective Alsop, who after a week had not yet managed to go home. They went farm to farm for miles around, interviewing every person they could. They used a helicopter to search the fields.

Only one mile away was a set of CNR railway tracks.

OCTOBER 13, 1969. Police found Jackie's violently ripped and discarded clothing only a short drive away, along one side of Culloden Road.[23] Strewn along the roadside were her white work

McBride and Alsop visit the scene where Jackie English was found.

---

22 Arab often served as a tool to garner positive publicity and support for law enforcement in the local press, a mascot of sorts.

23 County Road 46 near the village of Richmond in Bayham Township.

uniform with the orange stripes down the front, her bra, her panty-hose, and the bottom half of her dress, black with big white checks. Her underwear contained a sample of semen that did not match that found in her vaginal cavity. However, I could not determine if it was a different blood type or a different DNA profile. It's possible that both the semen in her panties and inside her vagina were the same blood type but belonged to two different people, and that this differentiation was only found through police examination decades later. It's also possible that the blood type of the second sample could not be determined, an issue of science that we will discuss later.

OCTOBER 18, 1969. A *London Free Press* editorial demanded action. Citizens of the Forest City knew — but would never admit — that they lived in a place where an uncommonly high number of sexual homicides were taking place:

> Too many children have been murdered in and around this city. It's certain that three children have died at the hands of one or more sex-mad killers . . . It could have happened that five persons chose this city to kill so many in two years. But it's unlikely. It's unreasonable to insist that it just happened that way in London . . . [There is] a curious and striking relationship between pickup points and where bodies were found . . . What does it mean? No one knows. But London may have a vicious murderer in its midst.
>
> At the moment, no parent in the city can feel secure that his child will get to school, to a downtown swimming pool, or to a movie . . . and back . . . safely. No one knows whose child may be next.
>
> It's easy to give advice when you don't have to do the work, but the *Free Press* feels it is time greater priority is given to the single killer theory.

Young people dance at All Saints Church, raising money to investigate the unsolved murders of young people in London.

London Free Press Collection of Photographic Negatives, [1969-10-31], Archives and Special Collections, Western Libraries, Western University.

Letters to the editor were plentiful.

Brent Bulani wrote, "Let us pray that Jacqueline English did not die in vain. These murders are much like threads. They begin to form a pattern which will one day unravel, and until that day — these threads will bind us together as one family and one closely knit home."

Mrs. D.E. Gartley wrote, "Are we going to have to face a Kitty Genovese case in London before we shake our apathy?"[24]

J.H. Peters wrote: "The people of London are wondering who the next victim will be."

---

24 Kitty Genovese was murdered on March 13, 1964, in New York City. The case became a notorious example of bystander effect, meaning a bad situation where people stand by and do nothing to help. While the story was later proven to be an untrue narrative created by the media, the general public believed that thirty-eight people had witnessed the attack and none of them had called the police or otherwise tried to intervene.

The most poignant letter to the editor was penned by Doris English while she was in the psychiatric ward and published in the *London Free Press* on October 22, 1969.

> What does it take to wake a city up? Does everyone shut their eyes to those who don't belong to them? Someone, somewhere had to notice Jackie getting into a car and they had to notice which way it went. Just suppose it was your daughter. I was in hospital and other people were there picking up their young ones.
>
> I have a small dig to throw the [police's] way. When a mother reports her child missing then, immediately, notice should be given over the radio, and every means used to draw this person to the public attention. This should be kept almost constantly before the public. Someone would see them. The police are not lazy workers and if they had a thousand tips, they would check them all out, until they had the answer or looked for something new.
>
> I have just read your article regarding "the murder [sic] in our midst" in the Saturday, October 18, edition. I feel free to write some answer, as the latest victim is my 15-year-old daughter. Here was one of the sweetest, most considerate, selfless persons one could find (not because she was my daughter, but because she loved people without any reservation). After 15 years — they were tough for her and us — she never complained. She took on two extra jobs to clothe her brother and herself and she did a fine job. Now my baby is gone forever.
>
> Some person is probably gloating and laughing to himself knowing how well he has fooled my

child, her parents, the many police. I am a staunch believer in Jesus Christ and I pray and ask fervently that God in his own time and fashion will repay this man a thousand fold for the anguish he has caused. May God show some mercy on him. He must realize he is too ill to be with human beings.

To the public, please let's start now — be a lot more observant, more attentive, copy licences down, see what direction they head. The police sometimes get impatient and short with you, but it could return a young happy person. Please God and Mr. Editor, impress upon people to keep their eyes wide open, be very, very observant, especially of women. Let's catch this maniac, before he catches and crucifies more daughters or sons. The police can't see everything but if they know about something they certainly can check it. Keep missing person bulletins on the radio, and bulletins on the TV. Keep it fresh and hard in front of everyone's face and thought. Murders are too frequent here, but people don't give a damn unless it's their own. Force it on their attention.

I must close. Please Mr. Editor, take this and write it the way it should be. I loved my daughter dearly. — Mrs. Doris English

OCTOBER 25, 1969. At the behest of city councillor Fred Gosnell, the *London Free Press* began a new program called Hidden Witness. The idea was that Londoners could share information anonymously. All they had to do was write down an eight-digit number twice on a piece of paper. They kept half and sent the other half along with their letter to the newspaper. If the information led to an arrest and the reward that city council had approved, they could come forward to claim their money with their half of the secret number. At the time, the amount of money was $10,000. The newspaper went so far as to distribute Hidden Witness forms to more than 15,000 students in London schools.

The police were working hard to find Jackie's killer. Perhaps they were getting too close. What happened next may have been a tactic of diversion.

OCTOBER 26, 1969. Joseph Varnagy took a walk in Wortley Village with his three-year-old son. Wortley, as it is often called by Londoners, is a quaint part of Old South, with its own charming main street, grocery store, and neighbourhood pub. The houses are old, brick, and large, and enormous trees shade the sidewalks that have been warped by time. On this day, Varnagy could tell a rainstorm was coming. He and his son walked by the historic Normal School, a landmark red brick Victorian building in the middle of the neighbourhood. At the time, it housed the Board of Education. The Normal School stood on one end of a large green space that took up a whole block, where people walked their dogs and children played tag. It was the perfect place for his boy to get some exercise.

They were heading home to 17 Elmwood Ave when Varnagy spotted a couple of colouring pencils on the ground. Being a thrifty dad, he picked them up to take them home for his son to use.

As they approached the house, he turned them over in his hands. The classic red Laurentian pencil crayon had a white field where someone could write their name. In red ink were the words "Jacqueline English."

He grabbed his son and rushed inside to call the police.

A detective came right away to see what Varnagy had found. There were two pencils, the red one and a light blue Sabra pencil with no name on it.

Detective Alsop joined a team of investigators to comb the area. He noted all the items uncovered around the Normal

School, which had presumably been the contents of Jackie's purse: the red and blue pencil crayons, a bottle of Tabu perfume, and a cosmetics case.

From the vantage point of the Normal School, Alsop could see the house where Jackie used to live on Elmwood Ave. This meant one of two things: either the killer had been watching her for some time or he thought he knew where she lived and somehow got her old address instead of her current one. The English family was not listed in the phone book. No matter what, the Forest City Killer was playing games. A cat-and-mouse game.

There was still no sign of Jackie's coat, purse, or the top half of her dress.

Alsop turned to the media to help find the missing items, publishing images of a coat like the one Jackie had worn, as well as illustrations of her purse, drawn by *London Free Press* artist Rita O'Brien.

Calls came in. There were leads. He got in the cruiser and went out to interview the people who had called in the most promising tips. For each one, he sat at his desk and made a report. It all led to nothing.

DECEMBER 29, 1969. It was snowing badly, but for some reason two teenage girls were out walking near Kilally Road in London's north end, alone. They noticed a brown car parked down by the riverbed, but didn't see anyone around. Then, as they continued their trek, a man came up behind them. He was in his late twenties with dark hair. He passed by, but as soon as he got ahead, he turned around and said something to them, described by the *London Free Press* as an "indecent proposal."

He hit one of them in the mouth, knocking her down, and grabbed the other by the arm. They fought back, screaming, until he gave up and ran away. When they got home, they called the police.

Walter English died in the spring of 1970 at the Henderson Hospital in Hamilton. Anne had not returned to visit him there since she left in October 1969 to look for her sister. Walter had gone to London for Christmas with Anne and Fred, but they had not spent very much time together.

The truth about her dad was right in front of her; she just couldn't see it. Maybe the idea of another loss was just too much for her to take. An ambulance pulled up to take him back to the hospital after the holidays, and Anne joked irreverently, "Sheesh, people would think you were sick or something."

Now, looking back, she sees how terrible it must have been for her father to have lost his daughter, to be hospitalized, dying, and no one seemed to care. His estranged wife was locked away in the psychiatric ward, and his children were trying to survive in the wake of a tragedy. He was alone and unable to do anything for himself or anyone else.

The kids were with him when he passed on. The last thing Anne said to him was, "Look for Jackie, Dad."

CHAPTER FOURTEEN

SIGHTINGS OF JACKIE ENGLISH

*"Weeks after the duck hunters made their grim find,
a small office at the London OPP detachment where
the murder-teams operate still bustles."*

— BILL MCGUIRE, THE *LONDON FREE PRESS*

There were sightings of Jackie in the days and weeks leading up to her disappearance. Each witness had to be interviewed. Somewhere, Alsop was sure, he'd uncover a clue.

OCTOBER 3, 1969. Diane Harding and her boyfriend, Hans Berthelsen, saw Jackie the day before she disappeared. The three of them were riding the public bus. Not knowing she had dropped out — that Friday was a PD Day[25] — they didn't think anything of Jackie being out of school. She had a bag with her, and she told Diane that she was carrying a bathing suit.[26] Diane, Hans, and Jackie were riding the 2 Dundas bus route heading east. All three got off at the Maitland Street stop, next to Beal Secondary School, which had a swimming pool. Jackie walked

---

25 Professional Development Day, i.e., a teacher training day, when students get the day off.

26 Friend Marilyn Hird and boyfriend David Papple also said they saw Jackie carrying this bathing suit in a bag that day.

south, while Diane and Hans walked north. They assumed she was going to the school to swim.

Later, she met up with her co-worker Marilyn Hird[27] and they went to the Metropolitan Store in advance of their shift to do some shopping. Jackie bought a new nightie and a pair of slippers.

At some point after her shopping, Jackie went in the side entrance of the Metropolitan Store around 5 p.m. She held the door open for Karl Schroeder, who was going for a leisurely shop and dinner with his four-year-old son.

"Thanks," said Karl, taking the door from her.

His excited son ran straight to the coin-operated mechanical horse and Karl went to buy cigarettes. He saw Jackie on the payphone, taking notice of the pretty young woman who had smiled at him. She was talking about someone not showing up to work, and while Karl and his son followed her, he heard Jackie repeat the information to a co-worker.

Karl went to shop for a doorbell in the Met store, leaving his son to play on the mechanical horse for a while longer, but when Karl couldn't find what he wanted, he went back to get his son. They headed into the restaurant to get a bite to eat. He saw Jackie again, this time staring out towards the parking lot as if she was waiting for someone.

While they ate supper, Karl's son (whom he referred to as "the boy" in his statement to police) spilled his milkshake. When he looked up to get help with the mess, Karl saw an exchange between Jackie and a man who was trying to get her attention. When she turned to him, "his whole face lit up" and "he looked much younger when he smiled," Karl would later tell police. He described him as a man in his thirties, around five-foot-eight and 160 pounds, athletic and with receding black hair parted on

---

27 Marilyn Hird was not interviewed for this book due to her health issues.

the right. He had dark eyes and a tan complexion, with a five o'clock shadow and sideburns.

He wore a green jacket.

———

Jackie's co-worker Linda Green came out of the Met after her shift in the children's wear department ended, just after 10 p.m. on the same night, Friday, October 3. She saw a maroon car with no lights on, parked parallel to the curb. She recognized the car and the man sitting in it. It scared her.

"I don't walk past cars that are parked alone like that," she later said. So she "walked into the parking lot in a roundabout way to my car. I got into my car and drove away."

She'd seen him the night before too, walking back and forth in her department. He had been smoking in the store, and this caught Linda's attention because she wanted to make sure he didn't burn any of the clothes on the racks. She had a poor opinion of him immediately. She had left work with Ruby Johnson, a co-worker to whom she was giving a ride, and she saw the creepy smoking man sitting in the same maroon car, parked parallel to the curb, just as she would see him the following night. He looked right past them, as if he was waiting for someone who was in the store. She said the car was clean and shiny and that the man had dark eyebrows and was clean shaven. He was of average height and build. When he smoked, he held the lit end turned towards his palm.

He had on a green jacket.

Linda did not see him at the store on the night Jackie disappeared.

———

During one of their many sessions over the past forty years, investigators asked Anne English if her sister was a smoker. Jackie was not a smoker, but Anne got the distinct impression that law enforcement had found a cigarette butt, or several, at Big Otter Creek, where Jackie's body was found.

When Jackie had started at the Metropolitan, a month before she disappeared, her mother was working at Northern Electric, just a block away from Treasure Island on one of the nearby industrial roads. The only problem was that Doris got off work at 11 p.m., and Jackie was off at 10 p.m. So Doris asked the Northern Electric security guard, Stanley Arthur Clarke, if it would be okay for Jackie to wait in his office until Doris finished her shifts, so she could give her daughter a ride home. Stanley agreed, and as a result, he saw Jackie regularly, until Doris went into the hospital.

On Monday, September 14, Stanley saw Jackie get dropped off by a young man who drove a maroon four-door Chevrolet, 1964 or '65. That night, the young man got out of the car and walked Jackie right up to the door. He dropped her off a couple of other times, but didn't get out, so this was the closest look at him that Stanley ever got. He noticed there was always another man in the car too. He said that the fellow who escorted Jackie to the doorway was about five-foot-eight, 150 pounds, and had sandy-coloured hair. He was about twenty years old, had no glasses or sideburns, and was dressed casually. These observations were made at a distance, in the dark.

Marilyn Hird also recalled Jackie getting rides to Northern Electric to meet her mom, but Jackie never told her who the driver was. Once, Marilyn had planned to get a ride with Jackie. They waited outside the Metropolitan for forty-five minutes, but the maroon car never came. Instead, they decided to hoof it and make it in time to get a ride downtown with Jackie's mom. While they were walking, the maroon car finally showed up. The driver asked if they wanted a ride and Marilyn said no. Afterwards, when they got to Northern Electric, they realized they had missed Doris, and Jackie was annoyed.

"We should have gone with them," she'd said.

———————

The bathing suit that people saw Jackie carrying around in a plastic bag is a point of much speculation. No one saw her with wet hair, and no one confirmed seeing her at Beal Secondary School's swimming pool or at the YMCA a few blocks west of there.

It's possible that Jackie was getting her picture taken in the bathing suit for extra money. Her sister, Anne, says that she doesn't think Jackie would have ever taken nude photos, but she might have been convinced to let someone take pictures of her in a swimsuit if it meant she would make some extra cash. This could also make sense of the unexplained extra funds police found in her bank account.

Both David Papple and Marilyn Hird remembered Jackie carrying the swimsuit with her on Wednesday, October 1; Thursday, October 2; and Friday, October 3. She told Marilyn she had been swimming at the YMCA, but Marilyn noticed her hair wasn't wet. Jackie told David she was planning on going swimming at Beal. He saw the swimsuit and said it was a very brief bikini that he didn't know she owned and had never seen her wear.

Marilyn and David both spoke to police about a man named Larry. He hung around the Wellington Square Mall downtown. Known to locals as "queer," Larry had asked Jackie on several occasions if he could photograph her. He promised her that, because of his sexual orientation, she wouldn't have to worry — he didn't want sex, just to take pictures. He gave Jackie his phone number, and both David and Marilyn remember Jackie prank-calling him.

Another potential photographer was Elmwood apartment resident Stanley Morris. He painted and photographed women in the nude. After the disappearance and murder, he told police he had never painted or photographed Jackie English. Detective Alsop would return to interview Stanley Morris some years later.

———————

In police reports and statements, Jackie's co-worker and neighbour Paul St. Cyr comes across as a bit of an odd fellow. He worked as a general handyman for the Downs family, who owned the Latin Quarter, washing Johnny Downs's car and taking care of whatever jobs came up. He drove the panel truck and helped the English family move from Elmwood Avenue to Kent Street. He also worked as a maintenance man at the London Psychiatric Hospital.

Detective Alsop interviewed Paul St. Cyr several times in the weeks after Jackie disappeared.

"About three times, she came to my apartment after work to watch colour TV," he told Alsop. "She would sit and talk to me, but I told her to not come so often, for her boyfriend was a very jealous man. Dave is a cook here and he was mad at me, for he's a very hard man to make understand."

It didn't make too much sense that David Papple would be jealous of Paul's time with Jackie. It was thought among the staff at the Latin Quarter that Paul was scared of women. He'd had his heart broken and, for all intents and purposes, he was off the market. His role with Jackie was more that of a big brother. He didn't like that she was staying late, alone, in David's apartment. This annoyed David Papple more than anything. He didn't want Paul's advice to get in the way of his relationship with this beautiful young girl who seemed eager to please.

"Jackie would talk more in confidence to me than any other person," Paul told Alsop. "She did not have a father, and her mother was working very hard. Jackie would seldom talk to her."

Because of his friendship with Jackie, he was able to offer Detective Alsop insights into her love life that even her family didn't know about. He told Alsop, "Jackie complained to me that

Dave [Papple] was a cheapskate and would never take her out. It was always a visit to the apartment."

David Papple wasn't the only young man with whom Jackie was entangled. There was also Greg Carter, who had walked in on Jackie and David naked during that first party in July. She had written about the moment in code in her diary.

"I knew Jackie had an eye on him," said Paul. "She told me that she liked Greg, too. I saw Greg last night for he is staying in Dave's apartment for he is going to the funeral. He is staying in London for the long weekend. I spoke to Greg last night and he was feeling very bad about Jackie's death. He said, 'I didn't think it would end like this.'"

Jackie also had a flirtation with Lloyd Lackey, the married kitchen colleague she had kissed and written about in her diary in code.[28]

"Lloyd [Lackey] said he would belt Dave if he ever harmed Jackie. When Lloyd knew about Jackie and Dave being in the apartment without any clothes on, Lloyd said it was too bad, he wouldn't ever think about fooling around with a girl fifteen years old, for she was too young and Dave doesn't realize what he can get if he is caught. Lloyd and I would both be keeping an eye on Jackie, and after he knew about Dave and Jackie, he said, 'How is the love life, Jackie?' Yesterday, October 11, 1969, Lloyd and I were talking about this death and Lloyd said, 'Dave really thought that he had the hang on Jackie. But he didn't get her after all.'"[29]

Even though the English family lived only a block away from the restaurant, Jackie still asked Paul for rides back to the

---

28 Michael Arntfield speculates in *Murder City* that the Lloyd mentioned in the diaries is actually Rick "Lloyd" Papple, David's brother, not Lloyd Lackey. Alsop referred to Rick Papple as "Lloyd" in his notebooks, lending credence to this theory.

29 This statement by Lloyd has relevance to a statement made by David Papple in 1978. See page 298.

Elmwood apartments on occasion, which surprised him. The last time, he said, was a week before she went missing. Jackie explained to him that she had a boyfriend there, even though he knew she was dating David Papple. He asked her about it, and she said, "I like David, and I like him. I can't make up my mind." She never told Paul the name of the other man in her life, and she never referred to him in her diary.

CHAPTER FIFTEEN

MEET MARILYN HIRD

"I didn't know they were going to kill her . . .
If she had only listened, she wouldn't have wound up dead."

— MARILYN HIRD

The Simpsons department store in downtown London is fondly remembered as a long-gone landmark of better days. Walking in off the southwest corner of the city's main intersection at Dundas Street and Richmond Street, shoppers were greeted with gleaming glass displays and countertops, smiling salesgirls offering samples, and classic services such as gift wrapping, registries, and delivery. Every year, the store's Christmas windows attracted crowds to see animated elves and Santas play in artificial snow under twinkle lights. It was the pinnacle of downtown retail. This classy, trusting, adorable department store in the heart of prosperous London, Ontario, was the stage for what happened next.

NOVEMBER 21, 1969. The night watchman of the Simpsons department store did his rounds. There was nothing out of the ordinary, as usual, but he still attentively checked every corner. He took pride in his uniform and his work, protecting one of the city's gems. He wasn't just a security guard — he was the night watchman of

Simpsons downtown. It was a good position, a bit of a cushy job, even if the nights could get awfully long.

Rounding the back loading bay at about 10:30 p.m., he saw a young woman, crumpled up and passed out. "Hey! Are you okay?" he shouted.

When she didn't respond, he found her to be unconscious, but breathing. He picked up her lanky fifteen-year-old frame and carried her to the security office, propping her up in a chair while he called the police and an ambulance. Her long brown hair drooped to one side.

The girl was Marilyn Hird.

She had taken sleeping pills and pain medication in an attempt at suicide. Doctors at Victoria Hospital found a wrinkled photo of Jackie English in her pocket. On the back were the words:

Let her killer remain a secret to be buried with me.

———————

The two girls met after Jackie started working at the Metropolitan in September 1969. While Marilyn would swear they were best friends, in reality, they had probably known each other only a month. Marilyn will tell you that they had met earlier in the summer, and that Jackie got her the job at the Met, but she cannot provide any details. There is no evidence to say they ever met before Marilyn's first shift on September 3. It's far more likely that Linda Hurst, who also worked at the Metropolitan, was the same Linda Hurst who can be found in Marilyn's grade nine class photo and was actually the person who got her the job.

Marilyn took rides downtown from work with Jackie and Doris, where she'd catch the bus to her east end home, but on the Saturday night that Jackie disappeared, Marilyn was not at work.

After Jackie went missing, Marilyn inserted herself into the investigation. She was photographed by the *London Free Press*, sitting next to David Papple, and identified herself to reporters as

David Papple and Marilyn Hird are interviewed by reporters in Agnes Murray's apartment.

London Free Press Collection of Photographic Negatives, [1969-10-10], Archives and Special Collections, Western Libraries, Western University.

Jackie's best friend.[30] She gave repeated interviews to police, each one different, each story shifting. She kept coming up with new information. They paid close attention to her despite her inconsistency — or perhaps because of it — particularly after her suicide attempt. However, she wouldn't talk to anyone about what happened in detail. Every time someone asked her a specific question about Jackie or the overdose, she became withdrawn and dodgy. Her psychiatrist was sure she was hiding something, but according to an OPP report, "The girl absolutely refused to talk to anybody."

---

30 Jackie's actual best friend was Vicky Larazavich.

A month or so before her suicide attempt, Marilyn had written to the Hidden Witness program at the *London Free Press*. The childish blocky handwriting and spelling clearly matched that of statements she had given police. Alsop kept this letter next to her statements in his file, inferring that he knew it was written by her. She wrote:

> Jackie English was worried about going to work on Saturday because the previous night a man who had been talking to her said he was going to meet after work on Saturday. She left me with the impression that she knew the individual and made me promise not to mention it to anyone so untill [sic] now I have not. I did reoganise [sic] the man in the composite drawing[31] as the one talking to her in her bay on Friday October 3. I did not say anything about it to the police since I would then have to revel [sic] the promise made to Jackie. I had see [sic] him before as the man who tried to pick up Jackie and I again at this time Jackie gave the impression of knowing the individual. The third time I saw Jackie with this man he was talking to her one day before work again. I promised Jackie not to say anything.
>
> I might seem ridiculas [sic] but promises made by me are ment [sic] to be kept and this is the only time I will revel [sic] promises made to her. You probably relize [sic] who I am but if asked about any part of this statement I would deny any knowledge of it. Sincerly [sic] Yours 67439676.[32]

---

31 The composite drawing is included in a later chapter.

32 This eight-digit code was part of the instructions included in the Hidden Witness Program with the *Free Press*.

She would not speak directly about Jackie's murder, but she told lots of stories about what had happened before her co-worker's abduction, most of which could not be corroborated.

Marilyn Hird said she had spent time with Jackie on October 3, 1969, the day before the abduction. She told police that she got out of school early that day,[33] and Jackie met her at Beal Secondary School on Dundas Street. Jackie had a plastic shoe bag with her that Marilyn said contained a swimsuit. Jackie said she had planned on going swimming, but never did. According to Marilyn, the two girls went to the Simpsons department store and got something to eat before walking back to Beal to get Marilyn's uniform for the Met, which she had forgotten in her locker.[34] Then they took the Ridout bus before transferring to the Northern Electric bus, which took them close to work.[35] They arrived at 4:05. That was when Jackie did her shopping at the Met store at Treasure Island, buying a nightgown and slippers, before her regular 5 to 10 p.m. shift. Marilyn said, "Jackie was in real good spirits. She was laughing and joking."

That night at work was very busy. They were flooded with customers, and while they didn't have a lot of time to speak, Marilyn managed to tell Jackie, "I'm totally overwhelmed. I'm making mistakes."

"Don't worry," said Jackie. "I'm messing up, too. I forgot to get someone a glass of water they asked for."

Because Doris was in the hospital, the girls didn't have their usual ride downtown. Instead, according to Marilyn, they decided to walk to the bus stop on the other side of the overpass. There was

---

33 October 3, 1969, was a PD Day, so there were no classes that day.

34 Marilyn spent half a year at Beal before returning to Clarke Road Secondary School.

35 This bus route did not continue as late as 10 p.m., which is why Jackie could take the bus to work, but not home. Marilyn and Jackie could not take the bus back without having to walk over the bridge.

a long line of traffic stretching along beside them, moving slowly, as the crowd from London Gardens had just let out after a Boston Bruins exhibition game. According to Marilyn, one of the cars had two guys in it, Americans, who were drinking beer in the vehicle.

The girls figured they had already missed their bus when one of the young men called out to them from the passenger window, "You two going into London?"

"Yeah," said Jackie.

Marilyn said it wasn't the first time they had hitched a ride. She recalled that once they took a ride from a nice elderly couple, and the safe experience emboldened them to try it again. Now, the two-door car pulled over so the girls could get in. The young man who had called to them got out to let them squeeze in the back.

"I'm Ted," he said as he sat back down. He was in his early twenties, about five-foot-ten and heavy-set, with dirty blond hair and sideburns.

"I'm Bob," said the driver, who was about the same age and height, only skinnier. He had sunken cheeks and dark brown hair, parted on the right side, with skin blotched from acne scars.

"I'm Jackie. This is Marilyn."

"Where are you coming from?"

"Oh, the Metropolitan," said Jackie.

"Oh yeah? How much do you get paid?"

Jackie told them.

"That's better than what I make. I only make eighty cents an hour delivering groceries."

"You think that's bad?" said the other. "I make fifty-five cents an hour."

The car had a bottle opener on the dashboard that the boys used to open their beer bottles. There were piles of garbage and clutter, not just on the dash but also on the seats. They had the radio on. Traffic started to lift as they drove faster into the city. When Jackie told them what grade they were in, one boy whispered to the other, "*Sixteen.*"

"Do you work in the cafeteria?" asked Ted.

"We do," said Jackie. "Flipping burgers."

"So, do we get a free hot dog for giving you a ride?" Ted asked.

"Yeah, sure," she laughed. "Come in tomorrow and I'll give you a hot dog."

"If you do the dishes for me, I'll buy you a steak," said Ted.

"Ha," said Bob. "You'd have to come pretty far. We live in Michigan."

"Fine, no dishes. But maybe you can pass me a beer?" Ted asked Jackie.

She handed him one from the case on the floor of the back seat.

"I'm definitely showing up for that hot dog tomorrow," said Ted. "When can you be there?"

"I work five until ten," said Jackie.

"What about you?" Ted asked Marilyn.

"I'm not working," she replied quietly.

"How do you usually get home?" asked Ted.

"Like this," joked Jackie.

They dropped Jackie off at the corner of King Street and Wellington Street, turning east onto King Street. Ted had to get out and lean the seat forward to let them out. Marilyn took the opportunity to jump out with her friend, even though the boys told her they were going close to her house. She told them that she'd rather take the bus.

"Why, don't you trust us?" they asked her.

After they left, Marilyn turned to Jackie. "I wouldn't want to be in the car with them alone."

"I wouldn't either," said Jackie. "I wouldn't have gone if there weren't two of us."

"Safety in numbers."

"I hope they don't come to work," said Jackie, laughing.

Just as they parted, Jackie called out to Marilyn, "See you on Tuesday — no, I mean Thursday." Jackie had asked to have her hours cut back so she could return to high school the following week. She had been working full-time hours, against her mother's wishes, to save money and help out the family.

After saying goodbye to Marilyn, Jackie went over to David Papple's house, and so he was able to confirm Marilyn's story in part. He told police that Jackie showed up at about 11 p.m. with a story that she had gotten a ride home with a couple of fellows. "They seemed like nice guys. The only thing she was afraid of was that they had beer in the car."

Marilyn later amended her story, saying that Jackie was so worried about the boys in the car that after they got out of the vehicle, Marilyn volunteered to come to work the next night, even though she wasn't scheduled, just to help her friend feel safe. She said Jackie told her not to worry about it and that she had a date the next night after work with a guy named Mike who was thirty years old. Allegedly, Jackie swore her to secrecy because she didn't want anyone to know she was dating a much older man.

Who was Mike? Well, Marilyn gave a statement to police, describing a kind of double date that she and Jackie had gone on. Like the story of the two Americans in the car, the story of this double date is unverified, but mostly consisted of them driving to a back road and necking in a car. The first man was Mike, who was tall and slim, in his late twenties, with brown skin and slick black hair. He spoke with a bit of an accent. He had an oval face with sharp cheekbones and crooked teeth that embarrassed him, so he often spoke with his hand over his mouth. The other man was named Arney. He was also tall and in his mid-twenties. He was messy, blond, and wore clothes that made him look like he worked in a manual labour job.

Marilyn made a point of reporting to Detective Alsop that she saw Mike on the bus a week or so after Jackie disappeared. Mike had asked her the name of the street behind the Metropolitan Store and wanted to know where RR 3 London was. He could have been going to the outskirts of town for one of the many industrial jobs in the area.

There is no corroboration that Mike or Arney ever existed.

DECEMBER 16, 1969. Marilyn reported a threatening phone call to police. She said a man told her not to talk to the police, not to tell them anything.

Despite Marilyn's constant stream of bizarre stories, some of which were obviously untrue, Detective Dennis Alsop must have been sure that she knew something. He interviewed her at least five times over the years, interviews that he documented and kept in his personal files. "As stated previously, this witness is described as 'difficult,' 'reluctant,' and sometimes 'hostile,'" he wrote. "Any information obtained was as the result of lengthy interviews and information was gained with great difficulty."

He never gave up. In 1976, Alsop took Marilyn for hypnosis. He continued to talk to her, even after his retirement, and documented a conversation that took place as late as 1988.

———————

Marilyn wasn't at work on the night Jackie disappeared.

She told Detective Alsop she attended a sleepover after a Sadie Hawkins dance at Clarke Road Secondary School. For the past fifty years, this has been her alibi. Until now, no one studying the case was able to confirm that Marilyn was actually at that sleepover or that the sleepover even happened. However, the woman who hosted that sleepover agreed to an interview for this book — thanks to researcher Sharla Smith — and her information tells a different story.

The sleepover was actually a birthday party. Janet[36] was a student at Clarke Road Secondary School, and her close group of

———————

36 A pseudonym is used at the request of the interviewee.

girlfriends were in the school band together. This group included Marilyn Hird, whom Janet remembered as a very quiet, sheepish, and asexual teenager. Marilyn didn't tell them about a boyfriend, a flirtation, or even a crush. They were as nice to Marilyn as they were to anyone else, but none of them got really close to her. She didn't share any secrets. Then again, Marilyn didn't seem like the kind of girl who had many salacious stories to tell. In yearbook photos, her hair is cropped short and she wears baggy sweaters that cover up her burgeoning female form. She seemed like a quiet nerd. The girls were never invited to Marilyn's house, and they had the idea that life at the Hirds' place wasn't particularly wonderful. At the time, Marilyn lived at 245 Manitoulin Drive with her parents and two siblings. She had attended Clarke Road in the 1968–69 school year and transferred to Beal in September 1969. However, before the end of the year, she was back at Clarke Road, her neighbourhood school.

Janet told me there was no Sadie Hawkins dance that night — the school's "turnabout" dance was held in the winter months, not in October. Because it was her sweet sixteen (a memorable birthday), and because of Jackie's murder, Janet remembers details about that night. She recalls one of the party guests complained about the sheets and pillows they used to create makeshift beds in the basement. She also remembers that one of the girls, now deceased, had to wash her ballet uniform and hang it to dry so it would be ready for her dance class in the morning. She clearly hadn't washed her own clothes before, and so Janet's mom had to help her out. Janet remembers thinking that there was no way the uniform would be dry in time for the morning class.

This detail is very important. In London in 1969, no one had ballet class on a Sunday morning. No mistake, as Janet asserted in our conversation, the sleepover took place on Friday, October 3, the night *before* Jackie disappeared. This means that Marilyn's long-standing alibi was false.

Marilyn came to the sleepover late that night after work. Janet did not remember hearing a story about Marilyn hitching a ride with Jackie. In fact, she doesn't remember much about Marilyn at all from that night, just that she came late and then, in her customary fashion, blended in with the background.

Police came to Clarke Road Secondary School in 1969 to interview Janet about her sixteenth birthday party and to confirm Marilyn's alibi. They arrived when she was sitting in math class, and she was taken out by two intimidating officers in black suits. They escorted her into a private room, where she sat, terrified, wondering why her parents weren't with her while she was being questioned. I gave her a description of Detective Alsop, and she confirmed that he was not one of the officers. These were younger, aggressive. They scared her. Neither of them had the congenial approach that Alsop would have had with a sweet sixteen-year-old whose landmark birthday had now been forever tainted with crime. The information from their interview somehow never made it into Detective Alsop's notes or to his conversations with the English family. For the past fifty years, to anyone doing an independent investigation, including the victim's family, Marilyn Hird has been considered as someone who had an alibi.

No one knows where Marilyn Hird was on the night that Jackie was murdered.

———

Today, Marilyn Hird resides in an assisted living facility. After finding out from me that Marilyn's decades-old alibi was a lie, Anne English confronted her with this new information. She asked Marilyn to tell her the truth about what had happened to her sister. As always, Marilyn wouldn't answer directly. She said she couldn't remember. She guessed she was at home, watching the hockey game on TV. Anne was certain that Marilyn was keeping the truth from her, but decided she had finally had enough of being strung along.

Both Anne and Fred English have spent extensive amounts of time trying to get information out of Marilyn since first speaking with her in 2002. Their contact was precipitated by a letter Anne had written to the *London Free Press* two years before, regarding Project Angel. Project Angel was a too-short-lived attempt by the London Police to reinvigorate cold cases using new DNA technology. While several cases did find resolution, Jackie's was not one of them, and Anne wrote to the paper, lamenting this fact. Marilyn saw Anne's letter in the newspaper.

It took some time for Marilyn to get in touch with Anne and Fred, but she eventually did on July 22, 2002. They had long telephone conversations. She also spoke to them in person at the London Psychiatric Hospital while a resident there, and since then at her assisted living facility. Both of Jackie's siblings are certain that Marilyn holds the answer to who killed their sister.

During these conversations, Marilyn gave a lot of disjointed information. She told them about Rick Harrison, a student at Clarke Road who was supposedly a few years older than her, with whom she shared a birthday, May 23. She said he played the trombone and was on the yearbook staff. He was also supposedly a lifeguard and swimming instructor. She'd known him since she was six years old, and she adored him. She said he loved her back, and in some versions of her story, they were married. In others, they even had a child, Nathan Hird, born on November 4, 1975. No evidence can be found to back up these claims, and as such, this fellow might not have ever existed. In all of the versions of her story, Rick moved to Hollywood to become Harrison Ford, and Marilyn sees the Star Wars films as having direct messages to her embedded within them.

Her stories are confusing, convoluted. She told Fred and Anne that at Janet's sleepover, there had been a psychic who warned them about Jackie's death. She also said that her boyfriend Rick came to visit her at the sleepover. Janet did not remember any boys coming to the sleepover whatsoever.

Marilyn has suggested that Jackie may have been pregnant when she died. To this point, Metropolitan waitress Alice Faye Cox told police in 1969 that a week before she disappeared, Jackie had been joking at work about being knocked up. She was playing a practical joke and really hammed it up, but she didn't think that Jackie was actually pregnant. Boyfriend David Papple told Detective Alsop, "During the week just before she went missing, I didn't see any change in her. She never said that she was worried about being pregnant. She was only scared that I would tell her mother that she was missing school . . . I had intercourse with Jackie the first time about the middle of August. I knew she was a virgin at that time. She had her period in the third week of September and her next period would be due this week." The idea of Jackie having a secret pregnancy simply does not line up with David's statements to police or that of her colleague Alice Faye Cox.

There is a huge assortment of other tidbits that Marilyn has given out that could merit further investigation by police. These include names, scenarios, blackmailing, and family histories. Some of them seem pretty bonkers. Others have some credence.

Marilyn told the English kids that her mother had committed suicide. She also told them that her father was a drunk. On the weekends, things would get especially bad. Saturday nights were the worst. The dysfunction in the Hird home led to deviant behaviour in her brother, James "Jim" McKay Hird.

Jim Hird was arrested on June 28, 1966; he was eighteen years old. He was convicted of attacking five-year-old Bruce Shipley with an eight-inch butcher knife and injuring Bruce's friend, four-year-old Johnny, in the shoulder. The *London Free Press* covered the story on June 28, 1966. According to news reports, the boys were playing in the woods and then burst back into the neighbourhood. Mrs. Doris Rigg said, "I heard a scream . . . a real bad scream." There was blood running down little Bruce's back. Observing the emergency, neighbour David Hawley flagged down a passing car, driven by Mrs. Frances Scott, who lived down the street.

"A man stabbed him!" cried out Johnny.

"A man stabbed me . . . a man stabbed me!" repeated Bruce.

They put Bruce in the car and Hawley drove him to St. Joseph's Hospital while Mrs. Scott cradled him in a blanket in the back seat. On the way, they crossed paths with Fire Chief Frank Tambling, who escorted them to the emergency room.

"The boy was crying," Hawley said to reporters. "And blood was bubbling out of his shoulder blade."

Jim Hird was a genuine creep in the woods. Resident L.F. Parking told the newspaper that the field where he'd been hiding was known locally as a hideout for peeping toms who chased children.

More concerned with rehabilitation than punishment, the court sentenced Jim Hird to two years less a day in jail. After his release in 1969, he settled in at 18 Cornerbrook Avenue, in London. On the night of December 3, 1970, he got drunk at the Belvedere Hotel downtown, consuming about twelve shots of whisky, and attacked nurse Hazel Jean Miller with a knife in the Victoria Hospital parking lot. He wanted to hijack her vehicle and go to Windsor to see the horse races there, so he pushed her aside and got into the driver's seat. Inebriated, he figured she'd gotten out of the car — she hadn't.

With a terrified Hazel in the passenger seat, Hird led police on a high-speed chase exceeding ninety miles per hour, up and down Wellington Road. Along the big curve just south of downtown, he jumped the curb and nearly crashed into the Anglican church, grazing a tree. At the corner of Wellington and Southdale, he hit a brand new Oldsmobile and rammed his vehicle into a parked car in the Californian Restaurant parking lot. After all these shenanigans, he had flattened three tires and earned a dangerous driving conviction in addition to armed robbery and assault charges. On December 12, 1970, he was sentenced to three years in the penitentiary as well as psychological treatment.

The publicity of this case led people to wonder if he was

the same man who had attacked nurse Sharon Zappio one week before. She'd been walking from her apartment on Grand Avenue to work at Victoria Hospital on South Street, when she was confronted by a man with a sharp broken broom handle. With the tip against her throat, he pushed her down into the slush and told her not to scream as he grabbed her purse. That same day, Milena Vitkovic was mugged for the seven dollars in her purse.

Did Jim Hird meet Jackie during her short friendship with his sister? Clearly, Jim Hird had a problem with violence, but even if he is taken seriously as a viable suspect in Jackie's death, his attack style seems to be spontaneous and disorganized. He used a knife. None of these traits apply to the Jackie English murder.

There is one tangible connection between Jackie English and Jim Hird. According to Marilyn, her brother Jim had spent time in jail for sexually assaulting his neighbour.[37] Fred checked the guestbook from Jackie's funeral and discovered that this woman had signed the guestbook. Why would she have gone to Jackie's funeral? Fred knew all of Jackie's friends, and she wasn't one of them. Did she think that Jackie was also a victim of Jim Hird's? Fred called the family and spoke to the girl's father, who told him that Marilyn had spent a lot of time at their house as a child, hiding out from her abusive father. However, he didn't say anything about Jim assaulting his daughter. Fred then called the woman in question. She said that she didn't remember going to Jackie's funeral, and then got pretty upset when Fred brought up the assault. After that, she ended the conversation.

Marilyn's second connection to Jackie's murder would only be revealed during a trial in 1970.

---

37 I've kept this person's name out of this book. Sexual assault victims are traumatized enough, in my opinion.

PART III

THE FRYER AFFAIR

CHAPTER SIXTEEN

THE ATTACK ON BETTY HARRISON

*"Her story never ever made sense to me as a sixteen-year-old,
and it still doesn't all these years later."*

— ANNE ENGLISH

In the days after Jackie's disappearance, and especially after her body was found, she was the main story in the newspaper. Her picture was everywhere. This was how forty-two-year-old Elizabeth Harrison and her family got involved in the case, a choice that she would surely regret in the years that followed as her life was torn apart and her family, eventually, was utterly destroyed.

Elizabeth, or Betty as she was known, worked as the secretary for a chiropractor, Dr. Harvey Murphy. She was married to Verdun Harrison, a Parkwood hospital orderly. They had a son named Richard, who was twenty years old but gave the impression of being much younger. He was intellectually delayed and had a great deal of trouble keeping up at school, leading to counselling at CPRI and remedial classes. He worked a manual labour job at the Green Giant plant. The three of them lived in a tiny white-siding house in the east end at 171 Elgin Street. They were not the most likeable people, but for the most part, they seemed harmless.

The Harrison family home.

London Free Press Collection of Photographic Negatives, [1969-12-12], Archives and Special Collections, Western Libraries, Western University.

Another sibling, their oldest daughter, Sharon,[38] had left the family as a child and gone to live with her grandmother at 24 Mount Pleasant Avenue. Her grandmother's house was within walking distance of her part-time job as a switchboard operator at the *London Free Press*. No one knows why she left home, only that she had terrible misfortune, as did the rest of the family. The Harrisons seemed to be cursed.

OCTOBER 7, 1969. On the day that Betty saw Jackie's picture in the newspaper, she did not know what would become of them. She showed her husband the picture and asked him, "Isn't that the waitress that served us at the Metropolitan restaurant?" When she thought about it, she realized that they had gone there on Friday, October 3, the night just before the abduction. Betty was sure they must have some important information for the police. After she nagged Verdun for days, they finally went to see the police with their story.

---

38 Sharon also went by the name Joan.

The night before Jackie disappeared, the Harrison family had dinner at the Met. They sat at the counter where Jackie was serving. While they were eating, two men came into the restaurant and stood nearby to talk to Jackie.

"Did you tell her?" one asked the other. He turned to Jackie. "Are you going? We'll make it tomorrow then."

Betty said that Jackie was so upset by the confrontation, she dropped a glass and it smashed on the floor. Then one of the

LEFT: Composite image made with Verdun Harrison of a man seen at the Metropolitan restaurant the night before Jackie English disappeared.

London Free Press Collection of Photographic Negatives, [1969-10-19], Archives and Special Collections, Western Libraries, Western University.

BELOW: Detective Alsop (left) and Chief Inspector James McBride (right).

London Free Press Collection of Photographic Negatives, [1969-10-19], Archives and Special Collections, Western Libraries, Western University.

men put a penny on the counter and told Jackie, "This is all you're worth."

The London Police took Betty's story seriously and asked her husband, Verdun, to sit down with a sketch artist to put together a composite of one of the men he had seen that night. He obliged, and soon law enforcement had a person of interest to track down and question about Jackie's abduction.

OCTOBER 19, 1969. Betty was proud of the composite sketch, based on her husband's description, that appeared in the *London Free Press* that day. She was excited that her family was so important to the police and that they had helped with a very high-profile murder case. When she went to work at chiropractor Dr. Murphy's office, where she was a secretary, she told everyone about it.

NOVEMBER 14, 1969. Betty answered the phone just after dinner and heard a man on the other end. He spoke with a high-pitched voice, as if disguising himself, and used dramatic swells to make his point heard.

"Are you the lady who went to the police?"

"No."

"I want to talk to the woman that did."

She didn't reply.

"You had better not go. You had better cool it and not go again. We'll be watching you."

He hung up.

Responding to the threat, Detective Alsop sat in an unmarked car at the end of Elgin Street, keeping watch over the Harrison house. He was still sitting there when Betty answered the phone again at 6:45 a.m., just after Verdun and Richard had left to go to work.

"I told you not to go to the police. You've been to the police," said the caller, as Betty later recalled. "I saw you had the police over last night, just what we told you not to do. I'm going to cut you up good, and we will see what I'll do to your husband and kid. I am going to get you real good. I am really going to enjoy this one. What I tell you this morning, I am really going to enjoy this, baby. It will not make any difference where you are or what you are doing. It will be when you least expect it. I like to fuck dead women, and I'll do it with you when I'm through with you."

DECEMBER 7, 1969. It was midnight when the Harrisons heard a loud bang on their front door. They reached for the phone to call the police, just as they heard it again. Bang! Terrified, Betty looked out the window while Verdun called the cops. She saw a car pulling out of the driveway, which she later described a blue Ford with round tail lights.

Verdun didn't go back to sleep. He was up when there was another loud bang at 4 a.m. He went to the door and there was no one there, but he did see a car drive past his house — a Ford Falcon or Fairlane.

DECEMBER 11, 1969. Since her birthday had been the day before, forty-two-year-old Betty Harrison was looking forward to a relaxing weekend of celebrations. She left her job at Dr. Harvey Murphy's downtown clinic early and got home around 3:30 p.m. In the mailbox was a stack of birthday cards, which she opened one by one, smiling at the greetings from friends and family.

She pulled one card out of its envelope to see that it said *In Deepest Sympathy.* Thinking it might be a joke, she opened it up. Inside was a red ink stamp that read *Past Due* and the hand-written words, "We'll be watching you."

She didn't call the police. Instead, she took the family dog, Cindy, a forty-pound black Labrador, in her taupe[39] Volkswagen

---

39 Some reports list the vehicle as grey. The black-and-white photographs make it impossible to determine which report is correct.

Beetle and went shopping. She cut across the city to the shopping area at Wellington Road South that included the Metropolitan Store where Jackie English had worked.

She went to the Sayvette store where White Oaks Mall stands today and then the Towers store, across from Treasure Island on the west side of Wellington, next to the spot where there is currently a Value Village. When she got to Towers, she realized she didn't have any more money with her. In 1969, you had to make sure to visit the bank on Fridays if you wanted to have money for the weekend. That being said, people carried cheques for this exact reason. They were accepted at most stores, as charge cards were not as common. Cheques also proved where you had been and when, because people tracked them in their chequebooks. Presumably, Betty didn't have any cheques either, and she was therefore foiled in her attempt to go shopping that Friday evening. She decided to go home at around 6 p.m., and took the back roads heading east. These back roads were not, and are not, very populated at all, but home to industrial businesses and empty fields.

What happened next is uncertain. As defence lawyer A.J. Baker stated later in court, "She stopped at the intersection and there follows a long confused tale of a terrifying attack." I have tried to reconstruct what happened that night based on Betty's various reports to police and her court statements one year later.

Betty pulled up to the corner of Hubrey Road and Green Valley Road.[40] Before getting out of the car, she reached across and opened the passenger side door to let her dog out for a run. Cindy bounded out, and a man suddenly jumped in the passenger seat. Shocked and scared, Betty hit the gas. The car lurched forward, banking left and swerving onto Hubrey Road. She recalled, "there was a can of candies on the seat and he kept hitting me

---

40 Concession 4 of Westminster Township, one concession south of Wilton Grove Road, a more commonly used shortcut for Londoners.

The corner of Hubrey Road and Green Valley Road, where Elizabeth Harrison was attacked.

London Free Press Collection of Photographic Negatives, [1969-01-12], Archives and Special Collections, Western Libraries, Western University.

with it." She had hoped that the momentum of the turn would push the man out of her car's open passenger door, but as they careened over the bridge and into a snowbank, he held on tight.

While she was trapped in the car with him, he "got a knife from somewhere . . . he cut my face with it," she later said. "The knife seemed to have a blade about eight inches in length.[41] It was not like a butcher knife. It had a guard on the handle. I think he reached down and got it from his sock or boot." As she began to bleed, he turned on the interior light of the car.

"Look at yourself!" he demanded. "I like to see this sort of thing."

Instead, she turned the light off, and they began an agonizing game of turning it on and off as he attacked her.

He leapt out of the car and went to the driver's side, where he pulled the door open, and Betty desperately tried to keep him out. Her memory became foggy, but she recalled him driving her car south on Hubrey Road, away from London, as she was now in the passenger seat. He stopped more than once, continuing the attack each time. Cindy chased behind, trying to keep up with the car, her bark echoing in the night as the tail lights disappeared.

He became gentle "all of a sudden . . . After I was cut on the

---

41   The knife Jim Hird used in his attack on Bruce Shipley was also an eight-inch blade.

cheek, and blood was on my face he reached over and kissed me on the cheek," she remembered. "I felt sorry for him and touched his cheek. He immediately acted like a wild man again . . . He just went wild and he was terrible . . . He just was hitting me and hurting me . . . When he kissed my cheek, he became very kind and gentle and said, 'I like this sort of thing.' When he was violent, he said, 'I like to fuck a woman after she is dead.'

"This fellow was acting as if under drugs or maybe liquor. He was doing things as if automatic. When he was using the knife he kept saying, 'Fuck, fuck!' He grabbed my breasts through the blouse. He tore the button of my slacks. He kept trying to put his leg between mine . . .'"

He turned the car around and went north again on Hubrey, back towards London and Betty's loyal dog, who was waiting for her to return. The car stopped on the side of the road by a farm, and the two fought outside of the car. Then canine Cindy, brave black dog in the night, bounded up and tore into the attacker's leg, "nipping away at him." The attacker was trying to get Betty into another vehicle, driven presumably by a second man, but Cindy won the battle. The attacker loped ahead to the parked car, limping from the dog's angry bite on his leg, and collapsed into the passenger seat. A pair of tail lights disappeared down the long country road. Betty would later say it was a dark colour Ford Falcon.

She got back into her Volkswagen Beetle and rubbed snow on her wounds. Then, instead of going to the hospital, she drove herself and Cindy home. It was about 6:30 when she got in the door, and she could not recall the route she had taken to get there. She called the police from home. An officer came immediately and took her to the hospital, where she was placed under twenty-four-hour guard. She met with Detective Topham just after 8 p.m. to give a description of her attacker. She said, "'It was almost as if you were looking into a dead man's eyes. The blacks were very small. When he spoke they would get bigger and he had a way of flashing them . . ."

After speaking with Detective Topham, she talked to Detective Alsop and gave him another description: "The man was twenty-nine to thirty years old, one hundred seventy-five pounds, had dark hair, a sallow complexion, a dark leather jacket, no hat, may have had a tooth missing or a dark tooth." She said he was a head taller than the car, slim, had no accent and no glasses, and wore brown gloves.

Her injuries were recorded in trial records: "She had five small cuts on the front of her right shoulder, three cuts and two scrape marks on the back of her right hand, two small cuts on the back of her left hand, three scratches on the palm of her left hand and two on her right palm, five cuts on her right cheek, five cuts on her left leg. Nurse Linda Reid said she had numerous lacerations . . . most of them were superficial . . . two or three deep ones . . . mainly to the right side of her face, her right shoulder and some to her left thigh, indicating the main force of the attack came when the man was sitting on the driver's side. A doctor said the wounds must have been made by a very sharp, thin blade like a razor blade."

Detective Alsop had to wonder, why would the attacker have left her alive? Now she would be able to identify him.

She was in the hospital for twelve days and got out just two days before Christmas.

The Harrison family dog became quite the star after the attack. Cindy was featured in the newspaper by reporter Tom Williams:

> "That dog," said Det. Sgt. Dennis Alsop, "may have saved the woman's life." Cindy has been the Harrison's pet since she was a pup. Richard Harrison, 20, Mrs. Harrison's son, said she has been a good watchdog at their home, 171 Elgin St., but has never before had to defend anyone from serious

Richard Harrison admires his dog, Cindy.

London Free Press Collection of Photographic Negatives, [1969-12-12], Archives and Special Collections, Western Libraries, Western University.

danger. "She's still pretty shook up," Richard said. "Last night after the attack someone knocked on the door and she just threw herself at it . . . if the one who did ever came around, Cindy would sure know him." Cindy slipped self-consciously away from the picture-taking session and munched contentedly at a bowl of dog biscuits.

Detective Alsop cut out an article by Bill McGuire printed in the *London Free Press* about what it was like for the Alsop and English families over the Christmas season in 1969. He kept it with his files, which tells me it meant something to him. It must have been an accurate summary of how hard law enforcement was working on solving Jackie's case:

> Christmas Day will be little different from any other day since early October for the team of sleuths tracking the killer of Jacqueline English . . . From that night along the winding banks of the creek, 18 policemen worked 30 days, averaging 12–14 hours, without a day off . . . During the initial stages of the

murder hunt, some of the detectives would work for two straight days without sleep, grab a few hours' rest, then back to work . . .

[A] man pulled into a restaurant off a highway near Petrolia and bought a *London Free Press*. While reading it at home, he spotted a message scribbled on an advertising section saying: "We know who killed J. English." The paper was brought back to London and the police and Free Press officials traced the writing back to two youngsters in the mailing room. "It was a joke," they claimed, but police didn't find it funny. . .

Speaking with the eternal optimism of a murder investigator, [McBride] said: "The killer has to eat some place, he has to sleep some place, and he probably works some place. Somebody's got to know who it is. It's our job to find him."

CHAPTER SEVENTEEN

THE CONSPIRACY FORMS

"Never leaves me, my dear. Never leaves me."

— GLEN FRYER

Here's where the story gets pretty convoluted. I'm not the first one to try to iron it out. In his unpublished book, *Justice for Jackie*, Fred English goes through the entire investigation, every newspaper report, every piece of information he had at his disposal, to untangle the sticky mess that is the case against Glen Fryer, who was arrested for the attack on Betty Harrison. Even for someone well versed in the story, it's a lot to take in.

At first, I wrote about the Fryer affair very much like the way Fred English did. I showed all of that to my partner, Jason, and he said the amount of information was totally overwhelming. It's true. It is overwhelming. I've been researching the Jackie English murder for more than four years now, spending countless nights reading through documents and websites, looking up everything I could find in the archives. At this point, I am still confronted with details that are inconsistent from one report to another. I tried to sort it all out by finding the original transcripts for the Glen Fryer trial — yes, there is a trial forthcoming in this story — but was told by court officials and archivists that they are nowhere to be found. Carol Murray, daughter of Agnes Murray who identified Jackie's body, told me that they had been destroyed, as she was informed by an OPP officer some years ago. Glen Fryer himself has a portion of them, along with the notes his lawyer took during the trial. I told him I was trying to track them down but he didn't offer to share them with me.

So let me try to sort it out for you. I will give you the details, but I think it's best to start out with a cast of characters.

1. Betty Harrison: the eyewitness and attack victim
2. Verdun Harrison: Betty's husband
3. Richard Harrison: Betty's son
4. Glen Fryer: principal of CPRI, the accused attacker of Betty Harrison, and by insinuation, the murderer of Jackie English
5. Ruth Fryer: Glen's wife
6. Dr. Harvey Murphy: Betty's boss and friend of Glen Fryer
7. Dorothea Murphy: Dr. Murphy's wife
8. Dr. Dianne Johnson: Betty Harrison's psychiatrist and colleague of Glen Fryer
9. Reverend Gerald Johnson: Dianne's husband

First, it's important to note that all of these people are connected in bizarre ways. After her attack, Betty had therapy with Dr. Dianne Johnson, a child psychiatrist she knew from CPRI when her son, Richard, had treatment there. Since Betty's car was in police custody, her boss, Dr. Murphy, who was friends with Glen Fryer, offered to drive her to her counselling appointments. So, Betty goes to CPRI for counselling, to see a psychiatrist who worked for Glen, in the same building as Glen's office.

Further, Betty was surrounded by people who had fantastic reasons for disliking Glen Fryer. According to Alsop's notes, Dr. Murphy's wife, Dorothea, was rumoured to be having an affair with Glen, which her husband knew about[42]. Betty also spent a lot of time with Dr. Dianne and Rev. Gerald Johnson, socially, and Dr. Johnson hated Glen Fryer, although she never shared her reasons.[43]

As you will see, at Glen Fryer's eventual trial, there was no physical evidence to back up the story that Glen Fryer was their harasser, or Betty's attacker, or Jackie's murderer. He also had alibis — neither particularly great — for both the night that Jackie disappeared and the night that Betty was attacked. So why are we still talking about Glen Fryer?

Well, Glen Fryer is still an awfully suspicious character. There are so many circumstances and coincidences involved in the story that it's impossible not to give him the side-eye. I will go into all of that. It gets weirder, believe me.

In the end, someone really did attack Betty Harrison. Someone really did murder Jackie English.

Just because you are smart enough not to leave physical evidence and smart enough to have your wife give you an alibi, doesn't necessarily mean you didn't do it, right?

With that little introduction, let's jump down the rabbit hole.

———

When Betty got out of the hospital after her attack, she understandably had a lot of things to deal with. First, there was the physical pain. She felt disfigured and scars were developing on her face, so she was afraid to go outside. She didn't want anyone to see her. This was further complicated by her paranoia, insomnia, and depression.

---

42 In our interview, Fryer denied knowing the Murphys, so I was unable to ask him about their relationship. I was unable to track down Dorothea Murphy to ask her about it.

43 When I interviewed Fryer in 2018, he couldn't tell me why she hated him, either.

One of the first things she wanted to do was sell her car. The police had kept her Volkswagen Beetle, and she never wanted to see it again after the attack. She hoped she could sell it right off the police lot, as soon as it was released from evidence. With the car all ready to go, she prepared to make a sale, but could not find the insurance slip. This piece of paper was required to finish the transaction. Her son, Richard, assured her that he'd put the new insurance papers in the car that November, but no matter how hard they looked, the police could not find it. The insurance slip was certainly missing.[44] Betty had to call her agent to get a copy and make other arrangements, and she eventually sold the car.

In January, Betty went back to work. Dr. Harvey Murphy and his wife, Dorothea Murphy, had always been kind to her, and they were especially tender after the attack. Since Betty had disposed of her car, Dr. Murphy kindly picked her up and gave her rides when she needed them. They decided she should see psychiatrist Dr. Dianne Johnson, who was a colleague of Murphy's and whom Betty had known since her son had been a patient at CPRI. Harvey could drive Betty to her appointments at the Children's Psychiatric Research Institute. Betty agreed to go, and the visits became regular.

Dr. Harvey Murphy was friends with the principal at CPRI, Glen Fryer. One day, after he dropped Betty off at her session, he went to see Fryer, who suggested that the four of them, including Betty and Dr. Johnson, have coffee together after the appointment. Fryer sent the message by secretary, but as soon as Betty heard the invitation, she became distraught and refused. She was very upset. The four of them met in the hallway — meaning that Betty saw Fryer face-to-face[45] — and Harvey made the polite excuse that they didn't have time for coffee. He could tell something was wrong. He

---

44 The missing insurance slip will become an important point later on.

45 Betty's attacker had not been wearing a mask.

drove Betty home. He didn't recall Betty saying anything about the attack or illuminating her negative reaction to Fryer.

Betty Harrison later testified that at the beginning of February 1970, she received an envelope in the mail. The words were written with a children's printing stencil, and inside the envelope was a note that said, "We will be watching you. Final." She was terrified. She burned the letter and the envelope and immediately contacted Dr. Johnson for counselling.

FEBRUARY 16, 1970. Richard Harrison found the blood-stained scarf Betty had lost in the attack tied to their front-door handle.

Dr. Johnson and her husband, Rev. Johnson, later said that they experienced harassment of their own at their family home in Ilderton, around the same time as the Harrisons. The outdoor floodlights were smashed on three or four separate occasions. They saw footprints in the snow leading to their outbuildings. They came home late one night and found items of their children's clothing scattered in the driveway. Other times, they found the house open, as if someone had broken in, but nothing was taken. They felt like they were being watched. Someone broke into their car and moved things around. Dianne could swear there were cars following her. She could see them in the rear-view mirror. Once, someone even tried to run her off the road.

FEBRUARY 24, 1970. Betty visited the Johnsons' home. Betty, Diane, and Gerald started to talk about all the strange things they had experienced, and Dianne shared that she had seen some odd and unexplained happenings at CPRI, too — unusual phone calls and missing files. Dr. Johnson later related their conversation. She said Betty was "quite upset . . . I was attempting to calm her down . . . I said that not just a working man could be sick[46] but

---

46 Meaning deranged, disturbed, or deviant.

a lawyer, doctor, or teacher. I mentioned some of the difficulties we were having at the institute. I was talking about the fact that some of the teachers had been receiving threatening phone calls and some of them had received various things in the mail and that they were very frightened . . . I said that the principal was sick. I didn't mention any names."

"Are you talking about Glen Fryer?" Betty had asked.

"How do you know him?" she'd replied.

"He's a friend of my boss, Dr. Harvey Murphy."

Whoever had attacked Betty must have been motivated by her involvement in the case and the description her husband gave police, and if the Johnsons were getting harassed in the same way as Betty, they assumed that all of these troubles were caused by one individual. As the three of them talked, they became convinced that Fryer must be the guy who was harassing them all, and, by extension, must have been involved in Jackie English's murder.

FEBRUARY 25, 1970. The very next day, Betty sat down with Detective Alsop and his partner Detective Topham. That was the first time she mentioned Glen Fryer in association with her attack. The officers followed her lead and went to the school, where they interviewed a bunch of the staff, some who liked Fryer and some who didn't. Dr. Dianne Johnson was right. Strange things had been happening — unusual occurrences — and there were a lot of people who hated Glen Fryer.

Right around that time, Glen Fryer was asked to resign from his job, for probably unrelated reasons.

APRIL 4, 1970. Betty Harrison took it upon herself to do a little investigative work. She told Alsop she wanted to hear Glen Fryer's voice to see if it was the same voice she had heard in the threatening phone calls she got before her attack. She had Richard call the Fryer house, while she listened on another phone. "I realized that . . . if I recognized his voice, that he would recognize mine." This was why she got her son to dial. "I recognized his voice . . . the man that was in the car the night I was hurt."

The next day she drove past Fryer's house twice. The first time, during the day, the driveway was empty. When she came back after midnight, she saw a car that she later said looked just like the one she saw on the night of her attack. She told Detective Alsop.

Of course, if Betty had already met Fryer, she would already know if he looked like her attacker and already know if he sounded like the man who had been calling her house. Whether or not her phone call to the Fryers was actually made has never been confirmed by the Fryers, but the story would serve her by backing up her assertions that Glen was her attacker.

APRIL 8, 1970. Based on Betty's concerns, Detective Alsop dutifully went to interview Fryer a couple of days later at his home. He didn't realize that this interview was happening in the middle of Fryer's resignation. Alsop made sure not to mention Betty's name, but he asked Fryer if he knew anything about the attack on Dr. Murphy's secretary. Fryer said, yes, of course he had heard about it. He specifically said that Dorothea Murphy, Dr. Murphy's wife, would "confide" in him. They had just been talking the day before. He said that Dr. Murphy's secretary was attacked on a country road "because she had seen something she shouldn't have seen." When Alsop asked him about the strange things going on in the school, he joked that he saw lots of weird things at CPRI; after all, it was a school filled with "retarded" children.

Ruth Fryer came in then and asked why the officers were there.

"They came to take away your driver's licence," joked Fryer.

APRIL 10, 1970. The situation with Betty Harrison had caused a great deal of conflict between her employers, Harvey and Dorothea Murphy. A fight began that lasted at least two days and resulted in Dr. Murphy getting home at 1:30 a.m. and sleeping on the couch. The reason for the fight is unknown, but while Dr. Murphy was out of the house, his wife was on the phone with Glen Fryer. [47]

Dorothea Murphy was very good friends with Glen Fryer, and she told Betty Harrison, "He wouldn't do anything to anyone . . . he wouldn't kill that little girl or hurt you either."

Harvey Murphy must have been swayed by his wife. He knew Glen Fryer had polio as a child, and his disability was pronounced and obvious. Harvey called Betty and demanded to know if her attacker had a limp, pressing her on the issue. Eventually, Betty admitted that if the man had a limp, it was probably because the dog had bitten him. This was upsetting for Dr. Murphy, who now believed that Betty was lying, despite having every reason to want Fryer to be guilty. This was the man who had come between Dr. Murphy and his wife, putting their marriage in jeopardy.

APRIL 12, 1970. The day before Fryer's resignation, Betty Harrison and the Johnsons conspired to trap him in a letter-writing scheme. They were absolutely convinced that Fryer was guilty of harassing them, of attacking Betty, and of killing Jackie English. To prove it, they decided to send Glen Fryer a letter, described in court records as a red folder containing a *Life* magazine subscription renewal notice. It said in large threatening letters on the front, "You can't say we haven't warned you. Your subscription to *Life* will expire in a few weeks." This was the perfect device for their plan. They underlined certain words for emphasis and put it in an envelope addressed to Fryer. They would mail it to him and see if it triggered a response. They put the items together at the Johnsons' home in Ilderton, about a twenty-minute drive north of London. Betty took it with her and promised to put it in the mail, which she says she did on the way home to London. The post office outlet most

---

47 As per Alsop's notes.

conveniently located on her route home from Ilderton was Sub Post Office 18, which was in a convenience store on Dundas Street East.

At trial, Dr. Johnson recalled her conversation with Betty and Gerald that precipitated their postal scheme. "We had been discussing the various things that had been happening to Mrs. Harrison and also the various things that had been happening around our house," she said. She said their home had been broken into three times, the last time on November 19, 1970. Two clocks and an accordion[48] were damaged.

"We wondered in a sense how Mr. Fryer would feel if he received a similar type of notice [to the threatening letters Betty Harrison had received]," Dr. Johnson said.

"None of which . . . you know as a fact are attributable to Mr. Fryer?" asked the defence lawyer.

"I haven't one hundred percent proof, no."

"Do you have any?"

"Concrete proof, no."

"What other kind of proof is there?" asked the lawyer.

"Prior to any connection with Mrs. Harrison, we led a quiet life. Nothing was happening. Everything was fine," she asserted.

"Why did you send that letter to Fryer?"

"I was under a great deal of tension," she explained. "There was a possibility he might be involved . . . [and we did it] because I was probably acting in an emotional fashion."

Dianne went to bed, leaving Betty alone with Dianne's husband, Gerald. They stayed up late. Dianne said she did not know until two days later that the letter was mailed.

"I think we agreed we should send something to the accused," Gerald said under oath. "Partly as a release of our tension . . . and also to see what the reaction of the accused would be."

"Were you threatening him?" asked Fryer's defence lawyer.

---

48 It's funny. It's funny that an accordion was damaged.

"I would not say we were threatening him . . . in one sense."

"Do you think that was a rather horrible thing to do?"

"At the time, sir, with the things that were happening to us, which seemed rather horrible, it didn't."

"It didn't seem that way, did it?"

"No, it didn't. In hindsight, yes."

"He was doing these horrible things to you, so it was all right to do a horrible thing to him?"

"We didn't know if he was doing the horrible things," admitted Gerald.

APRIL 13, 1970. Suspicious of Betty Harrison's son, Richard, Alsop went to the Green Giant plant, where Richard worked, to see if the employees wore green jackets, like the man who'd been seen at the Metropolitan restaurant on the nights before Jackie's disappearance, and the man seen in the field near Frankie Jensen's school. He also uncovered confidential records about Richard that he thought could be misinterpreted and seem overly suspicious to the public. Alsop did not record what these confidential records revealed, but he dug deeper and found out more about Richard Harrison. He had been treated at CPRI and had taken remedial classes taught by Glen Fryer. This information made it very unlikely that Betty and Fryer hadn't had an interaction before her attack. If she had met him in the past, why didn't she recognize him that night and immediately identify him to police? When I asked Glen about Betty in our interview, he told me that he'd never spoken to her.

Fryer submitted his resignation to CPRI that same day. He later told the court, "I was fired because I felt within myself, and the Department of Education felt, that I could not administer the school with so many pressures both from education and health. I found the task for me was too great to cope with."

To his credit, the administration of CPRI had gone through a major shift that year, as did many similar facilities around the province of Ontario. About half of the CPRI staff left that spring during the administrative reshuffle, completely unrelated to what was transpiring with Glen Fryer.

However, there were definitely other factors at play that led to Fryer's dismissal. His colleague and fellow churchgoer, chiropractor Dr. Robert Dryburgh, explained at court that Fryer had talked to him about it. Fryer had said that he had tried to cover up a mistake made by his secretary that involved the cashing of some cheques. Dryburgh did not know the name of the secretary and said it could have been two or three years prior to the resignation. "Glen had apparently tried to protect his secretary," said Dryburgh.

APRIL 15, 1970. The *Life* magazine subscription card Betty had sent to Fryer on April 12, missing the envelope, had shown up in the mailbox of her home on Elgin Street. She later told police that she was scared, so she burned it. She thought she would get in trouble. "I shouldn't have mailed it to him, and I couldn't very well take it to the police and say I mailed him this and he brought it back."

Neither she nor the Johnsons told Detective Alsop or any other member of law enforcement about the results of their little test.

APRIL 20, 1970. Not knowing what Betty and the Johnsons had been up to with their letter-writing conspiracy — although he would find out later — Alsop went to the Harrisons' house to show her, Verdun, and Richard a series of photographs, hoping to narrow down his list of suspects. Since the attack, Betty had looked at about 1,200 mug shots. This time, Alsop showed her just twelve, a picture of Glen Fryer among them. She pointed out Glen Fryer, but did not say that she knew who he was or his name. Alsop knew she was lying. Though she wouldn't admit it, he knew she knew the name of the man in the picture, so he questioned her. His notebook recalls the conversation in detail:

"You pointed out the [third picture] from the top left-hand side."

She started to cry and nodded yes. "I don't want to talk about it."

"Why did you point him out?"

"Because he was the only one who looked familiar."

"Familiar for what?"

"He looks like the man I saw at the Metropolitan Store."

". . . Did you see him since that time?"

She started to cry again. "I think so."

"When?"

"In December."

"What happened when you saw the man in December?"

"I just know his face. I can't tell you how. I just remember it."

"What are you referring to, that you remember his face?"

"The night I was attacked in the car [and] at the Metropolitan Store, he was the one talking to [Jackie English]. He was the shorter of the two." She said she had never seen him before, except on these two occasions, which Alsop knew was untrue. She said, "I would like to know what it is that bothers me about that picture." She stared at it for half a minute.

"Got the answer?" asked Alsop.

"No," she replied. "Just his eyes."

All this time, Alsop was aware that Betty knew exactly who Glen Fryer was.

Dr. Dianne Johnson conveniently happened to be at the Harrison house during this interview. As Alsop discussed the photographs with the family, he noted that Dianne spontaneously began talking about the man in the photo. She told Alsop she had seen him on the previous Saturday at 3:30 p.m., with the detail that he was wearing dark brown trousers. The detective thought this was odd, that Dr. Johnson clearly knew who Fryer was and was offering information about him, but no one had stated that Fryer was the man in the picture. They all behaved as though they were oblivious. Alsop later said in court: "When Mrs. Harrison looked at the picture, she had had two or possibly three months of discussions with the Johnson family. Mrs. Harrison knew Fryer and certainly had seen Fryer before she saw the pictures."

Alsop also showed the folder of photos to Betty's son, Richard, who picked out Fryer, too, as the man at the Met. He also did not admit that he knew him, although later in trial he'd admit that Fryer had taught him remedial classes and had done developmental testing with him at CPRI.

APRIL 23, 1970. Betty Harrison reported more harassment. She said that someone had tried to break into her house and that she heard someone in the back shed.

CHAPTER EIGHTEEN

MEET GLEN FRYER

"The scripture says 'Vengeance is mine sayeth the Lord.
I will repay.' So, I left everything with Him as my advocate."

— GLEN FRYER

In August 2018, I sent a letter to Glen Fryer, hoping that he would agree to an interview for this book. I knew he was religious, and having grown up in an evangelical household, I felt that I could perhaps speak his language. He'd attended the Hamilton Road Brethren Church, where my parents also went for a brief time in the early 1970s. My mother remembers his good friend Dr. Dryburgh, a church elder there. Fryer also went to West Park Baptist.[49] My family is rooted in the Baptist church, and among us are missionaries and pastors. My childhood was steeped in religion. I knew exactly what I had to do. I wrote to Glen that he had been framed by Betty Harrison and the Johnsons and signed my letter "God Bless." This caught his

---

49 This was the same church attended by Helmuth Buxbaum, who famously had his wife murdered by a hit man in the 1980s. My grandmother lived in the Buxbaum-owned retirement home in Komoka, Ontario, which is really of no consequence, but just goes to further show how small the Forest City really is. To make it weirder, Anne English attends West Park Baptist today.

attention, but by the time he called me, I'd given up hope that he ever would. It turned out that the delay had been caused by the death of his daughter, Cathy.

He was much like I expected: charismatic, humorous, pointedly evasive. He joked about going jogging with his new knee, at the age of eighty-five. He laughed about the old story of him vacuuming dandelions on his front lawn, which you'll read about later. He told me how he wished he'd done things differently and ministered more to those who became his enemies. Loving his enemies was a big theme. He came across as open and friendly, forthcoming even, but at the end of our phone call, I was left with the realization that he hadn't really told me anything. At all. We were on the phone for more than an hour, and I'd barely learned a single tidbit of new information. This was very unusual for me. I've interviewed hundreds of people, for my books as well as newspapers and magazines. I could only remember one lengthy interview that had been so fruitless, and it had been with someone who was nearly incapacitated from old age. Somehow, Glen Fryer had managed to avoid saying anything while doing most of the talking. I'd hardly got a word in edgewise.

To be fair, he warned me there were certain things he wouldn't talk about. He referred to it as "the stop sign," and every time I got close to asking him a direct question — even about something that was not particularly incriminating — he put up his defences and changed the subject, usually to something religious. He quoted to me all the stanzas of his favourite hymn, which he told me he sings every morning. He gave me proverbial advice from the Bible. He tied together superficial biographical anecdotes with his seemingly complete devotion to his faith and constant references to Christianity. It was a beautifully crafted smokescreen.

In the end, I sensed that Glen Fryer had something to hide. I just wasn't sure what it was.

On November 25, 1932, Glen Fryer was born in Stratford, Ontario. His family — father Arthur, mother Alice, brothers Harold and Keith — lived in a working-class neighbourhood, and his father and grandfather worked for the Canadian National Railway.[50] From my interview with Fryer, I learned that at the age of three, he suffered from polio. His parents had told him that they had asked the police to drive them to London, where there was medication available,[51] but the police said no. They had no other way to get him there. As a result, Fryer blamed the police for the fact that he spent years in a brace, leaving one of his legs shorter than the other, which gave him a pronounced limp. He required continual use of the painful device even while he was sleeping. He developed an overly charismatic personality to compensate, and a lack of respect for cops — which would only be reinforced later. He had a broad smile, a symmetrically handsome face, and a thick head of dark hair. His lanky arms extended to expressive hands, and his face came alive when he had an audience. Everything about him was designed to make you look past his deformity.

He pursued a career as an educator and married Ruth, a girl with whom he had grown up in Stratford. She was a meek nurse, and the pair were very religious. They moved to London in 1955 for work, where they lived briefly at 31½ The Ridgeway, just two blocks from the Stanley Variety. They then moved to 320 Ridout Street in Wortley Village.

Glen Fryer presented himself as a ladies' man, a go-getter, and a leader in the community. When Amway, a popular pyramid scheme sales operation, moved their first international headquarters to London, Ontario, in 1962, he and Ruth were eager to get

---

50   I got these details from the archives, not from Glen.

51   There was no such thing as medication for polio until a vaccine was introduced in 1955, the year after Fryer was married.

involved. It was an easy fit for Glen, a man who liked to be wacky and make people smile. To some folks, he was just weird. A lot of his jokes fell flat, but he told them anyway, convinced that they had humour in them. He was the kind of guy who liked to laugh at his own zingers. In between smiles, his face had a dead quality, making *London Free Press* reporters George Hutchison and Isaac Turner think he matched Betty Harrison's description of a man with "dead eyes." He gave the impression of a void, an empty shell performing as the person he wanted everyone to think he was.

I received a phone call from a woman named Abigail[52] who knew Glen Fryer. Her account was fascinating, and while it is not something I've been able to corroborate, I'll present it unvarnished and allow you to decide what to make of it. She remembered a day in 1963 or 1964 when she was walking home from school. She was about 11 years old. As she went along the Wortley Village sidewalk, a station wagon pulled up next to her. In it was Glen Fryer. She recognized him as the father of Glenda and Ricky, who went to Tecumseh Public School with her. He snarled at her and told her to get in the car. Abigail was confused. She wondered if he was drunk and thought she was Glenda. He opened the passenger door for her, insistent that she come in to the car, but she didn't. Instead, Abigail turned tail and ran. [53]

She told me how she had dashed across Garfield Avenue to her friend Jane's[54] house, but there was no answer. She ran back across the street and banged on another door, but no one came. As she ran, she saw Fryer in his station wagon. He had turned his car around and was coming after her. Abigail knew he couldn't keep up with her on foot, because he had a limp, so she hid under a bush and waited for him to leave. As soon as she thought it

---

52 Name changed.

53 I have not spoken to Fryer about Abigail's claim.

54 Name changed.

was safe, Abigail sprinted home. Gasping for air, she told her mother what had happened, and her mother immediately called the police. An officer came quickly in case the perpetrator might still be in the neighbourhood, and while Abigail already knew who had tried to pick her up, he wanted her to make an identification. He got her in the cruiser and suggested they drive around Wortley Village to see if they could spot the car again.

They were driving up High Street when Abigail saw the car, heading straight for them. She reached up her hand and pointed her little pink finger at it, exclaiming, and as they passed him, she saw Glen Fryer turn his head and look right at her.

The officer took her home.

Later that night, her cousin, a rookie cop, was sent over to her house to give her an update. He went in the other room with her mother, and while Abigail wanted to know what was said, she couldn't hear. Her mother came to her and said, "You don't need to worry about that man anymore."

In 1966, Glen got his gig as principal at the Children's Psychiatric Research Institute, and in February 1968, one week after Frankie Jensen disappeared, the Fryers and their four kids moved out to the suburbs to be closer to the Institute. Their new address was 598 Headley Drive, at the corner of Plymouth, in a west-end neighbourhood referred to as Oakridge by Londoners, very close to where Jacqueline Dunleavy and Frankie Jensen lived. He moved there the same year they were killed. A family member told me he'd had the keys to the empty house one week before Frankie vanished. I asked Glen if he had helped look for Frankie — since many local teachers and neighbours had — and he was taken aback, as if this was a ridiculous question. It had nothing to do with him, he said.

While their split-level home looked outwardly like a happy place, inside was a different story. Glen and Ruth's marriage was fraught and violent, escalating over time. On one occasion, Glen hurt Ruth so badly that she stayed with a friend for two weeks. In another incident, Ruth saw her husband waiting to give a ride to a female teacher. She became enraged with jealousy, reaching in through the open car window to grab him, and Glen rolled up the window on her arm. She was injured enough that she reported the incident to police. These events were all detailed in the *London Free Press*, and Fryer didn't seem particularly interested in discussing them with me. From his point of view, his marriage to the now-deceased Ruth was a beautiful fairy tale.

Dennis Alsop leads Glen Fryer into the courthouse for his bail hearing.

London Free Press Collection of Photographic Negatives, [1970-04-27], Archives and Special Collections, Western Libraries, Western University.

APRIL 26, 1970. Glen Fryer was arrested for the attack on Elizabeth Harrison. Detective Alsop and his partner pulled up in front of the Fryers' split-level suburban home at around 9:45 a.m. During this arrest, Alsop took extensive notes. They read him the charges and he immediately denied committing the crime.

"Is that right? I wasn't even there."

"You're under arrest," said Detective Topham.

"All I can say is the charge certainly isn't right. I wasn't there. I don't even know the woman. This is a false arrest. Can I call a lawyer?"

"Do you want to do it at our office?" asked Alsop.

"I would rather do it here," said Fryer.

"Well, you will be going with us," said Alsop.

"That's all right. Can I shave first?"

"Yes, you may."

He came out in a white button-up shirt, a blue striped tie, dark blue pants, and a grey sport coat. The kids came into the room — or were sent in — and innocently asked if they'd be going to Sunday service. Obviously, they would not.

"Can I have any breakfast?" asked Fryer.

"Yes, you may," said Alsop.

"Do you fellows want any coffee?"

"No, thanks."

As he made his food, he chatted with the officers. Fryer was always on the lookout for someone to converse with, and his game of shifting perceptions was already afoot.

"You mentioned last time [I was interviewed] that Mrs. Murphy was to contact me. She didn't."

"We thought she might. Can we have the keys to your car and office?" asked Alsop.

"Yes, they are in the car. I always leave them there, so if anybody took my car I wouldn't know it."

They left the house and stopped at Fryer's office at CPRI to get his briefcase and some work he had to complete. The main red brick buildings, covered in ivy, were quite empty on a Sunday morning, as the full-time residents lived in cabins at the back of the property. Fryer told the officers which keys to use to get inside.

"Will my office be searched?" he asked.

"We have a search warrant," said Alsop.

"Oh, have you? When will it be searched? I would like it done today, to save any embarrassment."

"It will be done today."

"Oh, good. There is certainly a lot of gossip here. One thing disturbs me: who of the officials will be notified?"

"We have someone in mind to let us in to search your office," said Alsop.

They watched as Glen Fryer gathered up his papers. He was giving a seminar the following Tuesday and commented, "That is ironic. I am supposed to speak on aggression. Do you want to check my datebook?"

"We can do it later on."

"I just wonder where I was [on the night of the attack] myself. Can I go in my secretary's office to see the datebook?" He went into the office and checked the records. "It is open, it is blank. I had no appointments on that day."

While they were driving, Fryer commented, "You fellows woke me up. I am so tired." He was very talkative as they went along. He made observations about what he saw along the drive, a bump in the road, his old car. The trademark Fryer humour was on full display, as he chattered throughout the journey.

After Glen was taken away, other officers searched his house for evidence. They gave Ruth Fryer their warrant, hoping she could help them locate two specific items that were listed there. The first was an eight-inch knife with a guard on the handle. She couldn't help them with that. The second item was the insurance certificate for Elizabeth Harrison's 1966 Volkswagen, which was still missing. The presence of this insurance certificate, a presumed trophy taken by the attacker, would go a long way towards Fryer's possible guilt.

"It came in a green[55] envelope," Mrs. Fryer placidly told the officer. "In the morning, in the mail a week or two ago."

She told officers that it was addressed to Glen so she had put it on the piano for him to open when he got home. He did so, told Ruth it was just an advertisement, and dropped it in the garbage. Nevertheless, Ruth thought she might still have the card and envelope. She had scooped it out of the garbage after Glen threw it away, because the Fryers were thinking about changing insurance companies. They had even contacted Abstainers' Insurance for information about rates.

She went upstairs and returned shortly, handing over the missing evidence to Detective Alsop with seeming ignorance. Ruth Fryer said she thought it was advertisement, but it didn't look like one. The insurance card was tucked inside a greeting card. On the outside was printed, "I don't feel safe around you," and on the inside flap it said, "You've got my combination."

They asked her if the envelope might still be around. She went on the back porch to grab a garbage bag. Digging around, she found the corresponding envelope. It looked identical to the threatening letters Betty Harrison had received, the name and address printed with a child's stencil set, except for the street number, which was printed by hand. It seemed that the same person who was sending threatening letters to Betty was sending evidence to Fryer.

While officers searched the house, they asked Mrs. Fryer where her husband was on December 11, 1969, the night of Betty Harrison's attack. She went and got her chequebook to jog her memory. Chequebooks used to a be great way to track your own whereabouts, a kind of financial diary, much like looking at online

---

55 Some reports say the envelope was blue.

bank statements would be today. Ruth Fryer found a receipt for a purchase she'd made on December 11 at Kmart. She remembered the shopping trip and said she'd taken three of their four children with her. The fourth child had been ill and stayed home, which worked out because Glen was busy with some paperwork that had to be handed in the next day, Saturday. She said when she got back at 10 p.m., he was there with their sick child. The December 11 entry showed a $93.24 cheque to Kmart for clothing, a large purchase that would equate to about $600 in today's currency. This seemed to provide a plausible alibi for Glen Fryer.

I'd like to take a moment to address the issue of "the Porn Man."

Many amateur sleuths were interested to find out about the Porn Man in Michael Arntfield's book, *Murder City*. According to the legend, the Porn Man's house was searched by police, who allegedly found child pornography and a steamer trunk containing mason jars filled with human feces. Many people from the Unsolved Canada community have assumed that this Porn Man was Glen Fryer, as is inferred in some sections of Arntfield's book but questioned in later chapters.

Detective Alsop made detailed notes. There is no mention of this evidence being found on the day of Fryer's arrest, nor any mention of a previous search. There is no mention of the Porn Man at all, and no reference to clogged toilets, child pornography, or poop jars.

I decided to track down the source of the Porn Man legend, and I discovered that it had come from the *Toronto Star* in 1992. A series of articles were written by Nick Pron and John Duncanson about cold cases in Southwestern Ontario; they were on to the Forest City Killer before anyone else. They mentioned the Porn Man in one of these articles, but they didn't say who he was or when the search took place. They didn't even say it was in relation to the Jackie English murder, but simply gave it as an example of the kind of grotesque stuff happening in London at the time.

The name Nick Pron stood out to me. I had coincidentally just finished reading his book *Lethal Marriage*, about Paul Bernardo and Karla Homolka. I decided to try to track him down and I sent him a Facebook message. I was excited to talk to a veteran crime reporter, and the author of a book that I had found incredibly compelling.

One of the most fascinating aspects of *Lethal Marriage* is that Nick saw the videotapes of Paul and Karla's victims. The court banned them from ever being screened outside of the courtroom and were later destroyed. Only a select group of journalists were allowed to see them, and that included Nick. The court order did not forbid him from writing about what he saw on those tapes and, within the boundaries of good taste, he did, insofar as the descriptions were necessary to the story. I think he did a great job of balancing the reader's curiosity with what was appropriate to share — I'm sure there are others out there who would disagree and say that no description of the events on those tapes should have been made in any media, ever.

Nick Pron couldn't help me find the source of the Porn Man story. Short of digging around in his files myself, there is nothing more that I or anyone else can do to figure out where the story came from, unless one of the officers present at the search comes forward, or the Porn Man himself. Nick Pron's writing partner, John Duncanson, is deceased.

The second source of the Porn Man story is a passed down community rumour that the groundskeeper of CPRI, who was called to do some plumbing at the Fryer household, called police when he found kiddie porn 8mm film jammed in the pipes, resulting in the search that found the mason jars of feces and child pornography. That story would have to be confirmed by police reports in the London Police archives, to which I am not allowed access. However, when I spoke to Glen Fryer, he told me a story meant to illustrate his great relationships with his co-workers at the Institute: "My sewer plugged up once, and we were only a block away [from CPRI]. And the head of the maintenance, I told him, 'We're going to have to get somebody to look after my sewers. It's got to be dug up and replaced.' He got the guys together, they went over to my house, dug it all up, fixed all the plumbing, and went back home again. Didn't cost me a penny. We had a beautiful relationship."

He volunteered this story without me ever mentioning the Porn Man. I didn't press him about it, because I had more questions about the Forest City Killer, not the Porn Man, and I didn't want to compromise the interview. Someone, however, should ask him.

Detective Alsop sat across from Glen Fryer in the interrogation room. It was the evening of Fryer's arrest.

"What can you tell me about the attack on Mrs. Harrison on the evening of December 11, 1969, in the area of Hubrey Road on the Fourth Concession of Westminster Township?" Alsop asked.

"I was not in that area, or involved in this incident . . . I was not involved in this incident in that area at that time or any other date . . . [Dr. Murphy] has a secretary and I believe the secretary is the woman named by you, Elizabeth Harrison."

"Can you remember Mrs. Murphy telling you anything about Mrs. Harrison involved with the police?" asked Alsop. He knew that Glen Fryer had a particularly close relationship with Dorothea Murphy. It would track that he'd heard about the drama.

"You mean the bad experience she had in which she was attacked?"

"Yes."

"Yes, on one occasion, Mr. and Mrs. Murphy and I discussed this incident in their home in their kitchen . . . it would have to be after Christmas."

Fryer asked if he could call his wife. Afterwards, he said, "May I make one more statement that would make all of this unnecessary? The day of December 11, I went home from school between 4:30 and 5, helped get supper, and was with my family until a while after 7. My wife was there and my four children were there. Around 8, they went shopping."

He volunteered a sample of saliva and made eight handwriting samples, copying out the address of the Harrison home. These would be compared to the threatening notes that Betty Harrison had received. Afterwards, Alsop and Topham drove him to OPP headquarters, where he was held in custody. Later, he was released from custody on $5,000 bail.

MAY 6, 1970. Betty had a conversation with her boss, Dr. Harvey Murphy. He had lost trust in her almost completely and relayed his conversation to Detective Alsop, who recorded it in his notes.

"How did [the police] get onto Mr. Fryer — was it because I took you out to the Institute [for counselling]?" asked Dr. Murphy.

"No, things started happening after I went out there."

"You mean your scarf being tied to your doorknob?"

"What do you mean?" asked Betty.

"You know, your scarf was tied to your doorknob."

"Who told you that?" she asked.

"I think Vern [Verdun] that told me."

"It wasn't Vern, I know that."

"It was Richard. He told me the night it was found," remembered Dr. Murphy.

"Listen, Harvey, Vern and I have made it a point to be around Richard so that he won't say anything."

"You told me," replied Dr. Murphy.

"What a ruddy lie," she said.

"Is it true? Did it have anything to do with taking my fingerprints?" Apparently the police had taken Dr. Murphy's fingerprints.

"It might interest you to know that they found a lovely set of fingerprints," she said threateningly. No other mention of these fingerprints is made in any of the files available, and so there is no way to know whose fingerprints she was so confident about. The conversation with Dr. Murphy did betray Betty's desire to keep things secret, and to hide things about her family, particularly regarding her son, Richard.

Dorothea Murphy got in touch with Detective Alsop, as she had forgotten to mention that Glen Fryer had borrowed her car on occasion, and she wanted to make sure that they had it on the record. She didn't want to be implicated with the attack on Betty Harrison or the murder of Jackie English.

Dr. Harvey Murphy assured Detective Alsop that the police had the wrong impression about his wife: she was rumoured to have had extramarital affairs with more than one man.

MAY 7, 1970. As the domestic battle between the Murphys unfolded in daily dramatic shifts, Harvey Murphy changed his story. He told Alsop that he suspected his wife could have been having an affair with Glen Fryer after all. The couple, who had been plagued with problems in recent weeks, had just fought over Dorothea's relationship with another man, and Dr. Murphy suspected that this "other man" was simply a cover for Glen Fryer, and his wife was trying to hide her relationship with him. When asked about it, Dorothea told Detective Alsop that she hadn't told police everything about her relationship with Fryer because she thought he was just using her. Alsop did not specify if she was actually having an affair with Fryer or if they were just close friends and Harvey was jealous.

MAY 14, 1970. Betty found another threatening letter. She was shopping, and when she came out to her car in the parking lot, she found a greeting card on the seat. It said, "Since I last saw you I've been doing a little bit of this, that and the other thing. Mostly the other thing." She reported it to Detective Alsop.

JULY 6, 1970. Another threatening letter was intercepted at the post office, where Alsop was having all of the Harrisons' mail checked. The envelope contained lined paper, the words formed by letters cut out of a magazine: "Coming soon. Your death. Not today perhaps, not tomorrow, but soon, very soon. Whether you spend it at the beach or in the backyard, get the most out of your summer. After all, it's short enough."

Superintendent McBride sent a report to his superiors at the OPP sometime in late 1969 or early 1970: "If one can believe any of these deaths are related to the English murder, coupled with the manner of the attack of Mrs. Harrison, e.g. the stabbing, the kissing of her bloodstained cheek, the remark, 'I like to fuck a woman after she is dead,' one can only conclude that in all probability we are searching for some form of (sexual) psychopath(s). I make this last remark as a layperson, although several psychiatrists in London that I have had occasion to interview, concur with this possibility."

Whichever psychiatrists spoke to McBride would have been privy to details about the unsolved murders in London that were not available to the general public. Could McBride have consulted Dr. Dianne Johnson or one of the other psychiatrists at the Children's Psychiatric Research Institute?

Meanwhile, the drama leading up to Glen Fryer's trial continued to unfold.

Police were called to Betty Harrison's house when she discovered that Jackie's boyfriend's brother, Richard Lloyd Papple, had shown up at her house to deliver a typewriter. It seemed like a bizarre and troubling coincidence, and that's soon what the police decided. Rick had simply been given the wrong address, possibly as a prank.

On September 25, 1970, Detective Alsop wrote a report detailing Betty Harrison's increasingly erratic behaviour. Her tales of harassment seemed to escalate as the trial approached. On October 4, she said her car was tampered with. On October 6, she found another envelope in her car, which led to surveillance at the scene of her attack. On October 14, a man was questioned after being found prowling around the Harrison home, but no charges were laid. Most oddly, on October 19, police officers keeping track of the Harrison family made reports complaining of fleas at the Elgin Street house.

A lot of resources were being used to make Betty Harrison feel safe.

CHAPTER NINETEEN

THE TRIAL OF GLEN FRYER

*"Someday, someone is going to write a book about
this English case, as we are dealing with some of the
wackiest people that existed. Mrs. Harrison and
Glen Fryer were both insane. Even a TV drama
could not come up with weirder people."*

— DENNIS ALSOP JR.

NOVEMBER 23, 1970. Almost a year after Betty was attacked in her car, the trial began at the old courthouse on Ridout Street, one of the oldest buildings in London. It was built to look like an old castle, with crenellated towers and Gothic arched windows and ivy climbing up the sides. In the basement are old jail cells. Today, the courthouse is located in a much larger building across the street, and the old courthouse is home to administrative offices for the county. There is a grand hall that is rented out for events and weddings, and you can find plenty of photographs online of bridesmaids with goofy looks on their faces, drunkenly posing in those creepy old jail cells. The obvious pun, that marriage is a life sentence, lends itself to the revelry. I've always found the whole place unnerving, especially the solitary confinement cell with its well-worn stone floor. The London and Middlesex Historical Society holds their monthly meeting in the courtroom, which is also used for Middlesex Council Meetings. There are wooden pews staggered upwards in amphitheatre-style seating.

The ceiling is high, with thick wooden beams from pioneer times, and tall windows let in the light.

Betty Harrison was the first witness called to the stand. She testified for two days. Her story had shifted many times over the previous year. It was also contradicted by other witnesses. The events of October 3, 1969, the day before Jackie English disappeared, had been related by Karl Schroeder, who saw the man in the green jacket at the Met; Linda Green, who also saw the man in the green jacket, sitting in a maroon car; Marilyn Hird, who described her hitchhiking adventure with Jackie on the way home from work; Linda Hurst, a waitress who confirmed Marilyn's statement that they were very busy that night and had no time for conversation; and David Papple, who saw Jackie after work and didn't remember her acting strangely at all. None of this aligned with Betty's story that Jackie had been confronted by two men who told her she wasn't worth more than a penny. No one remembered Jackie being so upset that she dropped a glass full of water.

In fact, when the Harrisons had first gone to police, they did not mention any of the dialogue between the men and Jackie. They only said that the men were there and that Jackie was upset. This scant information nonetheless seemed to be enough for law enforcement to use Verdun's description to create a composite sketch on October 19, 1969. All police could say was that the mystery man was wanted for questioning in the case. The man in the composite hadn't even been seen the night Jackie disappeared, he'd been seen the night before, and only at the word of Betty and Verdun Harrison. The sketch was also pretty terrible, but it was still published widely and generated hundreds of leads. It probably helped police soothe an anxious public.

"The only description [Verdun] could give was of a man wearing a dark green or black jacket," the newspaper reported. "Dark trousers and dark, long hair. Mr. Harrison, who was questioned about the man's features by a police department artist, said he was five-foot-eight to ten inches tall, slim, about one hundred sixty-five pounds, between twenty-five and twenty-eight years of age, dark complexion, dark hair, narrow eyes, high cheekbones, a fairly large nose, and somewhat protruding ears."

Of important note here is that the man wore a green jacket. Linda Green had also seen a man matching this description that night at the Metropolitan, so this gave some credence to the Harrisons' story. The composite may have actually captured the likeness of the man in the green jacket, even if the story became warped in the following year.

Regardless of the description, the image it resulted in came under fire. The same court record states: "The composite picture . . . was not, according to Mrs. Harrison and Richard, a very good likeness of the man they had seen at the Met store." It seems difficult to understand why police would feel that this sighting, rather than that of Karl Schroeder or others who saw the man in the green jacket, was considered important enough to create a sketch that would be published in the local paper on October 19, 1969.

When it came to her attack on December 11, 1969, the only source of information on the incident was Betty herself, who relayed a non-linear, often nonsensical, version of events. The description she had initially given of the perpetrator in the hours after the attack was very specific and quite different than the description she gave of the man she saw at the Metropolitan Store in October. However, now both descriptions had become compatible with the accused. A damaged tooth and sallow skin had given way to straight teeth and pale skin, like Fryer's. Her description of the attacker's car shifted too. She initially told police that it was a dark-coloured 1964 to 1967 Ford, but later said it was a light-coloured vehicle, which would make it easier to match with Fryer's car.

Betty could not explain why she would be tender with her attacker and touch his cheek, which sent him into a rage. She could not explain if her attacker limped because he'd been bitten by the dog or because he'd had a limp from the outset.

The defence asked her why she would go out into the dark, alone, to let her dog go for a run after she'd been receiving threatening phone calls and letters. Wasn't she scared? And they asked why she had insisted on saying her stop at Hubrey Road was spontaneous, when a local farmer said she stopped there so regularly that he recognized her Volkswagen Beetle?

If it was spontaneous, and the farmer was mistaken, then her route still did not make sense. Many Londoners will tell you that the quickest way to get back to Betty's home on Elgin Street from the Wellington South shopping area would be to hop on the east-west stretch of Highway 401 and get off at Highbury Avenue, a north-south thoroughfare. This is the closest thing London has to a freeway system, and the little cheat of using the 401 across the south end of town means that many Londoners can commute quickly, skipping over the clog of traffic on city streets. In 1969, this stretch of highway had been around for at least a decade, and this pattern of driving was already well established for people who lived in the Forest City. However, Betty did not take the 401 to Highbury to get home.

It was very curious that she had driven home before calling police and had not driven directly to the hospital for help.

Why did Betty pretend that she didn't know Fryer? Surely, she would have recognized his picture on the day Alsop showed it to her. During the attack, hadn't she recognized him from when her son attended CPRI? Why hadn't she named him immediately? She had no answer.

The defence pummelled her with questions. After Betty was done on the stand, she went home and refused to return to court, saying she was unwell.

Richard Harrison testified, saying that he not only recognized Fryer from remedial classes and CPRI, but that he used to go around to schools collecting science reading labs as a part-time job and had seen Fryer ten years earlier at Chesley Avenue Public School and Trafalgar Public School. His identification of Fryer as the man he saw at the Metropolitan was then totally compromised and useless to the prosecution. However, his connection to Fryer and one other person was still important.

Marilyn Hird took the stand. Marilyn had been assigned remedial classes for kids who needed extra help. These classes were taken downtown. It was in this class where she met Richard Harrison, Betty Harrison's son.

Rick. Harrison.

Could this be the Rick who would later become Harrison Ford, according to Marilyn's dark fantasy?

The teacher of their remedial classes was Glen Fryer.

It turned out that the Hird family and the Harrison family lived only blocks away from each other. The kids likely knew one another from the neighbourhood. Marilyn knew the accused, Glen Fryer, and she knew the victim of the crime, Betty Harrison, the mother of her classmate and friend. She also knew Jackie English, the murder victim associated with the case. Her suicide note had said she knew the killer, who was presumably Glen Fryer if he had indeed attacked Betty. Perhaps she was put on the stand in the hopes that she would finally reveal the secrets she claimed to keep and point the finger at Fryer, but her usual evasiveness persisted. She gave the court no new information that would help the case, except for solidifying a connection between the parties involved, a connection that seems like more than a coincidence and is hard to ignore.

Dr. Dianne Johnson testified, saying, "As far as I am concerned, Mr. Fryer is two people. There are times when he is calm and cool and collected and there are other times when he is irrational."

Fryer's defence lawyer, A.J. Baker, asked her, "What does he do that is irrational?"

"I wouldn't say what he does. It is his conversation."

"His conversation is irrational?"

"Yes."

"Mr. Fryer is mentally ill? Do you consider him to be insane?"

"There are times when I think he could be classed as mentally ill, yes."

"You have thought that for some time, haven't you?"

"Yes."

"You don't particularly like Mr. Fryer, do you?"

"He isn't one of my personal friends."[56]

"And you didn't get along particularly well with him in your job as coordinator [at CPRI], did you?"

"We had our disagreements."

The defence lawyer asked Dianne Johnson if she approved of how Fryer managed CPRI, and she said that she did not. She said that several of the teachers were afraid of him. She could count four.

"Afraid for what?" asked the prosecution. "Their lives? Their safety?"

"Their sanity," she said. "One of them mentioned receiving a phone call."

"Did she know who the phone call was from?"

"No, she didn't . . ."

"She thought it was from Mr. Fryer, didn't she?"

---

56 Despite me asking him more than once, Glen Fryer could not explain why Dianne Johnson disliked him so much.

Other staff members from CPRI testified as well. Former teacher Laura Charlton stated that Fryer had a poor reputation for telling the truth and a poor reputation in how he treated women. Former teacher Doris Terry agreed that his reputation was not good. Terry had received her own threatening letters and was under the impression they had come from Fryer. Doreen Florence, a member of the Liaison Department at CPRI, said, "He did not tell the truth at all times . . . I would say he is thought to have a reputation with some women . . . of going out possibly with other women." Myrna Eamer, another former teacher, said, "He was not considered to tell the truth . . . yes, he could become very angry with women." Fryer's part-time secretary, Margaret Collins, claimed he was even "violent towards younger women," and former teacher Jack McVey agreed, saying, "He had a reputation of becoming extremely upset with women."

The defence brought Dr. Robert Dryburgh forward as a character witness. He was a well-known chiropractor in London, whose son continues the practice today.[57] Dryburgh went to the Hamilton Road Brethren Church with the Fryer family, and so he knew him both professionally and through their faith community, where they served as elders. Fryer still speaks highly of his friend today and asserts that they stayed friends up until his death in the 1990s.

"He's made a number of commitments to me and every one of them he has kept," said Dryburgh. "I would say he is a peace-loving type of man."

Dryburgh also knew Dr. Harvey Murphy and Betty Harrison, who had each called him individually to talk about the attack. "I think Mrs. Harrison knew I had worked with teens at a coffee house,[58] and I spend a lot of time in conversation with people about

---

57   Dr. Dryburgh's son declined to be interviewed for this book.
58   Dr. Dryburgh volunteered with troubled youth.

their problems," he explained. He met with them for counselling at Dr. Murphy's office where they "just talked in generalities about the attack . . . In my thinking, I just figured she had . . . been scared and needed to talk to somebody." When asked if he spoke to Glen Fryer about this meeting, he said, "I never did."

When Ruth Fryer's psychiatrist, Dr. Ross Gillman, was asked if the Fryer house was a happy home, he said it was "not particularly . . . There was a little friction . . . There were disagreements and arguments." While he believed that Glen Fryer had a good reputation in the community, his wife, Ruth, had been hospitalized for two months in 1965 and for six weeks in 1967, both times for suicide attempts. While she told her doctor that she was simply overworked and overtired, and perhaps her suicide attempt was an accidental overdose of sleeping pills, the doctor did not buy her excuses. Ruth swore to him that things were better at home. However, just two months before the trial, she'd spent time in the psychiatric hospital after taking an overdose of tranquilizers. She said again that she was just overworked and worried about money. During her own testimony, she told the court that she had really just "wanted a good sleep."

DECEMBER 7, 1970. Detective Alsop testified, stating the OPP suspected that Glen Fryer was somehow connected to the Jackie English case. He hinted that they may have evidence that they could not bring to court. This additional evidence is nowhere in his files.

The star witness was Fryer himself. He denied all the charges levied against him and said nothing that contradicted any of the evidence previously given.

According to his testimony, Fryer had attended a conference in Windsor from October 1 to 3, 1969. He got back to London at 6:30 p.m. on Friday, October 3, three hours before Betty

Harrison and her family had dinner at the Met. Fryer arrived at his family home to find his wife in a state.

That afternoon, Ruth had gotten a call at work that their fifteen-year-old daughter, Glenda, was caught smoking at her school, Mount St. Joseph Academy. Glenda was suspended for a week. When Ruth got home from her job at 5 p.m., she found that Glenda had not come home and that evening, the Fryers frantically called around, trying to locate their rebellious teenager. At around 11 p.m. they spoke to Dr. and Mrs. Valentine, whose daughter was also missing. The Valentines assured the Fryers that both girls were safe and were staying at a friend's house.

On October 4, the day of Jackie's disappearance, Ruth went to work at the hospital and hoped that Glenda would come home while she was gone. Glen waited at the house with the other children, hoping his daughter would return. However, when Ruth got home at around 5 p.m. that night, their daughter was still missing. The Fryers made a couple of calls, but eventually gave up and got in the car at around 5:30 p.m. to head to Stratford for a family dinner for Ruth's sister, who was celebrating a birthday. Before coming home, they made a few calls to London, hoping to track down their daughter, but it was still no use. On the drive back home, they stopped at a garage in Hyde Park around 9:30 p.m. and Ruth called someone again, hoping to find Glenda.

Then something weird happened. Ruth Fryer said she dropped her husband off at home and went to look at a real estate property all the way back on Hyde Park Road at 10 p.m. First of all, that's a tough drive to make in thirty minutes. According to her court testimony, during their stop at the service station, she had called about seeing the property. She could not explain this event: why she was viewing a house, and why she would do so at 10 at night. Her responses on the stand were murky.

I asked Glen Fryer about this information, in hopes of getting some clarity. He told me that Ruth would have manic episodes and do things like buy boats and cottages — big purchases, like the $600 at Kmart — without talking to him. This was how he explained her going to view a house after dark. He said he couldn't remember the specifics.

He also told me that he owned European and classic cars and had stored one of his vehicles in a garage in Hyde Park. The garage operator would have known Glen Fryer on sight.

DECEMBER 16, 1970. Fryer and his wife had testified that on October 4, 1969, at about the same time that Jackie disappeared, they stopped at a garage in Hyde Park on their way home from a family meal in Stratford. This amounted to an alibi for Glen Fryer. However, a surprise twist caught everyone's attention when the prosecution petitioned Judge Colter to include new evidence from George Morris, who owned that garage in Hyde Park where Fryer told me he also stored his classic cars. Is it possible that Morris would testify that Fryer was not with his family that night? While community rumors persist to this day, Morris is deceased and can never confirm what his testimony was supposed to entail.

While Ruth's initial testimony about the events of October 4, including the Hyde Park stop at the garage and the unusual real-estate viewing, had snuck its way into trial, Morris's new evidence was only in regards to Fryer's alibi for October 4, and since the trial was about the attack on Elizabeth Harrison on December 11, Judge Colter would not allow Morris's testimony to be presented in court.

Still, Colter allowed George Jorgensen, who had known Fryer for fifteen years, to testify that he was at the Metropolitan on October 4 between 8:30 and 9:30 p.m. and did not see Fryer there.

Information about the rest of the weekend likewise made it into the trial. Glenda came home Sunday, October 5. While Jackie's co-workers and friends were frantic, worrying about her disappearance, the Fryers were dealing with the family drama of their prodigal daughter.

Glen Fryer's recollection of what happened on October 5 did not match Ruth's. She told the courts that a man named Mr. McKellar brought Glenda home to them that Sunday night and that Glen was there when she arrived. However, Glen said that the Valentines brought Glenda home and that he missed them because he had decided to drive to the Valentines' house and see if they had any information about Glenda's whereabouts. He said they crossed paths en route, and that when he got home, he found Glenda safe and sound.

When it came to December 11, the night of Betty Harrison's attack, Fryer stated that he had been at CPRI finishing an assignment for a presentation he was to give on December 13. He got home at about 5 p.m. and finished supper around 6:30 p.m. Mrs. Fryer stated it was close to 8 p.m. that she and the three children had gone shopping, leaving Fryer and their youngest son at home. School records confirmed that the boy was absent for illness on December 11, and Mrs. Fryer produced her chequebook indicating the enormous purchase of children's clothing she'd made at the Kmart on December 11. She also had hospital records to show that she had been at the Ingersoll hospital until 3:30 p.m. that day. Glen swore he didn't leave the house and that Mrs. Fryer left home after 6:30 p.m. and was back around 10 p.m. The attack scene was some distance from their home, on the opposite side of the city.

Fryer's part-time secretary, Margaret Collins, testified she worked until about 4:25 p.m. on December 11, which was later than usual, to type an assignment that Fryer had to hand in the next day. Although there were only seven or eight pages, and she said she spent all day typing them in addition to her regular duties. She was sure she was in the office until 4:25 because she was waiting for Fryer to give her the last handwritten page to type. She remembers the date because she was going to a Lodge Christmas party that night and had to finish the typing because she would not be in to work the next day, a Saturday.

There was also the physical evidence to consider.

Police found Betty's glove at the scene of the attack. They also found a local property owner, Kenneth W. Laidlaw, who testified that he saw her car driving erratically along the road that night. He recognized the Volkswagen, as he'd seen it in the same spot before. He had not seen another car. Was it possible that there was no other car and that Betty knew her attacker? Is that why she had driven home and not straight to the hospital?

Exhibits were presented with testimony from OPP Identification Officer MacNally, who described photos of Betty's attack scene, including the footprints left behind by the perpetrator. These photos had been taken at 3 a.m. It had taken the police nine hours to get to the scene of the attack against a witness in a high-profile murder case. During that time, rain had disintegrated the footprints, so they were not of much use. Nevertheless, MacNally took the judge through twenty-two photographs of these melted footprints and compared them with plaster casts made of a pair of boots found in the Fryers' basement. The family said they belonged to their oldest son, Rick, who had gone shopping on the night in question. They were about the same size as the footprints, but MacNally admitted, "I could say, in my opinion, they were similar, but I could not say they were definitely made by that pair of boots." Undaunted, MacNally had even taken measurements of Glen Fryer's footprints in the snow outside the courthouse. They were very close in size to the ones found at the scene, but about half an inch longer.

Fryer's family doctor gave evidence that Fryer's right ankle was surgically fused as a result of polio, so that the joint was rigid and his right leg was one and a half inches shorter than the left, causing a pronounced limp. This detail could rule out a match between Fryer and any description of a perpetrator that did not include a visible walking impairment. The prosecution refuted this by having teachers from CPRI who had seen him playing basketball in special shoes testify. They said he was actually incredibly agile.

Dr. N.E. Erickson from the Centre of Forensic Sciences in Toronto gave testimony about blood evidence. Betty Harrison's car and clothing had been examined, and both contained large blood stains of Type-A blood. Betty was Type A, so this blood was probably hers, but experts at the trial testified that 40 percent of the population is Type A, so the blood could also have come from her attacker. Fryer gave a spit sample to investigators and was found to be also Type A.

It's important to note that you can't tell everyone's blood type from saliva. There is a relatively small percentage of the population called "non-secretors." That means that their blood type is not "secreted" into other bodily fluids like saliva or semen. You could only determine their blood type from an actual blood sample.

This is very, very important in this case, because a cigarette butt had been found in Betty Harrison's car that may have been left behind by her attacker. The saliva on the butt was left by a non-secretor, meaning that blood type could not be determined by the trace amounts of spit on the cigarette. Glen Fryer, as a secretor whose blood type was determined by saliva, could not have left that cigarette butt in her car.

The cigarette also raises the question of how on earth her attacker had time to smoke during what she described as a very physical, abrupt, and vicious attack.

Glen Fryer was not a smoker anyway. In fact, he was so opposed to smoking that when his daughter Glenda had been caught smoking at school and suspended, she was so terrified of her father's reaction that she had fled home.

Richard Harrison, however, was a smoker. His blood type is unknown.

As mentioned earlier, the man in the green jacket was also a smoker.

It is unknown whether or not the cigarette butts found near Jackie English's body at Big Otter Creek offered any saliva samples or whether they indicated if the smoker was a secretor. If they belonged to a non-secretor, however, that would increase the likelihood that whoever was smoking while observing Jackie's body in the creek was also in the car when Betty Harrison was attacked.

———————

There were no fingerprints left in the Harrison's Volkswagen, which Betty explained by saying her attacker wore gloves. If he wore gloves, how were his hands so easily wounded by his own knife?

Glen Fryer's fingerprints did not match any found on the threatening notes sent to Betty Harrison. A handwriting expert, Jeffrey Brohier from the Toronto Centre of Forensic Sciences, compared samples of Fryer's writing with that on the envelopes and letters Betty had received, and the results were inconclusive.

Fryer's home and car had also been searched, with the evidence analyzed by Dr. Erickson of Toronto. Some trace blood had been found on a floor mat that had come out of his white Chrysler and was stored in the trunk of his aquamarine 1961 Ford Fairlane. The blood could not be identified by type and could not even be identified as human.

It is interesting that Ruth Fryer owned a white Chrysler station wagon, which had also been identified as a vehicle of interest in the case of Jacqueline Dunleavy. The 1968 eyewitness had called police and reported the vehicle, which had led to the examination of every white Chrysler station wagon in the city. Presumably, the Fryer station wagon did not have the mismatched tires that the police were looking for or contained no physical evidence of Dunleavy's abduction and attack. As I do not have access to London Police files, who had jurisdiction over the Dunleavy case, I can't confirm if they searched Fryer's car, or if they found anything.

Another key piece of evidence was the insurance certificate, which, during the trial, Betty Harrison revealed she had sent to Fryer. While it had seemed incriminating when Ruth Fryer first handed it to Alsop, it was now pretty much evidence to the contrary. It proved that Betty was doing her best to pin her attack on Fryer, at the very least because she didn't trust detectives to do it.

It is also awfully interesting that the lettering on the envelope Fryer received matched that of the threatening letters Betty received and turned in to police, each one addressed using a child's stencil set. As the judge said, "There can be no logical explanation why Fryer would mail [the insurance certificate] to himself." Had Betty sent those threatening letters to herself? If the insurance letter that Betty admitted to sending matched the letters she received, didn't that mean that she had created them too?

The judge also noted that the envelope that had supposedly contained the insurance card was postmarked April 14,[59] and he wondered if it had been sent in place of the *Life* subscription. Perhaps the *Life* subscription card had never been sent at all, and Betty's story about burning it was completely fabricated. It is at least a coincidence that the *Life* folder and the green card, allegedly containing the insurance certificate, were both mailed so closely together.

The green envelope containing Betty's insurance certificate had been postmarked to the Fryers on April 14 and came from Sub Post Office 18, an outlet located on the route between Betty's home and that of the Johnsons.

If Fryer had attacked Betty, then, according to her story, he would have to bear injuries from where he was bitten by the dog and where Betty had hurt him with his own knife.

---

59 Some records give this date as April 12.

The office manager for CPRI testified that she had not seen any injuries on Glen Fryer. "I feel I can say he did not wear any bandages." She went further to call him a "peaceful man . . . some of the teachers were unhappy . . . maybe half." She'd heard the rumours about strange things happening at the school, and when the prosecution asked her if these problems stopped after Fryer's arrest, she said, "Well, I didn't hear anything more."

Dorothea Murphy, a former confidante of Fryer, now testified against him, perhaps to win the favour of her jealous husband. She said that Fryer came over to visit her on the night of December 13 or 14, 1969, and had a bandage on one of his hands. Her daughter Virginia was there, too, and she couldn't tell the court if she'd seen these bandages, but she certainly remembered Fryer complaining of having a sore leg. She remembered because she had joked that perhaps he was bitten by a dog.

Dr. Dianne Johnson testified that she saw a bandage on Fryer's left hand on December 15, 1969. He told her he'd hurt his hand playing with his son. Later, she said that Fryer's explanation for the bandages wasn't playing with his son but hitting his son when he caught him smoking. Other CPRI staff, including teacher Jack McVey, testified that they saw Fryer with bandages on his hands and Band-Aids on his face, at or around the time of the attack.

McVey had first gone to law enforcement in February 1970, over the disappearance of notes from a locked briefcase he had kept in a locked room at CPRI. He had also had an important report disappear from his desk, only to reappear three hours later. He testified that the school had been full of rumours about telephone calls, strange letters, and more disappearing documents. Further, he said that in October 1969, "Mr. Fryer had marks on his neck, which I drew to Mr. Fryer's attention and he claimed they had been inflicted during a wrestling match with his boy."

School vice-principal Joseph Murphy (no relation to Harvey) also remembered Fryer having bandages shortly after the time of the attack on Betty Harrison. In court, he also relayed a conversation he'd had with Fryer about the trial:

"Mr. Fryer mentioned that Dr. Johnson was lying, that no hand had ever been bandaged. He had doctors as well as office personnel who would swear that he had no bandages. Mr. Fryer questioned me as to whether or not I saw a bandage on his hand. I claimed I did . . . At one point I asked Mr. Fryer if he ever received the article from *Life* magazine that I had read in the paper had been sent to him . . . [He responded with a] very quick 'Yes,' then 'No, no.' Mr. Fryer said, 'We have it all figured out. Mrs. Harrison never mailed the letter. She took it home and destroyed it.'"

The defence asked Murphy, "What was the point in asking him that question?"

"I was interested," replied Murphy. "I asked Mr. Fryer why, when he received [the insurance certificate] he did not take it to the police. He said he felt it was an advertisement . . . I recall Mr. Fryer stating that he knew who was trying to frame him."

The judge then asked Murphy, "Was there any suggestion that you were the one who was trying to frame him?"

"No, there was no suggestion," he replied. "He mentioned Dr. Johnson's name in relation to that."

Fryer declared that he couldn't remember these bandages.

What about the weapon?

Police found a carton knife in the trunk of Fryer's Ford car, and it had a blade that could have made Betty's injuries, but it didn't match Betty's description of an eight-inch blade with a guard. In fact, it had blue paint on it that forensic experts were sure would have flaked off in Betty's car during the attack, and no blue flakes were found. While the weapon could have, in theory, caused the cuts, Dr. S.G. Henry had reservations. He thought the knife was probably "a sharp instrument . . . a razor blade, something of that nature . . . [a] very sharp knife, a very thin bladed knife, I would think."

Essentially, not one piece of physical evidence tied Fryer to the crime.

Dr. Harvey Murphy testified that he knew Betty had gone to police and had helped them with the composite sketch. Had he told Fryer about it? "Not that I can remember," he said. "I don't think I mentioned a thing about that to anyone . . . [unless it was] people that knew her well and were concerned about her health."

The Glen Fryer trial had so many people crowd into the gallery that the judge let them sit in the jury box. The old courthouse, with its none-too-large chambers, was packed with people from all over the Forest City. Not only was Doris English there every day, but so were the family members of the many other murder victims. Fifteen women and children had been the victims of sex-related murders in London, Ontario, since 1956. The majority of them, eleven in total, had taken place in just the past four years. At the time, the city had a population of about 160,000 people. It was a statistical anomaly, to be sure, to have that many serial sexual homicides in that size of a city in such a short period of time.

Everyone was looking to Glen Fryer's trial for answers. They wanted it to be him. They wanted to solve the puzzle and finally put it to rest so they could go back to ignoring the bad things. People tried their best not to talk about it at home. They wanted London to be the safe, picturesque little city they had imagined it to be: a good place to raise kids, not rape and murder them. Londoners still apply that same lens retroactively. This is why, fifty years later, it could seem to even enthusiastic local historians that the 1960s were a relatively prosperous, good time for the city. This is why it might be hard to find out that a serial killer, the Forest City Killer, had put a target on London and made it his hunting ground.

Feeding the growling masses, the local newspaper opted to print the entirety of the closing statements made on December 18, 1970. Mr. Baker spoke for the defence. Crown Attorney Martin also gave his final arguments. These were all printed in the *London Free Press* in full. It was clear from interest in the trial that paranoia was at fever-pitch levels. One of the smartest things Glen Fryer ever did was choose to have a trial by judge, rather than a trial by jury. He affirmed this to me during our interview. If he'd stood before twelve of his peers, he absolutely would have been convicted, probably regardless of the evidence.

Londoners were ready for blood.

According to Abigail, she was eighteen years old when she watched the news coverage of the Fryer trial. It brought up the terrifying memory of his attempted abduction of her. She was sure that the police would come and ask her to testify against him, but they never did. It was all she could think about. She talked to her mom about it, and recalls her telling Abigail that the police had "beaten the shit out of Fryer." That was what her cousin the police officer had said when he dropped by that evening, almost ten years ago, her mom said. It had seemed like a bad dream. Instead, the reality of what happened to her was on the front page of the newspaper, Fryer's face looking straight into her just as he had on that day.

DECEMBER 21, 1970. Glen Fryer sat in the prisoner's box while the judge addressed the court. This took two hours. Some excerpts of the judge's final remarks are below. Judge Colter had been the police commission chairman during the late 1960s and had seen first-hand the results of the Forest City Killer's reign of terror. He wanted justice as much as any of the citizens who sat in the gallery that day.

It has already been said a number of times that probably this 140-year-old courtroom has not before heard as bizarre a case, nor as long a one, as this has been . . .

After a particularly unrewarding cross-examination, lawyers often say in frustration that it was like trying to nail jelly to the wall, and I must confess that phrase has kept recurring to my mind throughout this case. And perhaps there is a weakness in the law in a case such as this. The law is based on logic, and when dealing with a sick mind, as unquestionably is this case here, it is perhaps impossible to explain the actions of such a sick mind logically or for one trained in the law to place himself in the mind of a person who is doing such illogical things, and yet in law proof is expected to be logical.

Throughout the evidence I waited for some single bit of evidence on which an unchallenged verdict could be given as to either guilt or innocence. Fingerprint evidence did not materialize, and the handwriting evidence simply fizzled out . . . And as strong as the circumstantial evidence is . . . in order to banish any reasonable doubt from my mind I would have to completely disbelieve the alibi evidence. Suspicious of it, I am. But the greatest suspicion is not sufficient for conviction in a criminal case . . .

Stand up, Mr. Fryer. You may never realize how very close you've come to being convicted. You are the only one who truly knows whether you are innocent or guilty. If you are innocent, this trial has been a terrible injustice to you. But if you know of your own guilt, then I implore you in the name of God to seek treatment for yourself. I hope that if you are guilty that you can realize it ... The person who is guilty of this crime has to be a psychopathic monster ...

That's all, and the accused is entitled to be discharged.

Glen Fryer was given a form of a Scottish verdict: Colter was not convinced of his innocence, but Fryer was still acquitted.

Glen Fryer smiles for reporters after his acquittal.

London Free Press Collection of Photographic Negatives, [1970-12-22], Archives and Special Collections, Western Libraries, Western University.

Glen Fryer kisses his wife, Ruth, after his acquittal.

London Free Press Collection of Photographic Negatives, [1970-12-22], Archives and Special Collections, Western Libraries, Western University.

Fryer told me that he noticed a man sitting in the gallery taking a lot of notes during the trial. He was about thirty years old, six feet tall, and had thick dark hair.

On Christmas Day, the Fryer family celebrated at home together. The ever-charismatic Fryer spoke openly to reporters about being on the other side of the trial.

"I'm thrilled that justice was being done . . . that a judge can come up with the proper and correct decision."

Then he showed off with his corny sense of humour. "I've got a '53 Chevy, and with all the publicity I might be able to get a good price. How shall I advertise it — one of the remaining assets through Fryer's trial, a '53 Chevy?"

He really thought he was hilarious.

"There was another time, I could talk about this all day, when I knew the house was being watched by the police and I had to cut the lawn. Well, it was in the fall when all the dandelions are going to seed — you know, you can blow all the seeds off. I decided to get the vacuum cleaner out and go over the lawn and suck up all the seeds, and you can just imagine what the policeman thought — but it was all fun . . .

"I've always said to people, you only live once and to get the most varied experience you can — not knowing that it could come to my own doorstep."

In 1974, Fryer earned his bachelor of arts from the University of Waterloo. Afterwards, he moved to Toronto for work. His wife, Ruth, and the children stayed behind in London, where daughter Cathy graduated from Oakridge Secondary School in 1977. After the kids had grown up and finished school, Ruth joined her husband in the "Big Smoke," where he found employment as an educator with special needs children. He retired in 1994 and focused on his hobby, classic cars. He was a co-founder of Citroen Autoclub Canada, and in retirement he had the time to serve as its president.

In the late 1990s, London Police checked Fryer's DNA against evidence found at the scene where Jackie was discovered. It didn't match. When I told Fryer about this, he was totally unaware that the testing had taken place and asked me to repeat myself. He assumed that the police used a sample of saliva from an envelope he licked while in custody, back in 1970. They never asked him to provide a fresh sample and did not inform him of the results — at least, according to him.

Margaret Collins, Fryer's former secretary at CPRI, told two stories after her time working there that have been passed along to Anne English. She said that Fryer had a drawer in his desk at work that was filled with women's jewellery and when police searched his office after his arrest, all of that jewellery was gone — the drawer was empty. She also told a story about driving with Fryer one day, and they took the exit off Highway 401 at Wellington Road South, where Jackie went missing. She said that Fryer pulled the car over to the side of the road to say a prayer "for the English girl."

This does not conclude Glen Fryer's part in this story.

The day after the trial ended in 1970, Elizabeth Harrison called Detective Alsop and told him she had received another threatening phone call. She called him again to say she had found a mysterious ring in her car on January 13, 1971. Her requests for his attention seemed to be never-ending. She showed up at his office and asked him to come to her house for interviews.

On February 9, 1971, she reported finding suspicious papers in her mailbox. It was the straw that broke the camel's back. Alsop's superiors ordered him to have nothing more to do with Betty Harrison. They wanted to move on to other things, but the murder of Jackie English remained ever-present in Alsop's mind, and Betty Harrison a thorn in his side.

CHAPTER TWENTY

THE DISAPPEARANCE OF
SORAYA O'CONNELL

*"In other circumstances, her disappearance might be treated as
a routine case of a missing girl, of a runaway — in an era when
transient teenagers are commonplace — but not in London today."*

— AUGUST 21, 1970, THE LONDON FREE PRESS

In the midst of pre-trial preparations for the Glen Fryer/
Elizabeth Harrison affair, Detective Alsop went to the London
Police station on August 24, 1970, to assist with a missing persons
case. Fifteen-year-old Soraya O'Connell had disappeared. This
was the first time that Alsop got directly involved in a missing
persons case. The law enforcement community knew there was a
serial killer on the loose.

AUGUST 14, 1970. The old one-room schoolhouse on Fanshawe
Park Road, just east of Highbury, had been built ninety-nine
years earlier, and still very little had sprung up around it. There
were no streetlights to soften the dark country road; the parking
lot next to the schoolhouse was lit by one solitary security bulb.
Teenagers stood under its glow to smoke cigarettes outside of
the Friday night community dance. Their shrieks of laughter
crested in sharp crescendo over the din of music from inside the
small brick building. Rich kids from Old North, known as "Pill
Hill," drove up in their cars, loaded with friends who wanted a

lift to the party. The less affluent young people, including Soraya O'Connell, got dropped off by their parents.

Soraya was different from the others. Most of the students at Lucas Secondary School didn't even know what a Pakistani was, so explaining her biracial parents would have been impossible even if she was able to overcome her crippling shyness. She hid behind the curtains of long dark hair that she inherited from her mom, Daphne.

The idea of the drop-in centre and the Friday night dances was a measure to keep things under control. Too many hippies were running around, going to coffee houses and standing around in gas station parking lots. Parents feared their children falling into that trap. They didn't want peace, love, and, particularly, drugs, in their homes. London had earned the moniker "Speed City" honestly. Keeping teens in the suburbs on the weekends, instead of having them head downtown, was a brilliant first step in avoiding this catastrophe. The Northridge Community Association decided to start a place for teenagers to hang out — a recreation centre — and the old schoolhouse was the perfect spot. Closed in 1955, it was still owned by the school board and was cheap to rent. They began hosting events in February 1970. Soraya went there and learned to play bridge. As school came to an end, the Northridge parents recruited their daughters to run Friday night dances during the summer. The decorating committee chose "Flower Power" as their theme for the first Friday night dance. They created huge, colourful tissue-paper blooms that would serve double duty as party favours. They set up punch and baked goods for sale to raise money, as well as a coat check. The music was very important, too. It had to be hip enough to bring in the young people but still appropriate.

Their first dance was a success. It drew such a crowd that the organizers got sponsors to provide refreshments for the following week. At first, Soraya said she wouldn't go. Finally, the girls talked her into it. She put on some beige bell-bottoms and plain brown shoes. She wore a white long-sleeved shirt and buttoned it up to her neck, even in the August heat. The only extra splashes were her oversized pink sunglasses and the key she wore on a chain around her neck. She looked positively dowdy next to her new friends, whose bikini bathing suit tops showed through their unbuttoned, waist-tied blouses. Their belly buttons hovered over huge belt buckles wrapped around their little hips.

"Come on, Soraya. Loosen up! Have fun!" they encouraged her.

She stood against the wall of the small schoolhouse, hoping to blend in. The night passed by around her. Everyone was having a great time, swaying to the beat and smiling. Once or twice they looked over at her, encouraging her to join, but when she didn't move, they quickly gave up. She passed the time listening to stray bits of conversation and wondering what the magic trick was to be part of the fun. Soon the night would be over.

Sometime around 9:30 p.m., the DJ announced a ladies' choice dance. A slow song started to play. The girl standing next to Soraya told her that she should be brave. She should ask someone to dance and put herself out there. Otherwise, she'd just have stood next to the wall all night, and that would make the whole thing a waste.

Soraya knew it was true. It was time for her to make a move, be brave, and take action, so slowly, timidly, she walked over to Lenny,[60] the hottest boy in school. He was a big fish to catch, but her eyes were only for him. He positively glowed. Tall, muscular, popular, he drove his own car and lived in the wealthy neighbourhood. Naïve Soraya thought that ladies' choice simply meant asking the boy she *wanted* to dance with, not the one she was *allowed* to dance with. Her voice was quiet as she looked up at him with her big brown eyes.

---

60 Name changed for privacy.

He laughed, loudly. "On what planet would I ever . . . I mean . . . *really*?"

Her eyes widened as she realized what was happening to her. His friends started to laugh at her, pointing and guffawing.

"I would never dance with a fat . . . ugly . . . pimple-faced . . . smelly immigrant! Where do you get off?"

The room closed in on her. She could feel all the blood in her body rush to her head. She grabbed her bag and ran away as quickly as she could. She wanted to be alone, in her room, where no one could hurt her. Her feet carried her outside, where a group of shocked and appalled white girls clamoured around her with their skinny waists and bright, skimpy clothes.

"What an asshole!" exclaimed one.

"Oh my God, Soraya, are you okay?" asked another.

They handed her a Kleenex and stroked her hair as she struggled to control herself in front of them. What had happened was terrible, and this wasn't helping. They treated her like some kind of pet, their little pathetic project. She would never fit in.

At 9:45 p.m., she decided she'd had enough.

If you were crouched in the historic Siloam Cemetery across the street from the drop-in centre, hiding behind one of the large marble stones, you could watch the gaggle of pretty teen-aged white girls comforting the little brown one. She was so distraught and so tiny. So malleable. They tried to help, pawing her with their feminine consolations, but she broke away and said she was going home. It wasn't too far to walk. Maybe she'd hitch a ride.

"Wait!" one of the girls called out after her. "Billy can drive you!"

You could follow her silhouette as she began to disappear into the dark and the other girls turned away and went back inside to the dance.

You'd have a moment, just a moment, before one of the boys got in his car and went to look for her at the urging of his empathetic girlfriend. You'd have just a moment to hop in your car, creep up the road, and offer the girl a ride. She'd trust you, with your handsome face and your charming smile.

I grew up just a few blocks away from Soraya O'Connell and the area was much the same in the 1980s as it was in 1970. Since then, new neighbourhoods full of suburban sprawl have built up. However, just north of Kipps Lane used to be wild territory. We played there as kids. The river cuts through the valley at the bottom of a moraine and it was the perfect place to experience nature. Mom called it "the ravine." While we went down there a lot with her to explore, the truth is that even in the late 1980s, I was going down there by myself. A lot of other kids did, too. You could see leftover campfire spots on a regular basis, the charred remains of a weekend party hosted by teenagers from nearby Montcalm Secondary School. There were makeshift houses for the homeless, too. I'm sure lots of crazy stuff was happening there after dark, but little pre-teen me was totally oblivious.

All of this context is to explain that while it might seem completely foolish to some people that Soraya would walk forty-five minutes to her Kipps Lane home from the outskirts of the city, the farthest northeast edge of town, the truth is that it probably didn't seem that far to her. She had probably spent time in those woods like the rest of us. In fact, there was a well-trodden series of unauthorized trails that created an easy network for her to get home. The assumption is that she headed to Highbury Avenue to hitch a ride, but as a kid from the neighbourhood, I can tell you that her plan may have been to cut through "the ravine" and head home that way. If she caught a lift, it could have been a last-minute decision, although some of the kids at the dance told police

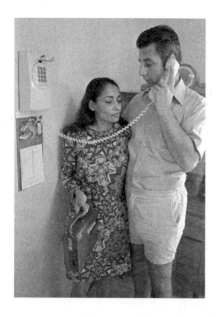

Soraya O'Connell's parents wait to hear news of their missing daughter.

London Free Press Collection of Photographic Negatives, [1970-08-19], Archives and Special Collections, Western Libraries, Western University.

she said she was going to hitchhike. This would have fit in very well with the prevailing narrative at the time: that hitchhiking girls disappeared. The weather that night was cool, not too humid. It was nice out, a good time to walk, but perhaps the idea of walking through the woods after dark, getting bitten by mosquitoes or flashed by creeps, was not as appealing as the ride offered to her by a handsome stranger who pulled up next to the easy prey of a teenage girl walking along what was essentially a dark thoroughfare.

Mr. O'Connell was home from Toronto that night and called police just before 1 a.m. to report his daughter missing. A constable came immediately to get a description of Soraya, and officers checked the area of the Fanshawe drop-in centre right away. The next morning, a province-wide alert was sent out to law enforcement agencies and the investigation began.

The all-too-familiar story hit the local news by the following Tuesday. On Wednesday, August 19, the *London Free Press* reported:

> Det.-Set. Bryson said Tuesday night "an important clue" may involve a brown and white tote bag the girl was carrying with the word 'Cyprus' written across the side . . .

The search for Soraya — described as not the type to stay out late — is concentrated in the London area. The dark-complexioned teenager wore her dark hair "almost waist-length," said Det.-Sgt. Bryson. She was described as four feet, 10 inches tall, 135 pounds in weight, with brown eyes.

Sgt. Dan O'Connell, who has served almost 20 years in the army, has offered $1,000 for information leading to the whereabouts of Soraya . . . He said she would never stay away this long without calling. He has exhausted all possibilities — called friends, relatives and drove the streets of the city at night.

A week after her disappearance, the *London Free Press* printed an editorial that seemed distressingly routine:

Another teenage girl vanishes and fears and anxieties heighten in a community where the ugly pattern of disappearance and violent death is all too familiar . . .

Police published this image of a bag similar to the one Soraya O'Connell was carrying the night she disappeared.

London Free Press Collection of Photographic Negatives, [1970-08-29], Archives and Special Collections, Western Libraries, Western University.

For more than two years, Londoners have lived with the harrowing realization that one or more madmen, vicious killers, are loose in the community and with painful awareness that an absence of witnesses and clues has frustrated police investigation of the murders. Until they are solved, no parents will be confident of their children's safety. London's anguish has no parallels in other communities.

The Forest City Killer had everyone running scared.

Police officers began a widespread search for Soraya, going from property to property, hunting out nooks and crannies in barns and farmers' fields. German Shepherd Arab once again joined the team, as he had in the search around Jackie English's remains and in the search for Frankie Jensen, hunting in the sweltering August heat. Over days and days, they went as far as nearby Thorndale, possibly due to the connection with the Jensen and Leishman murders, to see if they could find answers for the desperate O'Connell family.

Police dog "Arab" assists in the search for Soraya O'Connell.

London Free Press Collection of Photographic Negatives, [1970-08-20], Archives and Special Collections, Western Libraries, Western University.

The search for Soraya O'Connell.

London Free Press Collection of Photographic Negatives, [1970-08-20], Archives and Special Collections, Western Libraries, Western University.

Two women and a man said they saw Soraya hitchhiking on the night she disappeared.

The O'Connells began to receive suspicious phone calls. "It's pretty depressing that there are so many warped minds. Some of the remarks are pretty outlandish," said her father.

While the disappearance was outside of his jurisdiction, Detective Alsop nevertheless worked on the case. It was his suspicion that they would find Soraya outside city limits, putting her probable murder under his purview after all.

PART IV

WHERE IT ALL BEGAN

OCTOBER 1969. Out by the pond on his property, a farmer discovered a pair of battered brown leather penny loafers on the edge of the water. He thought they belonged to one of his twelve kids and took them home. It wasn't long before he read a description in the *London Free Press* of what Jackie English had been wearing the night she disappeared. These shoes were an exact match. He called the police, and soon OPP cruisers were pulling up the dirt laneway of the farm at Glencolin Line and Springer Hill Road, where neighbourhood kids sometimes parked late at night. It was a bit of a lover's lane. These ponds, this patch of land, the farmer never really figured out what to do with it. For the most part, nothing really happened there outside of area kids playing and swimming, and teenagers messing around in their backseats.

Detective Alsop stood near the pond, watching scuba divers search the water for more evidence. Turning the shoes over in his hands, he looked closely at the deep scuff marks on the opposite sides of each shoe. It looked like they had been dragged along a rough surface, weighted down.

He could imagine Jackie, slouched unconscious in the passenger seat. The passenger door opened and someone scooped her out, holding her under the arms, pulling her along, her shoes scraping against the stones.

Officers crawled around the pond like ants, searching for any other clues left by the killer, who had presumably dropped Jackie's shoes while he was here. Alsop walked away to take in the landscape. This area of land and the fields around it were familiar to him. It was the hunting ground of a predator he'd encountered before. Down the road was a dense bush of maple trees, where he had examined the body of another dead girl, another unsolved case that he realized was uncannily similar to that of Jackie English.

OPP Constable Henry Harley Heal points to the spot where Jackie English's shoes were found.

London Free Press Collection of Photographic Negatives, [1969-10-23], Archives and Special Collections, Western Libraries, Western University.

Alsop took the brown penny loafers to Anne English at the apartment on Kent Street, where she still lived with Fred.

"That looks like them," she said.

There was one way to be sure. Anne and Jackie had the same size feet, so she took her dead sister's shoes and slid them on one by one. She took a few steps.

"They must be hers," she said.

I asked Anne if it had bothered her to literally walk in her sister's shoes. She hadn't really thought about it, she said, until I asked.

Alsop asked Anne to take him into Jackie's room. He wanted to know if she might recall any other items from Jackie's wardrobe that might be missing. Anne ran her fingers over the garments hanging in that closet. No one had touched them since Jackie disappeared. She'd frankly been too busy to clean up, working and taking care of Fred.

Red, orange, pink, and yellow. A bright royal blue.

CHAPTER TWENTY-ONE

THE DISAPPEARANCE OF
GEORGIA JACKSON

"Somebody's got to do something about this thing;
but everyone's too afraid of becoming involved."

— HOWARD ZIMMER

An hour's drive southeast of London, Aylmer is a small town. It serves as a hub for summer tourists at nearby cottages, where city dwellers vacation along the shores of Lake Erie. The population swells during hot weather. Crowding the sidewalks in their swimsuits and flip-flops, families check out little boutiques, get some beer at the LCBO for a campfire, buy some bug spray at Shoppers Drug Mart, and grab four litres of bagged milk from the Valu-mart. The atmosphere is the perfect antidote to metropolitan living. Parking is free, and you feel safe leaving your purse on the passenger seat. It's a place with a strong religious bent, long-time residents, and a homespun feel. Antiques and apple fritters.

If you're from London, you may have gone there as part of a trip to Port Bruce. There are some really charming cottages along the rocky shores of Lake Erie. To enjoy it, though, you have to be the type of person who will sacrifice a sandy beach for the other charms that Port Bruce has to offer. Not everyone would be willing to do that. It's quiet, peaceful, and left alone by college students. There is a lot of driftwood. Nearby Aylmer is only a

Aylmer, a good place to live.

London Free Press Collection of Photographic Negatives, [1966-03-18], Archives and Special Collections, Western Libraries, Western University.

ten-minute drive, and is a must-stop for any cottagers or beach-goers who are in need of any sort of supplies.

In addition to its charming village façade, Aylmer dons a veneer of real safety. In 1961, it became the home of the Ontario Police College, located in the old WWII RCAF station off Hacienda Road. You can often see young recruits and a denser presence of squad cars. Law enforcement grows there, just like the corn and barley and soybeans of the surrounding fields. Those fields are tended by large Old Order Amish and Mennonite settlements, exponentially adding to the feeling of old-timey nostalgia in the area. They frequent country roads with horse and buggy, coming through to sell their goods at the weekend farmers' market.

You could hardly find a place that spoke to a safer, happier world than Aylmer, Ontario.

In 1966, Georgia Jackson would have stuck out in school as the girl who didn't stand up for the national anthem and never had a birthday party. She didn't drink or smoke or swear — those kids who did

Georgia Jackson.

Courtesy of the Elgin County Archives. *St. Thomas Journal-Times* Fonds.

weren't her friends. Her friends and family were all part of her church, a tiny group that tried hard to be in the world, but not at all part of it. While Christian, the Jackson's branch of faith was very different from that of the pervading ones in Aylmer. They often found themselves the objects of discrimination from the Baptists, Presbyterians, and United believers who made up the rest of the village.

The Jehovah's Witnesses met frequently in a tiny red brick building, near the Aylmer Cemetery on Imperial Road, that served as their Kingdom Hall. Their Overseer[61] was Albert Crooker. Georgia looked up to him. He seemed to be a good family man and a wise spiritual leader. Every week, he urged his flock to stay on track, keep sin at bay, and encouraged them to spread the gospel to anyone who would listen. Georgia sat attentively, next to her parents and siblings on wooden stacking chairs. She was chubby cheeked and had wavy dark hair. Her countenance projected the sweetness of a young woman whose future was laid out for the

The Kingdom Hall attended by Georgia Jackson.

Courtesy of the Elgin County Archives. Harley Lashbrook Collection.

---

61   Witness terminology for pastor or reverend.

Lord's service. She wanted to be a missionary, and for most women that meant teaching or secretarial work. Despite being a quiet girl, she overcame her shyness to give lectures to the young people and aimed to be a good example to them by living a pure life. At the age of twenty, she still resided at home. Her father, who owned Spicer's Bakery, said, "We never forced her to stay home. She just did." She believed in saving herself until marriage and didn't have a boyfriend.

FEBRUARY 18, 1966. It was very cold and damp outside that Friday morning, but the Jackson house was safe and warm. The family lived in a red-brick house at 196 Sydenham Street, at the corner of Wellington Street, in Aylmer. Knowing her daughter worked hard, Georgia's mother let her sleep in until 10:30. Then Georgia had breakfast and went back upstairs to her room, where she puttered about until it was time for her shift at noon at the Dairy Bar,[62] located just north of Talbot on John Street North. It was a short walk of four blocks. She wrapped herself tightly in her blue winter coat, gloves, scarf, and hat before saying goodbye to her mother.

It was the last time Virginia would see her daughter alive.

By the time Georgia finished her shift at 6 p.m., the wind was blowing the snow around in gusts and the temperature had dropped to negative 12 degrees Celsius. She called her mother before heading out into the storm, and Virginia asked her to get a pound of butter on the walk back, but then her mother corrected herself. "Forget it. Just come home."

The conversation had reminded Virginia that there were a few things she needed to buy, and she might as well go to the grocery store. She figured it was too late to call Georgia back and offer her a ride, so she called out to her other kids to get their coats on. They bundled up in the family vehicle and headed out to the

---

62 A Dairy Bar was basically a malt shop, or a neighbourhood diner. Its name came from milkshakes and ice cream, but it might have also served fast-food items like hamburgers. Some Dairy Bars also sold cigarettes and newspapers.

store, not picking up Georgia. They didn't see her on the way there, or on the way back.

It was only a short walk home from the Dairy Bar, about four blocks, so despite the snow, Georgia decided to stop at the Metropolitan Store on Talbot Street. Linda Holmes was working when Georgia came in. She remembered selling her a bottle of shampoo, but not the butter her mother had requested.

Georgia crossed the street and waved at a car that stopped for her. Inside was twenty-seven-year-old Terry Robinson, Georgia's neighbour. His young daughter sat next to him in the passenger seat. He recalled, "[Georgia] looked up at me, smiled, waved, then put her head down against the wind and continued on towards — I assumed then — her home. I recognized her by her blue coat — she was walking westward across John Street — her head buried in her collar for protection against the snow and wind. It was a miserable night. I knew her quite well, so I playfully edged my car in front of her. I knew her from the Dairy Bar." Robinson saw her carrying something white, probably the bag with her recent purchase. His later statements put the time of this sighting at 8:30 p.m., but he may have been mistaken as that was two hours after her shift had ended, and search parties were already out looking for her by then. It was hard to gauge the time when night fell so early.

Just two blocks away from home, Georgia passed by Marilyn Fisher's house at the corner of Sydenham West and Centre Street. Inside, Marilyn was watching TV and knitting. She heard a sound outside, like a woman being hurt, and a man yelling. She heard a car door slam. Later, Fisher explained why she didn't come forward with this information right away. "My husband was working nights at the time . . . I was alone, and I was afraid that if I spoke to the police, someone might think I knew more than I was telling."

Around 8 p.m., a girl fitting Georgia's description was seen at a community hall just outside Aylmer. According to a woman who was there playing cards that night, she saw someone she thought was Georgia come in and sit in a chair in a corner. The girl took off her coat, and revealed a soiled uniform underneath. The girl didn't talk to anyone, and after sitting there for a few minutes, got up and left.

Another man would later tell police that he was driving along the country roads near the Aylmer Police College when he noticed a car pulled over to the side of the road. He said that the windows were steamed up, and he could see two men inside. There was a woman too, and as his car got closer, he thought he saw them push her down to hide her, out of sight.

Virginia got home from the grocery store and unpacked the groceries, calling out to her eldest daughter. There was no answer. By 8 p.m., Georgia's mom knew something was up. It was totally out of character for Georgia to stay out and not call. She'd been on her way home. What could have kept her? She called the Dairy Bar, hoping that unforeseen circumstances had held her up at work. Owner William Broad answered the phone. Georgia had left at 6, he said. He hadn't seen her since.

When they realized that Georgia was missing in inclement weather, Broad and others got out in their cars and started to drive around Aylmer, looking for Georgia's black hair and blue coat, a silhouette in the cloud of snow. It was almost a new moon and completely dark. Aylmer residents would later call it the coldest night of that long winter.

The Jackson family called the police, panicked and terrified. She would freeze to death out in the storm. Chief Harold Henderson told them that she "probably has just taken off for the weekend and will be home Monday."

Virginia got on the phone and started making calls. Soon she had gathered a group of people to search for her daughter. Getting in their cars, a small army of Jehovah's Witnesses and neighbours began combing the streets, looking for Georgia. They couldn't find her. Arriving home shortly after midnight, cold and wet and utterly discouraged, one of the searchers made a phone call to their local councilman, Eugene Dopp. Woken up out of his sleep, Councillor Dopp was asked to make two long-distance calls to London, Ontario. It was only because of these calls that news of Georgia's disappearance reached London Police that night.

FEBRUARY 19, 1966. As soon as it was light enough to look again, the beleaguered friends and family of Georgia Jackson headed out to look for her. They had no idea what they were doing, no officials to help them, and there was no sign of the lost young woman. Resigned to what would probably be a tragic ending, the weather being what it was, they called off the search for the rest of the day, with the intention of getting organized and starting fresh tomorrow. This gave Bert Crooker, the Overseer at the Kingdom Hall, a chance to call in all of his reinforcements.

FEBRUARY 20, 1966. More than 300 volunteers showed up the next morning, the majority of them members of the Jehovah's Witness community who drove in from all over the region, to find Georgia. They spent their Sunday prayerfully checking anywhere they could think of in Aylmer and the surrounding countryside, hoping for any sign of her.

FEBRUARY 21, 1966. Georgia's uncle Russ Piggot drove in from London. He wasn't a Witness, and as such there was a schism between him and his family in Aylmer. But schism be damned, Russ wanted to find little Georgia. By now it was the workweek, so a lot of the volunteers had to go back to their jobs. Numbers were small and Uncle Russ found himself horrified that the police had not come out to assist those who remained or help them organize the search. They didn't help whatsoever. Russ told the media he thought it was because of religious discrimination, but Chief Harold Henderson (a Lutheran) told the press, "I'm not prejudiced towards anyone's religion — I've never had any quarrel with them."

FEBRUARY 23, 1966. One of the Jackson kids answered the phone.

"Hello, Jackson residence."

"This is your sister."

Virginia Jackson immediately jumped on the call. She was sure it really was her daughter. "Where are you, Georgia?"

"Help me, Mom. I'm being held downtown . . . I'm being held prisoner by two men."

The phone went dead. She shook the receiver.

"Georgia? Georgia?"

There was no answer. She yelled for her husband and he found her gripping the receiver in terror. He took it from her, hung up, and then called the police. His daughter had called, he told them. She said she was in danger. He gave them all the information, every detail he could get out of Virginia. There was still time to save her.

Chief Henderson thought it was a prank, some foolishness. Mr. Jackson later recalled that Henderson "never really appeared to be convinced that anything was wrong." The family would have to rely on the determination of their religious community and the sympathy of the residents of Aylmer if there was to be any hope of finding Georgia, whom they were convinced was still alive.

That same day, Aylmer's Mayor Russell McKibbin called Chief Henderson and offered to put out a $500 reward for information about Georgia's disappearance. Chief Henderson told him it would be a waste of money.

FEBRUARY 27, 1966. In the '60s, it was pretty normal to chuck your garbage out the window as you were driving, which made it mildly lucrative to hunt along the roadside for empty bottles. Two boys were out in the morning, hoping to collect a few extra bucks, when they found a blue coat in the snow along Concession 8 near the Ontario Police College. It was neatly folded, lying under a birch tree. When they saw it was bloody, they called the police.

There wasn't just blood on it. There was semen.

Virginia looked at the bloodied coat and knew it was her daughter's. In the pocket was a receipt for shampoo.

MARCH 1, 1966. The Ontario Provincial Police Criminal Investigation Bureau, including Detective Alsop, finally got involved in the case. They immediately offered a $500 reward for information regarding Georgia's disappearance, but were not in charge of the investigation. Local police were in command, and they still weren't convinced that it was even a case of foul play, despite the discovery of Georgia's bloody coat.

MARCH 2, 1966. The first official search for Georgia involving law enforcement finally took place almost two weeks after she had disappeared. In addition to the efforts of the OPP, Jehovah's Witnesses gathered all of their resources again through community leaders Michael Verbrugge and Howard Zimmer. "We covered the area pretty thoroughly with no results," said Zimmer.

A fellow Witness named Charles Oldham let them use his helicopter, and farmer Bob Plato let them use his plane. Overseer Albert Crooker and his son-in-law David Bodemer joined in to comb the fields, hoping to find some sign of Georgia Jackson.

MARCH 3, 1966. The OPP took over. Their patience with Chief Henderson had run out.

MARCH 4, 1966. A local couple spotted a man running out of the bush along Springfield Road. He jumped into his car and sped away.

MARCH 8, 1966. A search party led by Michael Verbrugge found Georgia's scarf, frozen into the shoulder of the road just one mile east of where they had found her coat. It was also stained with blood.

CHAPTER TWENTY-TWO

THE BODY OF GEORGIA JACKSON

*"They expected us to pull her out of a
hat before she was murdered."*

— CHIEF HAROLD HENDERSON

MARCH 14, 1966. Local farmer Bob Heffren usually tapped his trees
to make maple syrup, but not in 1966. "This is the first year in a
long while I haven't tapped the trees for sap," he said. Instead, he
found himself in the bush on his property, looking for poles to
build a greenhouse, his latest project. He didn't see anything out
of the ordinary.

MARCH 16, 1966. A conservation officer for the Department of Lands
and Forests, Lawrence Kelly, was driving about the countryside
on duty at about 2:30 p.m., almost one month since Georgia had
gone missing. He was heading down Springfield Road towards
Summers Corners when he stopped to take a leak — although that
wasn't what he'd write in his official report. "I don't know what
prompted me," he said instead, to be polite, "but I stopped my
truck, backed up and took a look. When I saw it was a body, I
took care not to disturb the scene and then drove to Aylmer where
I notified Aylmer chief of police, E.H. Henderson."

The site where Georgia Jackson was found.

Ah, old reliable Chief Harold Henderson. Something had been wrong after all.

After all the terror and chaos and confusion, there was Georgia: still, quiet, and lifeless. She lay under the shadow of a thick tree in Bob Heffren's maple bush, wearing her dishevelled waitress uniform, stockings, and winter boots. Around her pale thighs, her underwear clung frozen and torn. Her dark pubic hair was crusted in Type-O ejaculate, her hymen broken and bloody, exposed to the elements. Her black curls were matted in a bloody mess at the back of her head where she had been hit by a blunt object. The impact was strong enough to knock her out and cause a lot of bleeding, but it lacked the amount of force needed to fracture her skull.

In the end, she died from being strangled. She had been raped in the moments of death, gasping for air either right before or as it happened. Some vaginal bleeding was pre-mortem, but there were also post-mortem bruises. One of her gloves and her red plastic purse, the last of her missing personal effects, were nowhere to be seen, presumably taken as trophies by the killer, who wanted to relive that exciting moment when he watched the life drain out of her dark brown eyes and felt her body go limp beneath his depraved thrusting form.

Her left arm was missing skin and flesh down to the bone and showed teeth marks. This may have been caused by animal scavenging, but as Michael Arntfield points out in *Murder City*, why would an animal go for the inside of her arm when it would be more attracted to the soft bloody tissue of her genitals? This arm wound showed no bleeding and was therefore caused after her heart had stopped beating, as was the oval wound around her left ear — which was completely missing down to the bone.

Chief Harold Henderson, suddenly an expert, was confident that the killer was someone Georgia knew, "someone from this area — a local person."

In 1966, Detective Alsop was mostly focused on bank robbers, but he still got called to murder scenes. The OPP had stepped into the Jackson case, subverting the authority of police chief Harold Henderson, and Alsop was needed because his level of forensic training was higher than most. He was among the first to examine the crime scene. Afterwards, he spent most of the month of March driving back and forth from London to Aylmer.

Relatives and neighbours came in and out of the Jackson's red-brick house on the corner lot, holding hands, hugging, and putting casseroles on the table. Women from the congregation did the dishes, swept the floor, and wiped down the bathroom. Still, no amount of scrubbing could remove the terrible grime of what had happened to the Jackson family. Virginia stayed in her housecoat, even when the reporter asked to take her picture, even when TV cameras showed up. Like her daughter, Virginia was a stalwart woman with a thick frame and pronounced curves. While Georgia had died with the soft features of a young woman, Virginia was a good example of how her daughter could have looked if she'd lived longer. Her face had become elegantly carved. Under the harsh lights of a camera flash, she looked positively gothic. In softer lighting, she could have been Katharine Hepburn's big-boned sister.

Virginia Jackson is interviewed by reporters at her home in Aylmer.

Courtesy of the Elgin County Archives. *St. Thomas Journal-Times* Fonds.

A journalist from the *Aylmer Express* came to the house on March 17 and found the bleary-eyed family sitting around their kitchen table, drinking tea. He pulled out his notepad and asked them how they were doing.

"The tension has built up and up so much during the past weeks that we've been unable to sleep," said father George. "Last night my wife and I were up the entire night."

"I can't imagine what you've gone through," said the reporter.

"It's even some consolation to know that she'll receive proper burial," said George. "All these rumours about her being fed up with home and taking off will stop now. They have hurt as much as almost anything else."

"It's very hard for an outsider to understand the closeness and simplicity of our family life," added Virginia. "So many people of our faith and outside it have been so kind to us. We don't want anyone's job taken away, but we feel the police are not experienced enough in this type of thing. The attitude of small-town police must be changed." Her face altered and for a moment, unbridled bitterness entered her features. "They just can't sit back and tell parents, 'She's twenty years old and has probably just taken off.'"

George held his wife's hand. "We'll never know whether speedier action when Georgia was first reported missing would have been enough to save her life or not. She's gone now and vengeance belongs to Jehovah." He sighed. "The only thing that really perturbed us was when the Aylmer Police Chief took no action after we received that phone call from someone who might have been our daughter."

The anger in the room was palpable but tempered by religious prudence.

"What happened to my daughter could happen to any person's daughter or wife here in Aylmer," he continued. "They must find whoever is responsible . . . Our daughter is dead."

MARCH 19, 1966. There was a crowd of one hundred soaked people standing in the rain, huddled under umbrellas and the small overhang outside the H.A. Kebbel Funeral Home. The crowd was so big, they couldn't fit inside. Georgia's funeral was packed. Her family sat in the front row together, facing the simple coffin. They chose to keep it closed. No one needed to see what had been done to her.

Albert Crooker took his place at the pulpit. This was an opportunity to not only comfort the Jacksons, but also to spread the message of Jehovah to a large crowd of non-believers. He told them that, "Georgia was a faithful servant who dedicated her life to Jehovah and finished her earthly course faithfully. She will be privileged to come back with the many faithful who will be coming back from the dead in resurrection."

The pallbearers came together and lifted Georgia's coffin. In the crowd was Albert Crooker's son-in-law, David Bodemer. He

Overseer Albert Crooker leads pallbearers as they carry Georgia Jackson's coffin from her funeral service.

London Free Press Collection of Photographic Negatives, [1966-03-19], Archives and Special Collections, Western Libraries, Western University.

was tall, his dark hair combed neatly to frame his handsome face. He had known Georgia. When he was courting his wife, Elaine, both girls had worked at the Dairy Bar. He stopped in often, and Georgia had always given him extra scoops of ice cream. Now he watched as they carried her body to her grave, where a flat, modest stone plaque eventually marked her resting place in the Aylmer Cemetery. That day, she was buried with no headstone.

Remarkably, Mrs. Jackson said she felt sorry for her daughter's killer. "He must be sick to do such a thing. We can't judge this individual. I would not like to think this is not forgivable."

One of the lead search organizers and one of Georgia's pallbearers, Michael Verbrugge, said, "The Jehovah's Witnesses will not rest until whoever is responsible for the slaying of Georgia Jackson is brought to justice. If it's one of our people, no Jehovah's Witness will harbour him. We will turn him over to the police and let justice take its course. 'Justice is mine, sayeth the Lord' and we will not attempt to do his work."

It took no time at all for a consensus to form. The Aylmer Police had done a terrible job. They had blood on their hands, and the day after Georgia's battered body was found, Attorney General Arthur Wishart demanded an inquest. Georgia's faithful uncle Russ demanded that Henderson resign. Chief Henderson had held his position for twenty-three years. He was a solid member of the community and was near retirement. It was in his best interest to defend himself, even though his decisions in the hours and days following Georgia's disappearance seemed indefensible and his excuses bizarre.

The chairman of the police commission seemed to think that failing to solve the case was a "feather in our cap. If you bring a professional in and he can't solve the crime, it indicates it's a tough case. Don't forget, police here have to do stuff on the QT. They haven't got credit for everything they've done."

The chairman of the police commission defended Henderson, making the outrageous statement that, "If three hundred men couldn't find anything, what good would three hundred and six men have done?"

The OPP Criminal Investigation Bureau responded by creating a new $1,000 reward for information leading to an arrest in Georgia's murder and gave the original $500 reward for finding her to Conservation Officer Lawrence Kelly.

Despite the financial incentive, no new information surfaced, but there were rumours galore. A reporter from the *Toronto Star* went to Aylmer in August 1966 to catch up with residents and those who were involved in the case. He spoke to Mr. Broad,

Georgia's boss at the Dairy Bar, who said, "We all played detective. You know you'd say things to an outsider you wouldn't say to someone in town. We came up with far-out suggestions." Two of his employees, sisters Judy and Janet Nevill, told the reporter they had sat down with police to review photographs of sex offenders in the area. Police wanted to know if any of them were regular customers at the Dairy Bar, and some of them were. The Nevill girls were shocked to discover that the men who flirted with them and called them sweetheart might have dangerous ideas. The veneer of safety in Aylmer was, for some time, shattered.

That December, less than a year after Georgia disappeared, the Jackson family moved to Stratford. Two years later, George Jackson had a stroke that left him paralyzed. When he died, the family buried him next to his daughter, whose death had been the real end of him.

———————

Detective Alsop continued to work on the Georgia Jackson case for years. He would one day be instrumental in its resolution, but in the meantime he spent hours and hours following up on leads and conducting interviews. He performed surveillance on suspected deviants and visited the London Psychiatric Hospital. Friends of the Jackson family who knew them when they lived in London came forward to give statements, including Pastor "Benny" Eckhart, who performed the eulogies for two other sex murders in the Forest City area. Another man claimed he had a vision of the killer. On July 5, 1967, Alsop visited Corey Auto Wreckers in London, still in business today, where he examined a car that was suspected to have been involved in Georgia's murder. In the months preceding Jackie English's 1969 death, Alsop was even then still actively conducting interviews on the Jackson case, following up on leads — no matter how absurd — and doing forensic examinations on cars. He tracked down all of the Aylmer Dairy Bar suppliers, found records on the employees, and checked out all of them to see if there were any viable suspects. In between tracking down armed robbery perpetrators and investigating other homicides, testifying in court, and doing all the things an OPP detective had to do, he never gave up on trying to solve Georgia's case.

———————

In 1954, the Jacksons lived at 387 Simcoe Street in London's SoHo (South of Horton) neighbourhood. In 1955, when Georgia Jackson was eleven years old, they moved south to 85 Jacqueline Street in what is now known as the Chelsea Green neighbourhood. It wasn't until 1957 that they moved to the red-brick house at 196 Sydenham West in Aylmer, Ontario.

That the Jacksons lived in London might be important. On January 18, 1971, Detective Alsop interviewed a woman named Mrs. Collins, who gave him information regarding Glen Fryer and Georgia Jackson. She, at least, must have thought they were connected. The Jacksons did live in London at the same time as the Fryers, albeit briefly. They also both had connections to Stratford, the Jacksons through the Jehovah's Witness church and Fryer through his upbringing.

Bill Trent's 1979 book *Who Killed Lynne Harper?* includes letters sent to the author regarding alternate theories about who killed Lynne Harper in 1959. One such letter, written by a Londoner whose name was withheld, states that while living in London, young Georgia Jackson babysat for the notorious Glen Fryer and his family. This report remains unconfirmed,[63] but when I asked my mother if an eleven-year-old could have been babysitting in 1955, she said absolutely, yes. If this is the case and the letter is true, Georgia could have babysat the Fryer children while the Fryers lived at 31½ The Ridgeway and the

———————

63 I could not, for the life of me, track down Bill Trent or his family.

Jacksons lived at 85 Jacqueline Street, in Chelsea Green just south of Victoria Hospital.

Is this mystery Mrs. Collins who spoke to Alsop in 1971 the same woman who wrote the letter to Bill Trent? Is she also Margaret Collins, Glen's secretary? The note Alsop made about visiting Mrs. Collins and the letter that Bill Trent received are the only mentions in records I could find that connect Fryer with Jackson. This stuck out to me, and in my mind, it makes sense that the information could have come from the same person: Margaret Collins.

I asked Glen Fryer when I interviewed him if Georgia Jackson had babysat for his family. He said no, and then repeated her name to himself three or four times, as if he was trying to remember who she was — or trying to convince me that he didn't know who she was.

In 1967, Alsop noted that he made a visit to the new International Amway Headquarters of London, Ontario, regarding the Georgia Jackson case. This was the same pyramid sales organization that Glen and Ruth Fryer had enthusiastically joined some years earlier. Why the visit to Amway regarding the Jackson case? Was there a connection?

——————

The number of bodies in the area resulting from sexual homicides had stacked up since Georgia's 1966 murder in Aylmer. Detective Alsop thought the killings must be related. Like a burglar, this psychopath had methods, but those methods were tied to a madness Alsop couldn't understand. While the killings had seemed to stop since O'Connell's disappearance in August 1970, months before the Fryer trial, there was a stillness in the air, like the calm before a storm.

CHAPTER TWENTY-THREE

MEET DAVID BODEMER

*"Me as a normal person, that has never killed anyone, if I had
gotten away with something, even say rob a bank, anything,
if I pulled something off for fifty years, I would want people to
know. Even at the last second. Hey, I outsmarted you all."*

— ANNE ENGLISH

He had been getting away with it. For years, it had been his secret.
There had been rumours, mostly pointed at someone else, and he'd
still felt safe until that Friday in 1972 when elder Arthur Powley
showed up at his house. Now the walls were closing in. The church
elder looked at David with compassionate but judgemental eyes.
He reminded him that another man could suffer unjustly, under
the blame of the community. He reminded him that God could
see the truth of his soul and that the clock was ticking. In three years,
the world would come to an end. Only the chosen few would see
heaven.[64] The remaining people would reside on a restored earth,
and even more frightening, the unrepentant would go to hell.

It might seem contradictory for a killer to be influenced by
religion. After all, shouldn't his heart be cold and stony?

One aspect of growing up in an evangelical faith is that it can
breed duality in a person. It's easy to be someone different at

---

64 Jehovah's Witnesses believed the world would end in 1975.

church than you are during the week. I grew up this way. My family attended Faith Tabernacle, a Pentecostal-style evangelical church at the corner of Huron and Clarke Side Road in London, Ontario. The kids I first drank with, first smoked with, first tried pot with were all from church. We were filled with a potentially toxic mix of naïveté and repressed desire. We stuck together. For me, at least, I felt like an outsider to the other kids at school. It felt better to stick with my friends who shared this bizarre experience with me. We vacillated between fervent devotion and rebellion. The concepts of brotherhood and family that we were raised with only heightened our need to fit in, but I never felt like I could. My subversive desires had to be kept secret from my fellow Christians, but my religious ideas also kept me isolated from other teenagers who didn't go to church. It was a strange in-between place that I didn't conquer for a long time.

David lived in this no man's land. His blue-collar co-workers smoked, swore, drank. They laughed. They seemed free. He wanted to be one of them, and most of all, he didn't want to face the monster inside himself. Meetings at the Kingdom Hall forced him to do that, so he went as little as his wife would let him get away with. This made him seem childish to her.

He knew what he had done was wrong, but there seemed to be no consequences. He had gotten away with it and did what he wanted. It gratified him on such a deep level — other people didn't get it. They didn't get what it was like to be in total control of someone. They didn't understand the thrill of sex combined with the grimmest death, watching their empty eyes as he came. That kind of understanding required someone special, and David believed he was special, like the Biblical king he was named after.

———————

David was born on May 29, 1945, in Stratford, Ontario. Glen Fryer was born there, too, and as I've heard that it's the source for most of the crystal meth floating around downtown London,

I'm starting to wonder if it's also the gateway to hell. These two charming fellows shared some time in their small hometown, but with an age gap of thirteen years, it would require an exceptional circumstance for Bodemer and Fryer to have known each other. Still, anything is possible.

David's father, Leopold, was born in 1911. His mother, Jean Marie, was born in 1919. They moved to Perth County outside Stratford in the early 1930s. Leopold worked for the Whyte Packing Company and they rented a house in the country. He moved his family often, a behaviour his son would inherit. When their eldest son, George, was born in 1938, they lived at 565 Eerie Street in Stratford. By the time Lloyd arrived in 1942, they were on Trinity Street, and when David came along in 1945, they were living at 517 Ontario Street in a small cottage. Young Beatrice was born in 1948. The Bodemers' longest residence was at 298 Queen Street, a house that has been so redone over the years it's hard to imagine what it looked like back then. I think of this as David Bodemer's childhood home; he spent ages six to fifteen there.

Leopold then worked in manufacturing for Canadian Fabricated Products to pay for the one-story bungalow, which stood within spitting distance of a CNR railway yard. Whatever was happening at home, it was all overcast by the sound of the trains running day and night at the end of the street. David Bodemer would be attracted to trains again in his later employment with the CNR as a section man, a job he may have gotten with connections from his hometown. CNR was the major employer in Stratford for most of the twentieth century. Glen Fryer's father and grandfather worked there, too.

The Bodemer family of six attended services at the local Kingdom Hall. The small congregation had many homes during the years, but in the late 1950s, when David was held back a year in grade school, they met on the second floor of 90 Ontario Street. This space has been renovated into apartments above Fanfare Books today, a charming bookstore that I highly recommend.

This second-floor space is where the Bodemers may have first met the Crooker family and other Witnesses from Aylmer, as they visited regional congregations (Stratford is an hour from Aylmer). Bert Crooker may have even preached there.

Around the time that David started high school, the family moved out of Stratford to Alliston, Ontario. The motivations for this move are unknown.

———

David Bodemer's teachers at Banting High School in Alliston treated him like the stupidest guy around. Standing in the back row of his grade nine class photo, he towered over the rest of the students, fully grown. He was slim, dark-haired, and in his own opinion, pretty good looking. His striking eyebrows gave him a serious countenance. He had no trouble getting the attention of the girls, especially while playing the part of the badass. Those other grade nine boys had no chance; just a glance from him would make them scatter. He was a man and they were just children. One of his classmates[65] remembers him as a bully. He seemed like a "biker" type, perhaps "from the wrong side of the tracks." He picked on the kids who were smaller than him — which was pretty much all of them — and became isolated when they went out of their way to avoid him. He could be violent, scary.

He dropped out of school and left all that hassle behind with a flick of his cigarette.

When he moved away to work for the CNR in Ingersoll, Ontario, it's easy to imagine that a less-than-exemplary home life was what motivated him. He earned a good reputation with his co-workers and was well liked, but there were rumours that he stole copper from the railway to sell on the black market. He was also known as a source for stolen goods, which he could easily peddle all over

———

65 This classmate asked to remain anonymous.

Southwestern Ontario, unknown to authorities as he was always on the move. His job as a section man took him across the region and introduced him to off-the-beaten paths, lonely lovers' lanes, and back roads. Many of the locations he saw near railway lines were low-income, ghettoized areas that were home to those who became criminals out of necessity as well as by choice. He might have felt at home there. These places were just like where he grew up.

To Elaine Crooker, David was an underdog. The Dairy Bar where she worked was the perfect place to flirt. At first, he went there with his mother on her visits to see him. Jean-Marie knew the Jehovah's Witness owner of the Dairy Bar and his mostly Witness staff. She was the one who introduced him to Elaine, and her trips there with him were a bit of a matchmaking attempt. It worked. Later, he'd go in after a long workday on the rails, his youthful muscles and swagger impossible for Elaine to resist. He used his dark eyes, flitting in her direction, to court extra big scoops of ice cream and a little conversation, while her co-worker, Georgia Jackson, took care of the rest of the customers.

He had a lot to prove. Marrying Elaine, the pastor's daughter, would make up for everything. And it would make his mother so happy. He'd finally set his path straight, have kids, a job — everything he was supposed to have. And, like so many young Christian men, getting married young would allow him to express his overactive libido without sin. David had a very active libido. He had to satisfy it constantly, even though masturbation was a guilt-ridden act.

Their nuptials were held at the small red-brick Kingdom Hall on Imperial Road. His new father-in-law, Bert Crooker, conducted the service, and all of the Witnesses were there, including Elaine's co-worker Georgia. In that brief, shining moment, David was finally one of them. He'd scraped the dirt off his shoes and could hold his head up high.

But they had to live with her parents for a while.

David's libido was no joke. They had a lot of kids, very

quickly. He needed sex all the time, but not just any sex. He wanted specific kinds of sex, the kind he saw in the contraband magazines he got through the guys at work. He wanted oral sex, and Elaine hated giving it to him. He wanted her to lie still, not look at him, to be silent, his servant. He wanted to dominate her. When she objected, he threw violent fits. The bully emerged. He'd storm out of the house and disappear for days at a time. As a devout Witness, what was Elaine supposed to do? The book of Ephesians instructed her to submit to her husband as to the Lord.

Even if Elaine had spoken up, the Jehovah's Witness congregation had a habit of overlooking sexual crimes within their flock. London media personality and former Jehovah's Witness Donald D'Haene released a memoir in 2002 called *Father's Touch*, in which he detailed sexual abuses he'd suffered from his father, Daniel. He writes that right after he was baptized into the faith in 1973, he told an elder in the Aylmer Jehovah's Witness church about what his father was doing to him. This led to an internal investigation. When his father confessed to the elders that he had been abusing his children, he was excommunicated, but no one called the police. He couldn't go to church, but he could keep molesting his kids. His wife, Jeannette, finally had enough and left him in 1976.

Daniel D'Haene suffered no real consequences until the early 1980s, when Donald went to the police himself and reported the crime. As Donald wrote in his memoir, "Religion doesn't create monsters. Monsters use religion."

For the members of Aylmer's Jehovah's Witness congregation, there was very little they could effectively do to stop the sexual predators among them.

His two selves lived side-by-side for a time, but the dark part was taking over. He stopped going to meetings. He stopped going to Bible study and prayer groups. David had no ambition to become an elder of the church after all, much to Elaine's dissatisfaction.

Her disappointments with all of his little failures fuelled his growing rage. His wife later explained that David would get home from his job with CNR around 5 p.m. each day. He would head out again shortly thereafter. Sometimes this was to work with Bert at his after-hours cleaning business. Other times, he went out to his garage next to the house they'd finally rented in Avon, a small town just a short drive from their in-laws in Aylmer, up Springfield Road. The garage was his getaway, with no wife and kids to bug him, and could have been a safe place to store stolen goods and pornography under the guise of handyman projects.

Most evenings no one knew where he was.

In 1966, David decided the family needed to move. They moved many times, even after they landed in Kitchener, Ontario. They rarely stayed in one apartment for longer than two years. He got work where he could find it, at the CNR, the concrete factory, from his father-in-law. He had no career to speak of, and his involvement in their faith community was dismal. Elaine was horrified at how her marriage had turned out, and at just twenty-six years old, David already felt like he'd lost at the game of life. He worked hard all the time and the only things that made him feel good, that offered any relief from his shitty existence, were things he had to keep absolutely secret.

Two lives, existing side by side.

Starting in the 1960s, David Bodemer got in trouble with the law. His first arrest was in 1966, for public mischief. He was later arrested in 1968 on two counts of break, enter, and theft. In 1970, he was charged twice for committing an indecent act. The first charge fell under Section 159 of the Criminal Code,[66] referring to

---

66 Subsection A, Section 1, 115, 165.

anal sex. In homophobic 1970 cop-speak, this likely meant being caught having sex with another man. Homosexuality had been decriminalized only the year before, and cops were still eager to round up "perverts." His other 1970 charge was exhibitionism.

Around this time, he told Elaine that he didn't go to church anymore because he "had no right to go to assemblies." These petty thefts and break-ins weren't his fault; he'd fallen in with the wrong crowd. He was ashamed of his behaviour and laden with guilt. Whatever he was doing, he couldn't stop, even though he knew it was wrong. The sex was compulsive.

His charges actually led to a psychological evaluation. He was called a "pretty standard exhibitionist," lacking "any particular disturbance . . . [or] any major difficulty." He did it to "attract attention" because "there was no sexual adjustment in his marriage."

Elaine Crooker said her husband looked at a lot of pornography, both print and film. She admitted that he had sex with her without her permission, which was not then a crime. Of course, Elaine's refusal of sex with her husband was the reason the psychologist gave for his acting out. It was her fault. If she'd given him what he wanted, he'd have stopped committing crimes.

The psychologist finally assessed Bodemer as "immature."

His criminal activity wasn't just sexual. While working at CNR in the spring of 1970, he was involved in an investigation regarding stolen copper pipes and watches. In a report filed about the matter, his supervisor described him as "not too intelligent and very easily lead [sic]. It is a known fact other employees in his gang ask him to get them [stolen] watches, gloves, etc., and when he delivers the goods they cut his price in half. He usually accepts their offer and tries to be a good fellow to make friends with his workmates. However, this has been taken care of."

Could Bodemer have been selling stolen goods at Stanley Variety in 1968?

By the winter of 1972, David Bodemer found himself the father of five kids, working to support them in thankless manual labour, and living with a woman who didn't like him and couldn't sexually satisfy him. He'd gotten in trouble at work, in trouble with the police, and in trouble with his religious community, who saw him as a backslidden lout. There was perhaps only one thing he was good at, and he couldn't tell anyone about it.

CHAPTER TWENTY-FOUR

THE CONFESSION

"Thus sayeth the Lord, Behold, I will raise up evil against thee out of thine own house . . . For thou didst it secretly: but I will do this thing before all Israel, and before the sun."

— 2 SAMUEL 12:11–12

JANUARY 1972. The town of Aylmer was abuzz with renewed rumours about who killed Georgia Jackson.[67] As gossip circulated, the elders at the local Kingdom Hall decided to take matters into their own hands. They petitioned the national leadership of their church for assistance in rooting out the perpetrator of Georgia Jackson's 1966 murder once and for all. The church leaders took the matter very seriously, and they sent one of their best representatives to Aylmer: Charles Ross, a nationally recognized Jehovah's Witness. He was to work with elder Arthur Powley in finding the truth behind the whispers and backroom murmurings. Among the rumours was a story that Bert Crooker had been covering up for someone, but that person had gotten into a lot of trouble with the law over the past few years, and it was getting harder for Crooker to keep hiding the truth. It could have been the arrests and the psychological assessment that

---

67 The reasons for renewed interest in Georgia's murder are unknown and elusive.

got people talking, but there's no record or reference in available documents that tells us definitely what set off the following sequence of events.

JANUARY 21, 1972. Arthur Powley and Charles Ross drove an hour north to Kitchener to talk to David Bodemer. He let them in, and, somberly, they told him why they were there. As soon as they broached the subject of Georgia's death, David got upset, agitated. The tension was too much and he broke down.

"I'll tell you everything," he said. "Just let me talk to Elaine first."

JANUARY 23, 1972. Elaine was in bed next to her husband when he began to talk to her. He started to panic. It was hard to breathe. He couldn't stop the fountains of salt water streaming down his cheeks. Elaine looked perplexed.

"I killed a girl," he blurted out. "Six years ago."

At first she couldn't believe it, but, "when he broke down and told me — I believe he did it, for I never saw him so upset. He was near hysterical."

The pieces started to come together. Over the previous three weeks, Elaine had watched her husband sell off his possessions, including his hunting rifles and fishing gear. He'd spoken about suicide. Now she realized he'd been planning to confess. The rumours and the inquisitive Charles Ross had gotten to him. He had seen it coming.

She picked up the phone. "Dad," she said, "you have to expect the worst, about something that happened about six years ago."

They talked for only a few moments. Bert Crooker had expected the news, knowing what Charles Ross had heard and how the investigation was going. He promised to help. When he got off the phone with Elaine, he made arrangements to see David the next morning with Powley and Ross.

JANUARY 24, 1972. The next morning, Bert Crooker joined Powley and Ross on the drive to Kitchener, where they sat down with David at his apartment at 203 Chandler Drive.

"I did it," he told them.

"Did what?" asked Powley.

"I killed her."

"Who? Georgia Jackson?"

"Yes."

They sat down at the table and came up with a written statement, which was signed by Bodemer and the other three men as witnesses.[68]

This wasn't just rape or child molestation. It was murder. They had to go to the authorities. Bodemer's father-in-law stood slowly and looked up the number for the OPP. He dialed it on the couple's rotary phone. The sound of the phone dial's sliding clicks filled the chilly room.

———

Alsop was busy at work when he was interrupted late that afternoon. A man had called the station, saying he had just heard a confession to the 1966 slaying of Georgia Jackson. It could have been just another wack-job, but Alsop had a feeling. After six years of hunting a killer, he might finally have his man. Perpetually ready in his suit and tie, he jumped in his car and hit the highway. It didn't take long for him to reach the apartment in Kitchener.

There he found David Bodemer, his tall frame slumped over, his pale skin flushed with emotion. He had his shoes on and was ready to go. The church elders watched as Alsop slid his handcuffs over Bodemer's lanky wrists and escorted the twenty-six-year-old father of five out of the house and into the back seat of the OPP cruiser.

———

68 See appendix for a transcript of the confession.

They sat in an interrogation room at OPP headquarters.

"... the whole thing?" asked Bodemer.

David Bodemer's arrest photo.
Courtesy of Rod Keith.

Alsop looked at him from overtop his horn-rimmed glasses. "Yes, the whole thing. You will have to speak slow for I am going to write it down."

Bodemer began the second version of his confession.

"Left Avon after work to go to Aylmer to help my father-in-law in his cleaning business. I went up Talbot Street to the stop light. I noticed he was in the bank working, so I went straight through and went around the block to park my car. When I came around, I noticed Georgia Jackson in front of Spicer's Bake Shop.[69]

"I pulled over and honked the horn and she came over to the car. I asked her where she was going. She said she was going home, so I offered her a ride home. She said OK and got in.

"We went around the block to take her home and I was talking to her about her sister and her [sister's] husband, Dennis and Linda Sullivan. By this time we were at her place in front, and I had asked her where they had moved to. At this time I didn't have any thoughts of killing her or doing anything to her, or when I had picked her up at the beginning.

"She had told me where they had moved to and told me she

---

69 Spotting Georgia in front of Spicer's Bake Shop was inconsistent with the eyewitness testimonies of others who had seen her that night.

would show me whereabouts it was. So I said 'OK' and I drove away from in front of her house. It may have been four or five blocks away where they had lived.

"She showed me whereabouts it was, and I turned the car around to take her home. Driving down I am not quite sure what street it was, I think it was South Street I believe it is, I had stopped in front of an electrical company place and I had put my arm around her. She asked me why did I stop the car for. I told her that I was wanting to talk to her. I had pulled her over; we had started to — she started to pull away like. I had kept on pulling her, and she had started to scream and yell. I had told her not to scream when I put my hand over her mouth to stop her from screaming. I don't know what got into me or my mind to do this or to hit her on the back of the head with a pop bottle that was in the back seat. When I hit her she went kind of stunned and in the meantime she said her parents will be looking for her and for me to stop. We struggled and she passed out.

"I put my arm around her and her head right against my shoulder. Then I had pulled away, holding her up from falling over. I went south on 73 Highway to a sideroad on the left and went just about to the end of the road where I had stopped. She came to after and started to scream and struggle again.

"I had put my hand over her mouth and her nose to keep her from screaming. I had kept my hand too long on her and I noticed she was not breathing. I did this cause I did not want to see her cry. Certain times before I did this — I don't remember some things that went on.

"This is where I had sexual intercourse with her. When I had noticed her puffing up in the face, I knew she was dead. I was worried or scared what to do with her and myself. I know I had to get rid of her, so I left there and went to the end of the road and made a half-turn and started towards No. 3 Highway. I had turned right to Springfield Road, I went down Springfield Road a little way to the bush — where the bush is on the left-hand side.

"When I had stopped, I looked and wondered if I should have put her in there. There was no cars coming, so I picked her up and carried her part ways in the bush and dragged her the rest of the way, where I had placed her behind some shrubs. I went back to the car and started to drive off and I noticed her coat. I went to the next side road and turn left to go back into Aylmer, and just going down the road I stopped by a big tree and put her coat behind it.

"Then I left and went back into Aylmer to help my father-in-law. I went inside to help him, and I noticed different times looking at the window [that] Dennis Sullivan was walking up and down the street. I knew what he was looking for because Georgia Jackson said they would be looking for her if she did not come home soon. He came to the bank door and I answered it, and he asked me if I had seen her. I replied, 'No.'

"The father-in-law was in the basement at the time and he did not know he had come. Approximately a couple hours later, he came back to the bank. This time the father-in-law was upstairs and he answered the door. Dennis Sullivan told him what was wrong, so they decided to search for her. We stopped working and left the bank to search for her. Not too long later, we left the river there to go to the police station to see if they had heard anything. They had said no, but it was sent out about her disappearance. We left the police station and he said to me, 'If you want to go home, you can,' because I was not dressed for the weather.

"I forgot to mention earlier there — earlier when we went to the side road, I had noticed there was blood on my shoulder and arm of my coat. That is why he said I wasn't dressed too warm for the weather because I had taken my coat off before I had started to work.

"So I said 'OK,' and I left to go home. He had mentioned that there was going to be a search for her on Saturday, the next day, because it would be daylight. I had the next Saturday — Saturday I went out to the car to get in, and under the seat when I noticed her white glove in the front seat on the floor. I had taken both [Georgia's] glove and [my] coat and put them between the south wall of the garage or driving shed where I had kept my car.

"There was blood also on the front seat, so I got a rag and snow from the ground to wash it off as best as I could. There was not much blood left, more or less a ring on the outside of it. When I was finished, I put the rag with the coat and glove, and I went into Aylmer for the search. I helped them search for one day and one night."

Alsop cleared his throat. "You mentioned in your statement that, 'When we went to the side road, I had noticed blood on my shoulder and arm of my coat.' Who do you mean by 'we'?" asked Alsop.

"I noticed."

"Was somebody with you when you went to the side road?" he pushed.

"Nobody was with me at any time."

"What do you mean by any time?"

"Any time from when I had picked her up and went back to the bank to work."

"Who are you referring to when you say, 'when I had picked her up'?" asked Alsop.

"Georgia Jackson."

"So that is the same girl that is also known as Georgina Jackson."[70]

"Yes. That is what I always thought her name was, just Georgia Jackson."

Detective Alsop's moustache twitched thoughtfully as he watched the young man tell his story. Could this be the man he'd been searching for all these years? He had checked the records while the suspect waited to be questioned, and yes, Bodemer had

---

70 Some contemporary reports and files list her name as Georgina, not Georgia. She went by both names.

been arrested before. He'd committed sexual crimes. It was far from an outrageous idea. Still, it was always something to see a murderer in the flesh — especially one who could possibly be the Forest City Killer.

He slid a pen across the table and told Bodemer to sign his statement. With great satisfaction, he instructed the accused to stand up. Detective Alsop put him in cuffs and escorted him back to the holding cell.

There was no sweeter sound than those clanging cell doors slamming shut.

JANUARY 25, 1972. The next day, Elaine Bodemer came to the OPP station. She was not there to visit her husband, but instead to give a statement to Detective Alsop. He took her into an interrogation room, perhaps the same one where her husband had confessed, to share what she knew about her husband's crimes. They talked about his whereabouts, his general behaviour. She revealed that he'd gotten a few psychiatric treatments in 1971 at the Kitchener-Waterloo hospital. He was still an outpatient, supervised by a Dr. Muke.[71] She told Alsop what kind of person she thought her husband was, which was not a glowing portrait. She seemed thrilled to have him out of the house. She was deeply humiliated to be the wife of a murderer.

During this conversation, Elaine Bodemer said something quite startling. Unprompted, she brought up Jackie English. She told Detective Alsop that a few days before Jackie English had disappeared, she was with her husband at the Park Lunch restaurant, where they had seen her talking to a "negro."

Back in 1969, David Papple had told Alsop, "On [Thursday, October 2, 1969], Jackie came over to my apartment in the morning about 8:00 a.m., with a bathing suit in a plastic bag. She said she was

---

71 May also be spelled Moock.

going swimming in the afternoon with a friend at the Beal Technical School. On Thursday night, she was back at my apartment about 10:00 p.m. I asked her how she enjoyed her swimming and she replied that she didn't go swimming, for she met a friend uptown and walked around with him. She said his name was Bill Groat, [72] a coloured man who she went to school with. I'm not positive if it was Bill Groat, but she mentioned about Bill Groat, for she had a crush on him one time or another. That didn't bother me, for she told me that she didn't feel anything towards him now."

Was it possible that the man Elaine Bodemer saw with Jackie English was Bill Groat? Is it possible that she mixed up the Park Lunch diner in Byron with the Hi-Lunch diner near Beal Secondary School?

According to Fred English's research, Bill Groat attended his sister's funeral. Bill's parents, Jim and Willa, signed the registry. Their signatures were intermingled with those of Marilyn Hird and the girl her brother had attacked, leading Fred to wonder if they all knew each other and had driven together from the east end, where they all lived. If they did all know each other, it would make for a very interesting web of connections to unravel. Did Bill Groat know David Bodemer? And if so, did David Bodemer also know Groat's neighbours Marilyn and Jim Hird?

FEBRUARY 8, 1972. Alsop was energized by the arrest, and he was determined to nail a conviction. He tracked down the car David had been driving in 1966. It was a blue two-toned 1957 Ford Meteor that Bodemer had traded to Ted Berg, who was the mechanic at Gingrich Motors Victoria near Peterborough, Ontario, in 1966. In 1969, the car was sent to an auto-wrecking yard in St. Agatha, on the farm of a Mr. Holst.

---

72 Bill Groat did not respond to requests to be interviewed for this book.

Alsop found the car only two weeks after Bodemer's arrest. It took two days to dig it out of the snow. They found five or six spots of blood under the right armrest, where Georgia Jackson would have been sitting.

Detective Alsop also made a note, wondering if the car Bodemer was driving in January 1968, when Jacqueline Dunleavy was murdered, had faulty alignment.

———

As noted by Alsop during his interview with David on January 25, 1972, Bodemer owned two other Ford vehicles between 1966 and 1972: a 1965 Ford Fairlane and a 1967 model with a broken motor mount. During that time, he also owned a 1966 Peugeot, a rather rare European automobile. The company was later merged with Citroen, the same company for which Glen Fryer later became the Canadian club president.

There's something pretty interesting about that 1966 Peugeot. It has a feature called a "couchette." For those readers who are not European automobiles aficionados, let me explain: the front seats folded all the way down so that they were flat with the back seats, to form a double bed.

You could call it the perfect rape and murder mobile.

This vehicle was never recovered.

CHAPTER TWENTY-FIVE

THE TRIAL OF DAVID BODEMER

*"If one sat down to reason it out, you would have difficulty
in deciding how one could think that he would get eternal life
by lying about something that he hadn't done at all."*

— JUDGE BARNUM

When news got out that an arrest had been made in the Georgia
Jackson case, the community in and around Aylmer went crazy.
Of course, little Aylmer doesn't have its own courthouse. The
closest is in St. Thomas, the main urban centre of agricultural
Elgin County.

St. Thomas's claim to fame is that it's where Jumbo the
Elephant was killed in 1885, when he was hit by a train. There's
a statue memorializing the Barnum and Bailey beast that over-
looks the main thoroughfare of St. Thomas, the Talbot Line, so
that you pass by his feet every time you drive to the beach at
Port Stanley.[73] Inside a small red replica caboose beside the statue,
there's also a sporadically open museum where you can find out
interesting information such as this: when they examined Jumbo's
body — as he was an enormous and famous animal who merited
autopsy — they discovered a policeman's whistle in his stomach.

---

73 This was one of my favourite make-out spots back in the day. I used to ask
boys to drive out there.

The courthouse, a short ten-minute walk from the Jumbo statue, is a huge yellow-brick building that still stands today. It's been beautifully restored and preserved. For Bodemer's first day in court, people who wanted to lay their eyes on the vicious rapist and murderer who had killed innocent Georgia Jackson six years earlier spilled down the elegant front steps and into the square. Media hung around the side door where Detective Alsop tried to bring his perp into the courthouse with as little fanfare as possible. It wasn't a show; it was about justice. He took a brown scarf and draped it over Bodemer's head to stop photographers from getting a good shot.

In front of the aptly named Judge Fred R. Barnum, ringleader of an entirely different kind of circus, Bodemer stood alone. His lawyer, David Little, was out of the country. The accused was a solitary, leering figure. Tears streamed down his face as he was remanded and led away to his cell.

David Bodemer, hidden from view, is escorted out of OPP headquarters the day after his arrest by Dennis Alsop.

London Free Press Collection of Photographic Negatives, [1972-01-25], Archives and Special Collections, Western Libraries, Western University.

Each week, Detective Alsop proudly dragged Bodemer out of incarceration for a court appearance, during which he would again be remanded in custody, the status of his bail revisited. These short, fairly uneventful routine procedures still drew huge attention. The courthouse in St. Thomas was packed every seven days with spectators who wanted to see the killer, even for a moment.

Judge Barnum sent Bodemer to be examined at the Oak Ridge Hospital forensic psychiatric unit in Penetanguishene. Mental illness might lead to a not criminally responsible, or NCR, ruling. Courts had begun seriously experimenting with NCR rulings — Canada's version of the insanity plea — in the 1960s. In Ontario, NCR convicts were sent to Oak Ridge, now Waypoint Centre for Mental Health Care, for indeterminate periods of time. It could often be a life sentence.

The old Oak Ridge buildings closed in 2004, replaced by the adjacent Waypoint facility, but in its time they housed the worst of the worst. Among the long-term patients were two of the Big Three: "Bedroom Strangler" Russell Johnson and "Mad Slasher" Christian Magee. Magee would later protest that his NCR plea kept him incarcerated longer than a guilty verdict would have, as he is not eligible for parole or other benefits granted to non-psychiatric prisoners. These psychopaths had graduated from the London Psychiatric Hospital and found themselves in hell.

The story of Oak Ridge is a fascinating one on its own. There's an excellent fifteen-minute documentary on YouTube by CBC's *The National* that can fill you in on all the horrible stuff that went on. I don't know how long Bodemer spent there, but it's worth noting that Oak Ridge was not a place that made criminals better. If anything, it made them worse. Patients of Dr. Elliott Barker underwent psychedelic therapy, and in one type of treatment called "The Capsule" were chained naked together in a room for days at a time where the fluorescent lights never went off and they were fed through a hole in the wall, all while on LSD. Other treatments at Oak Ridge included electric shocks isolation, and hydropathy — which basically meant you took a bath for days, immobile, while fresh water was constantly pumped into a tub and the old water drained out.

Three psychiatric hospitals have appeared in this story — CPRI, the London Psychiatric Hospital, and Oak Ridge Hospital — and all three have been involved in separate class-action lawsuits from former patients who underwent abuse and sometimes torture. The patients of Oak Ridge won their suit against Dr. Barker in 2017.

At the advice of his lawyer, David Little, and his doctor, J.K. McNeil, Bodemer went to Oak Ridge by his own consent to be examined. This kind of cooperation would, in theory, help him with his defence; an NCR ruling could save him from the hangman's noose if the Crown found a way to prove premeditation. It was also, at first glance, a good way to avoid jail. That first short trip to Oak Ridge surely showed Bodemer instead that one was very much like, if not worse than, the other.

APRIL 27, 1972. Despite his two signed confessions, Bodemer pled not guilty to the non-capital murder of Georgia Jackson.

A grand jury hearing was held over two days at the St. Thomas courthouse to determine whether or not there was enough evidence for the Crown to go forward with a trial. There were twelve witnesses who appeared the first day before a full gallery, but a publication ban kept evidence presented under wraps. On the second day, four more witnesses testified.

Bodemer's lawyer suggested that he might ask for a change of venue, as the Georgia Jackson murder had been highly publicized and he wondered if his client could get a fair trial in Elgin County. Bodemer told him to drop the request.

The grand jury made up of seven men deliberated for only

forty minutes to determine that there was a true bill on the charge, and the case should go to trial. A date was set for June 19, 1972.

One of the witnesses at the grand jury was good old Aylmer chief of police, Harold Henderson. The court had to track him down. He had left town in disgrace after the inquest into Georgia Jackson's murder and was currently working as an ambulance dispatcher for Sudbury General Hospital.

MARCH 21, 1972. Detective Alsop pulled up at the farm of Roy Ferguson in South Dorchester. It was on this land where the refuse from David Bodemer's demolished garage had been dumped.

Starting in 1965, Bodemer had rented the garage next to a house he lived in with his family at the main crossroads of Avon, Ontario. After the family moved away, he continued to rent the garage. This might have seemed suspicious, but it's possible that, like Glen Fryer, he kept his various automobiles there, including the Peugeot with the couchette feature. That would be a good excuse to keep renting the property. It's also possible that he kept his continuing rental a secret from his wife so that he could use it as an escape from his miserable life.

He told Alsop in his confession that he had hidden Georgia Jackson's glove in the walls of this outbuilding. Finding it would offer fantastic proof of his crime. Unfortunately, by the time of Bodemer's arrest, the garage had been demolished.

In the trunk of Alsop's car was a shovel. The dirt on Roy Ferguson's farm was still mostly frozen as he plunged it into the ground, pushing through construction remains, cement, wood, and gravel. He was determined to confirm Bodemer's story: that he had hidden Georgia Jackson's glove in the walls of that building. He didn't record how much time he spent in that field, but it was the only task he'd completed that day, standing in the cold wind, fighting the frigid, rocky soil.

And then, there it was: Georgia's glove.

If he wanted to look for evidence from other unsolved murders in the area, he didn't search for them that day. The Ferguson farm has never been searched for other evidence.

Bodemer had another potential hiding spot for his treasured possessions. Behind the garage and the house in Avon was an old well. It's unused now, covered over for years. No one has ever checked its murky depths to see what it contains.[74]

MAY 1, 1972. Detective Alsop tracked down Bill Groat, who both David Papple and Elaine Bodemer said might have met with Jackie English days before her disappearance, as a suspect in the Jackie English case. He wanted to know if Groat and Bodemer were in cahoots. However, it was probably because of Alsop's suspicions, and that interview, that Bill Groat did not want to talk to me.[75] I had wanted to ask Bill if David Bodemer and his wife approached him when he had lunch with Jackie that day, and if he got the impression that Jackie knew Bodemer or recognized him from one of her workplaces. Alsop didn't keep his notes from their meeting, if he took any, so there is no way to find out aside from speaking to Bill.

MAY 24, 1972. London chief of police Walter Johnson recommended that City Council rescind the $50,000 reward they had established for information regarding the deaths of Jackie English, Jacqueline Dunleavy, and Frankie Jensen. It was as if the Forest City Killer had been removed from the streets and they thought he would never return.

---

74 I have confirmed that a proper excavation has never been performed on the Ferguson site to see if there is evidence on the property pertaining to other murders in the London area.

75 It would have been hard enough to live in London as a visible minority in the 1960s and 1970s without being connected to one of the most famous murders in the city.

JUNE 7, 1972. City Council, including London's first female mayor, Jane Bigelow, voted to rescind the reward offered for information leading to an arrest in the unsolved murders. It was determined that if someone did come forward in the future, they would come up with some kind of compensation then. They didn't think that was likely to happen, and it never did.

LEFT: David Bodemer is brought to trial by Detective Alsop.

Courtesy of the Elgin County Archives. *St. Thomas Journal-Times* Fonds.

BELOW: Virginia Jackson (far right) enters the court house for Bodemer's trial.

London Free Press Collection of Photographic Negatives, [1972-06-19], Archives and Special Collections, Western Libraries, Western University.

JUNE 19, 1972. David Bodemer's trial began. The jury was made up of twelve residents of the area and did not include a single woman, which was considered unusual even then.

Early in the trial, Georgia's mother, Virginia Jackson, took the stand and was asked to identify her slain daughter's jacket. The blood on the collar brought her to tears. Her emotional testimony was followed by that of other members of the family, including two of Georgia's siblings. As the trial progressed, the prosecution detailed Georgia's comings and goings on the last day of her life. They outlined her relationship with the defendant, and the court heard Bodemer's confession to Detective Alsop. Physical evidence, such as Georgia's glove, and the blood in his car, was presented to confirm his confession.

Virginia Jackson, at the rear of the group, leaves the courthouse with her supporters.

Courtesy of the Elgin County Archives. *St. Thomas Journal-Times* Fonds.

Since Bodemer's confession and arrest, Bert Crooker had been removed from his role as Overseer of the Jehovah's Witness congregation in Aylmer. He was also asked to testify but he had trouble with his story. He had initially told investigators that he had not been working as a cleaner at the Bank of Montreal on the night that Georgia Jackson went missing. This conflicted with Bodemer's confession. Crooker now conveniently remembered their shift at the bank. "It might have passed my mind" that Bodemer was with him that night, he said, and went on to offer specifics that his son-in-law had arrived at about 7:30 or 7:40.[76]

Constable Ronald Rupert of the OPP testified that he had run a test to see if it was possible for Bodemer to have committed the crime in the time between when Georgia had last been seen and when Crooker said Bodemer had shown up at the bank. The trip had taken Rupert only thirty-two minutes, leaving plenty of extra time for the crime to take place.

A forensic pathologist from Toronto, Dr. Frederick A. Jaffe, confirmed for the court that Georgia had been smothered to death. Jaffe was also the forensic pathologist who had worked on the 1959 murder of Lynne Harper in Clinton, Ontario. Around the same time as he was performing an autopsy on Georgia Jackson, he was defending his work at the 1966 inquest into Steven Truscott's conviction for the murder of Harper. His findings in the Harper case would be determined decades later to be bunk science. Taking this into account, it's impossible to tell how much of his autopsy report in this case was accurate.

The above information is based on newspaper reports and later appeal documents. The transcript for this trial has been lost.[77] However, the judge's final statements, made available in

---

76 It's remarkable that while he had claimed to have a blurry memory of that memorable night, when something so important had taken place, he could later narrow down Bodemer's arrival to a ten-minute window.

77 At least, that's what I was told by court officials. The OPP has a copy.

Bodemer's 1973 appeal, give us good insight into the events of the trial.

Jurors heard that on the night Georgia disappeared, the Bodemer family had been invited to have dinner with the Vandendriessche family in Avon. They never showed up. For the Crown, this broken dinner date offered an opportunity for Bodemer to have committed the murder. However, the testimony caused confusion, as it contradicted Bert Crooker's assertion that Bodemer had been working with him, cleaning the Bank of Montreal that night, which supported the confessions. Eventually, like Bert Crooker, the Vandendriessches changed their story and said they had gotten the date of their dinner invitation mixed up. The Bodemers had stood them up on a different occasion.

Perhaps the Crown had included the Vandendriessches because Crooker's testimony had originally refuted Bodemer's confession. He eventually changed his story to match Bodemer's version of events, and while the Crown may have worried this would make him look a liar, it ended up coming across as genuine. As Judge Barnum remarked, "he has lent his help here by telling the truth as best he knew it, whether it helps or hurt his son-in-law."

Defence lawyer David Little did his best to have his client's confessions thrown out. He first tried to show them as false because they were given under duress. The church elders, he argued, pressured the accused to admit to crimes he had not committed. Mr. Powley had even come to visit Bodemer in jail to intimidate him into sticking to his false confession, said Little. The accused could have gotten details about the crime from the newspaper. The facts surrounding Georgia's death had been extensively reported upon in the *St. Thomas Journal*, and Little argued that Bodemer had made up his version of events based on clippings his father-in-law Bert Crooker had kept, which would have been readily available for the accused to review even recently.

Many killers like to track the results of their murders in the press. It would have made sense for Bodemer to keep clippings of his crime. Perhaps the collection of newspaper articles found at Crooker's house were not even his, and David had left them or stashed them there. There is no way to know if the clippings found referred only to Georgia Jackson or if other murders were included, too.

Judge Barnum had to address the issue of whether or not Bodemer's confession to Powley, Ross, and Crooker should fall under the same kind of privilege one would expect from a priest. Barnum threw that line of questioning right under the bus, saying that the Jehovah's Witnesses did not follow that belief and that "there was nothing, nothing that one ought to criticize Mr. Powley about in doing his duty and turning over what information he had. I should think commendation is what he deserves for it."[78]

Judge Barnum excused the jury for some of these arguments and later explained to them that he wanted to be sure that the confessions were "made freely and voluntarily and not in response to any threat" before he allowed them in court. Barnum acknowledged that religious pressure could cause a false confession, but he pointed

Elaine Bodemer and her father, Albert Crooker.

London Free Press Collection of Photographic Negatives, [1972-06-22], Archives and Special Collections, Western Libraries, Western University.

---

78 In light of what was happening at the D'Haene home while this case was before the courts, Powley offered a rare example of the Jehovah's Witnesses bringing criminal activity within their ranks to the attention of the law.

to the physical evidence that lined up with Bodemer's statements to Powley, Ross, Crooker, and Alsop. Surely, the prosecution found it in the best interests of a conviction to downplay any discrepancies that could be found between Bodemer's confessions and the realities of the crime scene. Judge Barnum emphasized the similarities as well, and in the end, the confessions were kept in evidence.

The elders had suspected another member of the Jehovah's Witness community of the crime, and Judge Barnum wondered if this had affected Bodemer's desire to confess, rather than the religious pressure of Powley, Ross, and Crooker. The existence of this other suspect, whose name I could not track down, also encouraged rumours in the community that Bodemer had been a patsy.

When it came to the specific charges, there was an outrageous discussion about whether or not Georgia had been raped or simply murdered. These arguments were pretty horrifying in retrospect. I'll leave that to your imagination, but suffice it to say, the judge ended up explaining to the jury that if Bodemer had sex with her after he killed her, it wasn't really rape, so they'd best let that charge go to the wind and stick with murder. The sexual act wasn't part of the crime, he told them. It was part of the circumstance.

The fact that her hymen was torn and that she was a virgin prior to penetration also had nothing to do with it. The judge figured it would take the same amount of force to have consensual sex with her as it would to rape her, meaning the injuries to her vagina could have happened either way. But he did concede that consensual sex partners don't usually need to be beaten over the head with a blunt object in order to proceed with intercourse and that leaving her body out in the woods probably indicated that it was rape and not a mutual attraction.

A perceived lack of premeditation was also key to the defence. If Bodemer had planned the murder, he could be subject to a capital murder charge, for which there could be a death penalty sentence. While the death penalty had not been used in Canada since 1962, and a moratorium was placed on the punishment in 1967, it was still on the books. A hanging was still possible. Discounting premeditation was important to saving Bodemer's life. Defence lawyer David Little tried to show that the disposal of Georgia's body indicated haste and a lack of planning.

Remember, in 1972, they didn't have any understanding of behavioural sciences. The idea that the killer might have revisited the corpse for gratification never occurred to them. It was as foreign an idea as that of a serial killer taking trophies and hiding them in the walls of his garage. If part of a plan to revisit the body for gratification, Bodemer's body disposal method and choice of location would align with the report of a couple seeing a man around the bush where Georgia's body would eventually be discovered. The disposal site was right along his regular route between the house in Avon, and his work in Aylmer. It was, as Barnum said, "cold enough that the body hadn't decomposed, stormy enough at times that tracks can be readily covered over." These seem like ideal conditions for any sadist with necrophilic tendencies, but was played by the defence as a mistake made in haste.

Instead of damning a potential psychopath, these details were used to keep him from death row.

A capital murder charge would have also resulted if he confessed to any other murders, as a series of sex killings would infer premeditation. In that case, a psychological assessment leading to an NCR ruling would resolve a life-or-death situation. Bodemer already knew he had not received such an assessment. If he had committed any of the other killings, confessing to them would have absolutely put him in line for capital punishment.

Information about Georgia's autopsy, including scrape marks on her legs and buttocks that would indicate she had been dragged to where she was found, was used to confirm Bodemer's confessions with physical evidence.

One factor that played an important role in confirming Bodemer's confession was the weather. On the freezing winter night of February 18, 1966, Bert Crooker had said to Bodemer, "You are too lightly clad for such a cold night." The judge noted, "Why wasn't he wearing his coat? If he were an innocent man and had nothing to do with it, and there was no blood on his coat, why wasn't he wearing it on that cold night?" He had removed the incriminating coat and stashed it in the garage wall. As a result, Bodemer had been sent home early from the initial search for Georgia, while other men stayed out searching much later in appropriate winter gear. Bodemer joined them again the next day, in a different coat.

The confessions stated that Bodemer had hidden evidence of Georgia's murder inside the walls of his rented garage in Avon, which was also confirmed by testimony about the structure. It was described as a cement building, with outside boards attached to the uprights by two-by-fours, and another lining of boards inside of that, so there was a space in between. This would have given Bodemer the secret place he needed to hide his trophies, or what his defence described as hastily disposed of incriminating evidence.

No mention was made of the mysterious phone call Virginia Jackson had received from someone claiming to be her daughter. The assumption may have been that it was a crank call, rather than the actions of a sadistic torturer.

The defence used Bodemer's criminal history to actually refute the idea that he was a killer. Instead, Little argued that it proved he would *not* be a murderer. He called expert testimony to explain that exhibitionists were non-violent, something that behavioural scientists today would absolutely disagree with. It seems common knowledge to us now that crime escalates and that sexual assaults tend to become more severe the longer a predator continues to get away with it.

A psychologist named Dr. Evans testified that Bodemer had a high libido, and, laying the blame on Mrs. Bodemer, suggested that if this had been satisfied, he might not have committed this crime. The rape and murder of Georgia Jackson was only — as

Detective Alsop leaves the courthouse with a smile on his face after David Bodemer is convicted of non-capital murder and sentenced to life in prison.

London Free Press Collection of Photographic Negatives, [1972-06-22], Archives and Special Collections, Western Libraries, Western University.

Herb Jeffrey had stated after the murder of Jacqueline Dunleavy — the work of a healthy male.

JUNE 27, 1972. David Bodemer was found guilty of non-capital murder in the case of Georgia Jackson. As the verdict was read, reporters noticed a distinct lack of reaction in his face except for an almost imperceptible smile.

His sentence was natural life imprisonment to be served at the Kingston Penitentiary. He was never supposed to get out.

MARCH 9, 1973. The Ontario Court of Appeal denied Bodemer's appeal, and an application to further appeal to the Supreme Court of Canada never went ahead.

PART V

WHAT FOLLOWS

CHAPTER TWENTY-SIX

FIRE!

"Sometimes in the original investigation you can get too close to it and might not see things that are obvious years later. A lot of guys take it personally if they can't solve a case."

— POLICE SUPERINTENDENT DON ANDREW

AUGUST 6, 1970. Firefighters rushed up the stairs of 619 Dundas Street to the apartments above the storefront below. As they hurried up the narrow staircase, two unidentified men passed them coming down. One of the firefighters told them to get out, there was a fire. They laughed and said something snarky in response. They didn't say anything about smoke or flames. "They had to know there was a fire upstairs," one firefighter told reporters. "It must have been burning for ten or twelve minutes before we got the call."

The team burst into the apartment, where the door had been locked but was not otherwise impeded. The flames had been eating up the small residence unencumbered for about twenty minutes. Smoke filled the air, and the firefighter looked for a way to ventilate the space. It was impossible to see what they were doing. As they sprayed the flames with water, they could clearly see that the fire had started in the kitchen around the stove. The blaze was containable and relatively easy to control. Within fifteen minutes, they were looking through the apartment for evidence and survivors.

Room to room, no one was there. It seemed as if the apartment had been empty. One firefighter even told a journalist on the scene that there were no casualties.

Then, one of the firefighters closed the entryway door to see what was behind it. There was another door, one small enough to be a closet. He tried to open it, but the door swung inwards, not out. Something was blocking the way. A team of men went to work, and with great force, they cracked the wood and tore the door off its hinges.

It turned out to be the bathroom.

Firefighter William Burke was the first to step inside, and he immediately stumbled over something. Inside, curled up between the toilet and wall, was the naked body of eighteen-year-old Melissa "Cricket" MacIvor. She had suffocated in the smoke. Around her were her clothes, which she had removed. Apparently they were covered in hot grease. Her hands and shoulders were burned.

She had died just a few feet from escape. Her lifeless foot had jammed the door shut.

Cricket's handprints on the wall of the bathroom where she was found.

Outside on the sidewalk, Fire Inspector Keith Newman encountered two young men who said they had been in the apartment with Cricket. In fact, one of them, Chris Thompson, referred to Cricket as his wife. At the time, they had not found her body, so Inspector Newman had told Chris that no one had been in the apartment. His "wife" was presumably safe.

Chris Thompson told Newman that he had gone to the bank and left Cricket sleeping in the bedroom. On the way back home, he tried to enter the rear entrance of the building where he ran into the other fellow, James Smith, who told him about the fire. When Chris had left to go to the bank, James had been upstairs in Cricket's apartment making French fries on the stove. Smith had also, for an unknown reason, left the building and a pot of hot grease on the stove.

The two men stood out on the street, wondering where Cricket was, until a firefighter came up to them and told them she was dead. According to the newspaper, neither of them seemed particularly bothered by the news. It wasn't the reaction firefighters expected from her supposed husband.

James Smith later told the police his story, which contradicted Chris's. He said he did not meet him at the back of the building, but out front. Chris had been chatting with some friends. Then Chris went upstairs, and shortly after, the fire trucks arrived.

Chris would later say that Cricket had received a death threat from the Satan's Choice biker gang the day before the fire. The three of them had been crashing in the apartment, which actually belonged to a man named William Johnson.

The newspaper did not report who had called in the fire.

AUGUST 8, 1970. Cricket's unusual social crew made up the diverse crowd of funeral attendees who showed up to remember her. They were all hippies or bikers, like her "husband" Christopher

Thompson, who was a member of the Infernal Priests Motorcycle Club. Some of the mourners had bare feet.

The newspaper reported that the dead girl had actually been married to a man named David MacIvor, who lived in Hamilton. They had gotten hitched and left town in late 1969, shortly after Jackie English's murder. Cricket left MacIvor pretty quickly, relocating to Toronto, like so many young people, in search of a better life that would elude her. She had moved back to London just a few months earlier.

Cricket lived next door to the English family when they lived at the Elmwood apartments. The English kids remember their mother, Doris, tracking Cricket down after Jackie's death and asking her if she knew anything about it. Cricket didn't have the best reputation: she used drugs and hung around with bad boys. Police had her name in their files, and she could reliably be found hanging around youth drop-in centres and coffee houses downtown. Cricket was a bit sketchy to start with, and that might be why Doris asked her if she knew anything about her daughter's death.

During one of the many conversations the English siblings had with Marilyn Hird, Fred English heard her say that she knew Cricket.

The scene of the fire at 133 Elmwood.

London Free Press Collection of Photographic Negatives, [1972-11-16], Archives and Special Collections, Western Libraries, Western University.

NOVEMBER 16, 1972. Beth Grey's husband was ill and at a hospital in Toronto, so she was living as a single mom at the moment. She'd resided in their third-floor apartment of the Elmwood apartments for four years, supporting herself and the three kids on a government pension. It was a good neighbourhood to live in, especially considering their low income. Wortley Village, which has since been voted one of the top neighbourhoods in Canada, is dotted with century homes and heritage buildings. It is a tight-knit community with a local grocery store, pub, and coffee shop. If you were on a limited income in London, there were few better places to live. In the village, you could enjoy the atmosphere of traditional London culture, the scenic streets so similar to those in the prestigious Old North neighbourhood, without having to chomp a hefty mortgage bill off your monthly budget. Many of the old manors had been converted to cheap apartments, and there were early century walk-ups throughout. It was, and is, a desirable place to raise children, with its parks and overwhelming trees. Beth's kids attended the Wortley Road Public School and they regularly went to service at the village Presbyterian Church. It was a tough life with limited money, but they were happy. Her youngest, five-year-old Gordon, would be starting school in the fall and then maybe she would be able to find a job. Gordon shared bunk beds with eight-year-old Susan. Six-year-old Nancy had her own room.

The furor of the fire was loud and catastrophic. Of the twenty-five people who were in their apartments at the time, eleven of them were children, many of them in their pyjamas and ready for bed. A loud explosion, breaking glass, and screams brought them pouring out into the roadway, where they saw Beth leaning out a window upstairs, only a few feet above a balcony. If she jumped, she would be saved. The crowd yelled at her to move, leap, do anything to get away from the fire, but she would not leave her children behind.

After making sure her own kids were safe, downstairs neigh-bour and widow Emmaline McDowell rushed up the stairs as they awaited the fire trucks. Pulling open the Greys' apartment door, she was met with a wall of fire. There was no way to get in. Two men from across the street tried the same thing, but no one could get inside to help Beth and her children.

"There were terrible flames upstairs," one of them told reporters. "Oh God, it was terrible. I sort of like panicked. I didn't know what to do. We didn't know if she would jump or if we should climb up there. You don't know what to do when you get panicky."

They watched her waving a stove pot out the window, as the fire quickly consumed the building. By the time the fire crew got there, they could describe it only as an inferno. The roof was engulfed. The apartments were utterly destroyed. Standing outside in the cold night, Mrs. McDowell wept. Her neighbours were surely dead, and she had lost everything.

At first they thought it was a grease fire. Beth had been waving

Inside the apartment at 133 Elmwood where Beth Gray and her children died.

London Free Press Collection of Photographic Negatives, [1972-11-17], Archives and Special Collections, Western Libraries, Western University.

a pot, after all, and people wondered if she had been trying to rid the apartment of the culprit of the flames. But it turned out she was using the pot to throw water on the fire, which she had tried to extinguish herself. The taps were still running when officials got inside. They found Beth huddled with Gordon and Susan in the kitchen, their bodies charred from flame. The window that would have offered them a way out was in Nancy's room, where the kindergartner had died of smoke inhalation. The flames never touched her. The inspectors said she laid there "just like she was sleeping."

The cause of the fire was never determined. Fire Inspector Kaufman told the press that it had started at the bottom of a bunk bed, presumably in the bedroom that Gordon and Susan Grey shared. If Mrs. Grey had taken her children into Nancy's room, Kaufman speculated, they could have escaped and there would have been no casualties. Why they died, just a few feet from escape, is a mystery.

Another mystery is that Dan Kinsley, who'd been at the apartment building across the street, could have sworn he had heard an explosion. It was this sound that made him run outside, where he saw Mrs. Grey waving her arms out the third-floor window.

JANUARY 8, 1973. It was the night before Richard Harrison's twenty-fourth birthday. Firefighters arrived at 171 Elgin Street around 3 a.m. Inside, they found the body of Verdun Harrison just a few feet from the front door. Betty and Richard Harrison were nearby, inside Richard's bedroom. They had died of asphyxiation. Betty had cuts on her hands and bruises on her forehead, all injuries received before her heart stopped beating. It looked like she might have broken the window to escape and banged her head when she passed out from smoke inhalation.

The fire had started in the recent addition, a family room at the back of the house that had been constructed the previous September.

The scene at 171 Elgin Street after the fatal fire that killed the entire Harrison family.

Their dog died too, but it was not Cindy, the famous little black terrier-Labrador who had helped Betty when she was attacked on Hubrey Road in 1969. No, Cindy had been mysteriously poisoned on May 6, 1971.

Their current dog, Chimo, was a German Shepherd that Betty had gotten from the London Humane Society to replace Cindy. They wanted a dog to help them feel safe. Chimo was certainly a good security dog. She was known as an annoyance to the neighbours, as she barked at everyone who walked by, every car in the driveway, and every squirrel that dared to enter the backyard. Vera Norley, who lived next door, said she was surprised she didn't hear the dog barking on the night of the fire. The neighbours heard nothing until firemen knocked on their doors in the night.

All four bodies were taken to Victoria Hospital for immediate examination and then later sent to the Toronto Forensics Centre. None of them had consumed drugs or alcohol. The dog also had cuts and bruises.

One of my customers, a former London Police officer, told me that he was assigned to watch the house in the days after the fire, to make sure that the scene wasn't tampered with. Standing around in the cold with his colleagues, they had the understanding that the house had burned down because someone threw a Molotov cocktail through the back window.

Betty's sister told the press that not only had Cindy been poisoned, but someone had tried to set the Harrisons' car on fire. Chimo had been barking like crazy, so they went outside to see what the fuss was about. The car had been covered in a flammable liquid, and the only thing missing was a lit match. They'd scared off the culprit before he could strike it.

Fire Marshall Robert Kaufman determined that the house fire was not suspicious and ruled it accidental. There was no accelerant or any signs of a break-in. He suggested that the fire began on a piece of furniture due to a lit cigarette. The surviving member of the family was Betty and Verdun's daughter, Sharon, who said that her brother smoked and stayed up late, watching TV. She thought maybe he had fallen asleep.

The coroner told the press it was the most exhaustive investigation he had ever been a part of.

The Harrison family's funeral took place at the Needham Funeral Home, the same place where Jackie English's funeral took place. Reverend Hansinger of London Gospel Temple conducted the service.

In February 1973, there were two more funerals for the Harrison family. After her grandmother died, Sharon took her own life.

CHAPTER TWENTY-SEVEN

THE RESIDENTS OF 133 ELMWOOD

"I guess I suspect them all."

— DORIS ENGLISH

Dennis couldn't get it out of his head. The fires at Elmwood and the Harrison house were too much of a coincidence. There had to be a connection to Jackie's murder, and perhaps the other unsolved cases too. Taking note of the current list of residents in the Elmwood apartments just before the blaze, he began to track down all the tenants who had lived there four years earlier, setting up interviews with them and taking statements beginning in January 1973. Perhaps the killer's compulsion had led to a fatal error, and he would finally uncover the missing piece that could solve the mystery of Jackie's death. In these interviews, he uncovered some new details relevant to the English case.

Twelve-year-old Elmwood resident Deborah Anne Miller excitedly spotted Jackie English across the street on October 3, 1969, the day before Jackie disappeared. Debbie loved Jackie, the gorgeous fifteen-year-old who seemed the epitome of teenage style and confidence. She was always surrounded by friends, always smiling, always beautiful. Debbie didn't realize that the English family had moved two weeks earlier, and so she thought nothing was out of the ordinary when she saw her neighbour come out of the Elmwood apartments and head towards the shops in Wortley Village.

"It wasn't until after Jackie was killed and when a policeman came to the door and asked if I knew Jackie that I realized she had moved and didn't live in that apartment anymore," Debbie told Detective Alsop, in an interview at her family's home in Willowdale, Ontario, on January 23, 1973.

She had bounded up and joined her on a walk to Les' Variety Store, a regular hangout for kids in the neighbourhood.

"How are you?" asked Jackie.

Debbie told her all about school, how she was doing in grade five, about her friends at Wortley Road Public School. At the store, they both bought snack-sized bags of potato chips and munched on them as they strolled back to the Elmwood apartments. They made small talk, but Jackie never revealed to Debbie what she was doing in her old neighbourhood or even that she didn't live there anymore. Debbie later wondered if Jackie had been visiting her friends, Elmwood residents Donna, a black-haired short woman in her early twenties, and Cathy Vickers.[79] They were all very close and hung around together.

The Englishes lived on the second floor in the front apartment of the converted Victorian house that served as the Elmwood apartments, one of eleven units. The building was overcrowded, low-rent, and filled with questionable characters. Doris English later described living there to Detective Alsop as "a rather rubby-dub district and many of the tenants were . . . winos and alcoholics."

Doris remembered Stanley Morris, a professional commercial artist and high school art teacher whom Alsop had questioned

---

79 Cathy Vickers is the daughter of Beth Grey, who died in the fire with her children. Cathy, who had lived at Elmwood once, did not live there in 1972.

about photographing or painting Jackie in her swimsuit. "Mostly he would talk about boxing and how his hands were lethal weapons. I think that he was mostly looking for a bottle of beer." Doris was also suspicious of fellow resident Steve Bognar, with whom she asserted she had *not* had a romantic relationship. Suspicions that Doris English had had a relationship with Steve Bognar during her time at the apartments came from Stanley Morris's partner, Evelyn Buchanan, who told Detective Alsop that she saw Doris and Steve go out on dates. They'd get into his red Pontiac and go party downtown, returning around 2 a.m., after last call. She also saw Steve go into the English apartment on weekends, with a case of beer. There had been some drama around Doris rejecting Steve, and he'd complained about the English family to the landlord in retribution.

In 1973, Alsop spoke to Stanley Morris, who was suspicious of Steve Bognar, too, and remembered him trading in his car shortly after Jackie English was murdered. Stanley's biggest complaint about Steve Bognar was that he would never look you in the eye and had bragged about sleeping with teenage girls.

Alsop also found Steve Bognar's then wife and sat down with her for an interview in 1973. She didn't have much to say, except that she had no recollection of the English family and that "the people that lived in 133 Elmwood Avenue were mostly females and were pretty much living on welfare. Everybody in this house was living very poorly and were living in sin, always drinking and fighting. It was a very bad house."

Anne English believes that everything started to go "goofy" with Jackie when they lived at the Elmwood apartments.

She had heard an unsettling story from Fred. One day, Jackie said to her little brother, "Come upstairs and meet my new friend." They went upstairs to a room in the Elmwood apartments and there were two men. A younger man was standing, and an older man was sitting down. He could not remember what made him think it, but Fred could tell that the man sitting down was handicapped. Leaning in the doorway, Fred said to him, "Oh, you're crippled." He told Anne that the man shot him a look that made the hair on the back of his neck stand up. He apologized and walked away, leaving Jackie with the two strangers. He later wondered if his comment had cost Jackie her life. Even after being asked repeatedly, Fred couldn't remember what made him think this man was handicapped.

Thirteen-year-old neighbour Linda Jean Challis said she saw Jackie near the Elmwood apartments on Thursday, September 25. It wasn't until Jackie was killed that Linda realized that the English family had already moved by then.

Detective Alsop interviewed another woman who said that she had not realized that the English family had moved in mid-September 1969, because she saw Jackie at the apartment building during the weeks after. Jackie was hanging a swimsuit out on the line.

When Alsop questioned Stanley Morris to confirm whether or not he had painted or photographed a nude Jackie English, as he had other women, Morris denied approaching Jackie or her mother to pose. He admitted he had asked Beth Grey to pose before she was killed in the fire, but he never had a chance to take her portrait.

Alsop asked Stanley Morris if he had ever been to Aylmer, Ontario, where Georgia Jackson was from. Stanley said no, he had never been there.

But Alsop asked, and that tells us a lot about what he was thinking in 1973.

CHAPTER TWENTY-EIGHT

A STRANGE FRIENDSHIP

"She was just a beautiful person. She met the Lord,
got saved, and was baptized. The police tried to
twist her mind and drag stuff out about me."

— GLEN FRYER

After Glen Fryer's trial in 1970, Doris English began to act as a vigilante. According to Anne, Doris would go on road trips with friends Agnes Murray or Margaret Magee, armed with a large knife. At the time, Anne thought the knife was for protection, but now she wonders if the knife was intended to murder Jackie's killer. Doris would drive to Michigan, Windsor, and Toronto, following tips on where she could find the man who murdered her daughter. She didn't go to work anymore.

In 1971, Doris English sent out two odd dinner invitations. One was to Betty Harrison, who came over and made an interesting impression on the English family. They thought she was a real kook.

The other invitation was to Glen Fryer.

Doris asked him to come to dinner at her house at 54 Grand Avenue, right near Turner's Drug Store in London's Old South neighbourhood. Glen accepted her invitation and went to the English house, where he had dinner with Doris and young Fred. The three of them became friends. Glen took on Fred as his own project, a foster son. They worked on household tasks together and went golfing; the two spent so much time together that Fryer's own children became jealous of Fred English.

Years later, when Fred told Anne that he thought Glen had really liked him, she mercilessly said, "Fred, don't be so stupid. You aren't even likeable. Of course he didn't like you." Anne thought that Glen Fryer had remained friends with Fred so he wouldn't look guilty of Betty's attack or Jackie's murder.

Once, Fred was speaking to one of Fryer's children on the phone and said he believed that Glen was innocent. The Fryer kid said, "We always hoped he didn't."

They hoped, but they didn't know.

I asked Glen why he became friends with the English family. Wouldn't most people stay as far away as possible from the family of a girl whose murder you'd been associated with? He told me that he wanted to minister to them and show God's love.

As for Doris's intentions in regards to her friendship with Fryer, they may not have been altogether innocent. She stole his mail.

———

Anne always hated the Fryers. It became a major bone of contention in the family. She had particular friction with Ruth Fryer, who became closer with Doris as the years went on. Glen had moved away for school and work, but Ruth, left in London, spent a lot of time with Doris. She became one of Doris's best friends. While it's possible they first met while both were staying in the London Psychiatric Hospital in 1970, their relationship blossomed after Glen came over for dinner.

When Anne gave birth to her oldest son, Joe Duby, she stayed with her mother and became very ill with milk fever. Because Ruth Fryer was a nurse, Doris asked her to look in on Anne, who was bundled up in bed under a pile of blankets, shivering in the middle of a hot July. Anne woke up to find Ruth examining her and told her "basically to fuck off." Anne stormed out of the house and didn't go back until Ruth was gone.

When I asked her what Ruth was like, Anne bluntly responded, "Nuts. She was nuts. Nuts. Sweet goody-two-shoes. 'Simple' is the other way I could describe her. Just uninteresting, simple, Stepford, just blech. Take away all the players and the circumstances, Glen and Ruth Fryer are not my type of person. I wouldn't be that rude and nasty, but those are people that I don't waste time with. They're not my cup of tea." To Anne, they weren't her mother's cup of tea either, and she could never understand their friendship.

Doris and Ruth attended church together, including Wednesday night Bible study at Central Baptist Church.[80] Through this experience, Doris's Christian beliefs became fundamentalist. She accepted Christ in her heart and became "born again." This served as a coping mechanism for the unending grief she felt for Jackie, on top of whatever other mental health problems she'd dealt with for many years. While the connection with the Fryers was still troublesome to Anne, she and her brother agreed that their friendship gave Doris something she needed.

"Fred says it really nicely," recalls Anne, referring to his unpublished book. "[Christianity] let her stay in this world, because she was gone. It gave her grounding. But she never stopped looking [for Jackie's killer], she just stopped the craziness."

Her faith system, however, did not stop her from continuing to go out many nights, driving the city, armed with knives, maniacally looking for the Forest City Killer.

---

80 My own family has strong roots at Central Baptist Church. My grandmother took my mom and all of her siblings there, and I fondly remember going there as a kid. I even attended Christian preschool in the upstairs rooms of the church, which was built in an old converted mansion at the corner of Queens Avenue and Adelaide Street. The Sunday-school rooms were in the basement, where we learned the Bible via flannelgraph underneath a ceiling covered in pipes.

In the late 1970s, Doris became very ill. Her mind had begun to deteriorate and she became confused daily. She moved in with by-then divorced Anne and her son, Joe. When Anne got home from work, she would find her mother angry about being left home "with the children" all day, even though she had been alone — Joe was in school. Doris attacked a neighbour, grabbing them by the throat, demanding money she said they had stolen. Later, she threw her own purse in the garbage and Anne had to dig it out of a dumpster. Doris would eat only macaroni, so Anne would make Tupperware containers full of macaroni noodles for her mother to eat. Doris once started a fire when she used a stove element to heat up one of the plastic containers. She would wander, and Anne remembers sleeping in the hallway in front of her mother's door to make sure she didn't roam at night.

In 1981, Doris, who had been diagnosed with breast cancer, was admitted to palliative care. When Anne got the call to come to her mother's deathbed, she was shocked to find Ruth Fryer already sitting in her mother's room. She had somehow found out that Doris was dying and had arrived there even before the English children, who had come directly after getting the call.

Fred posted on the Unsolved Canada website about the night his mother died: "My mother, next to Jackie, was the ultimate victim. Maybe even more so than Jackie. When Jackie died, a very large part of my mother died with her. She was not only riddled with demons, but for a while she was actually taken hostage by them. It was only her hatred for Jackie's killer and her resolve to find him and make him pay that allowed her to escape [from mental illness] back into the real world. The fact that she later became a born-again Christian let her remain in the real world. Sometime in 1979, my mother was diagnosed with breast cancer and she chose to keep her breast; she chose death over life; she chose to be with Jackie."

Ruth stayed in the room with Anne and Fred, watching as Doris took her last breath. Then Ruth slipped away, unnoticed.

She came to the funeral wake with Glen. After that, Anne did not see or hear from them again for many years.

That was, until Fred got an odd invitation to attend the Fryers' fiftieth wedding anniversary celebration in Toronto in August 2004.

Fred called Anne on the phone. "We got an invitation to the Fryers' fiftieth wedding party."

Anne was taken aback. "Interesting."

"Ruth has enclosed a little handwritten note with the invitation."

Extend this invitation to Anne.

Anne was shocked but decided to go. She might be able to get a copy of the 1970 trial transcript from Glen, as she'd been trying to hunt down a copy for years.

The siblings drove to Toronto together. The anniversary party was held in a church basement. When the English kids arrived, they found out that no one had been expecting them. Their presence was a total shock to the Fryer children, and it set the family aflutter. A few of them kept to the kitchen, avoiding Anne and Fred. There was no confrontation, just polite discomfort.

Ruth sat next to Glen, wearing her original wedding gown with an otherworldly smile on her face. Anne got the distinct impression that she and her brother might have been Ruth's own twisted anniversary gift to her husband. Glen Fryer turned to them.

"I haven't seen you in a long time," he said to Fred. The two shook hands, and then Glen turned to Anne and said something very odd. He said, "I haven't seen you since you were a blonde."

"I was never a blonde," she said, redirecting her attention to Ruth.

"I'm so glad to see you guys," said Ruth. "You look so much like your mother."

"Fifty years," said Anne. "That's really something. I'm amazed you could get into your wedding dress."

"I'm amazed I made it fifty years," said Ruth.

When the time came to leave, Anne and Fred stood near Glen as someone brought him a piece of cake.

"It must be nice to be served," remarked Anne.

"We all get our just desserts," he replied.

In Anne's recollection, this final comment was made with a glint in his eye. "He took great delight in toying with us," she said. She had hoped the day might offer some revelation, and this was the closest thing she was going to get. "During our short meeting, I had, after years of no opinion, formed a very strong and unshakable conviction immediately." Ever since, Anne has been sure that Glen was somehow involved in her sister's murder.

Afterwards, Anne talked to lifelong friend Paulette Alloway about her encounter with Glen. The comment that seemed to stick with Paulette was Fryer's observation that he hadn't seen Anne since she was blonde. It was Paulette who remembered that Anne *had* been a blonde, in grade eight. She had pictures of them in Springbank Park for their grade eight graduation that showed her with blonde hair.

CHAPTER TWENTY-NINE

ANOTHER POSSIBLE CONFESSION

*"I have been haunted by the memory of what I done.
It has not been an easy thing for me to live with."*

— RICK PAPPLE

1978. Detective Alsop received a memo in the early weeks of the year that Jackie English's boyfriend, David Papple, had been arrested in British Columbia. He had been living in a trailer park with his common-law wife, Janice, when he bashed her head into a wall and threw her to the ground. He told her that if she was "good," meaning compliant with sex, then he wouldn't hurt her anymore. She had none of it and called the police. When officers arrived, they had to chase Papple on foot before they took him down. He was charged with assault and attempted rape.

Then he said something really odd to the arresting officers: "I know now what it is like for a girl to be raped because my girlfriend was raped and murdered, and I didn't get a chance to fuck her."

Had David Papple lied when he told police he had sex with Jackie on October 4, 1969? Had he been bragging to his friends about sleeping with her and had to save face with his buddies? I had always found it strange that Papple had admitted to having sex with an underage girl without protection, as though he wasn't worried about getting her pregnant.

Jackie never noted in her diary that she had had sex, even though she made coded entries about other sexual encounters. It seems strange to me that she would write about a French kiss with Lloyd but not her first time having intercourse. Anne and Paul St. Cyr both thought that her late-night visits with David meant they were having sex, but Papple's statements in 1978 indicates that it's possible that the semen found inside Jackie at the crime scene may have belonged to her killer.

The semen found at the crime scenes of Jackie English, Jacqueline Dunleavy, and Georgia Jackson were all Type O. As a non-secretor and a man with blood Type A, this seemed to rule Glen Fryer out as a suspect, even without DNA comparison, except for the semen found in Jackie English's panties. I have no idea which DNA samples were examined by Project Angel from 2000 to 2002.

Were the three victims assaulted by the same man who had Type-O blood?

While he was in jail, David Papple's brother, Rick, wrote him a letter, which was copied by jail officials and then sent to Detective Alsop. It seemed to indicate that something had happened between the brothers, or to the brothers, in the past. The note, just a page in length, spoke of keeping this event a secret between the two of them and mending fences in their sibling relationship. Adding this possible evidence to the revelation that Papple had offered at the time of his arrest — that he did not actually have sex with Jackie English the day she died — it is possible that Alsop may have thought the Papple brothers were somehow involved in her disappearance and murder.

However, linguistic analysis done by experts on the television show *To Catch a Killer* determined that this letter, while kept by Alsop in his files, is not a confession of murder. Based on the language used, it more likely refers to a family secret, some sort of trauma that both boys suffered. It has nothing to do with the Jackie English murder.

Still, it made sense that Alsop was watching Rick. He had kept an eye on him since he bizarrely delivered that typewriter to Betty Harrison in June 1970. When this happened, Alsop referred to him as "Lloyd" in his notes. Lloyd was Rick's middle name, and Alsop may have thought he was the Lloyd referred to in Jackie's diary, rather than Lloyd Lackey from the Latin Quarter restaurant. There is also the complicating story that Marilyn told about the mysterious Rick, which she may have related to Alsop and might have made him take note of any Ricks surrounding the case: Rick Papple, Rick Harrison, and Rick Fryer. Alsop had made a note of Rick Papple's car. It was a red 1966 Dodge with square tail lights.

CHAPTER THIRTY

SKELETONS

*"None — not even the largest metropolitan cities —
has experienced a comparable series of brutal killings.
None is enveloped by such deep fears and tensions."*

— THE *LONDON FREE PRESS*, AUGUST 21, 1974

As early as 1969, Alsop believed that the Jackson, Dunleavy, and English deaths were connected, and he continued to believe it in the following decades. While interviewing community members about one case, he often questioned people about the other girls, too.

He suspected Robert Bridgewater — a previously mentioned suspect who in 1971 would be convicted of raping and murdering a teenage boy — and executed a search warrant on his house on March 10, 1969. Bridgewater also lived in Aylmer for some time.

In January 1971, Detective Alsop investigated a "subversive group" in London, Ontario. He went so far as to speak about it with Agent Neil J. Welch at the Detroit offices of the FBI. He continued to investigate Jackie English's disappearance and murder in earnest while following up on subversive elements in the city, including a few specific individuals. He talked to city officials, doctors, psychiatrists, and specialists, and he visited halfway houses and shelters for the disenfranchised. Was he looking for one crazed killer? Or a malicious group of perverts?

In the summer of 1971, he began to get anonymous calls to his own home.

MAY 9, 1973. The body of Lynda White, the university student who disappeared after her exam in 1968, was finally discovered twelve miles southwest of Simcoe near the village of Walsh, Ontario, about ninety kilometres from where she disappeared.[81] Walsh is in the same general geographic area as Port Burwell, where Scott Leishman was found, and Aylmer, Ontario. Three men from the area — Charles Smith, John Prince, and Gordon West — were out looking for morels[82] on a lot owned by Mike Chwastiak, across the road from the historic Hillcrest graveyard, only a mile or so from now abandoned CNR tracks.[83] Lynda was found across from this graveyard, and Soraya O'Connell disappeared after being last seen across from another historic graveyard.

Lynda's remains were skeletal; she was lying on her back with her limbs splayed — all except for the lower part of her right arm, which was missing. That was the arm on which she wore her MedicAlert bracelet, which was nowhere to be seen. There was nothing else there — no clothing, no jewellery — just Lynda, alone and naked in the woods. Her body was identified by dental records. The findings were released to the public a month after she was found.

Little information is known about the autopsy, but no cause of death was determined. However, according to research conducted more than forty years later by Michael Arntfield, regarding adipocere — a waxy substance corpses create through decomposition — and bone whitening, her body could not have been there for the entire five years she was missing and could not have been deposited there in the winter months when she disappeared.

---

81 Walsh is in Charlotteville Township near St. Williams.

82 Morels are edible mushrooms.

83 These tracks were in use in 1968.

The remains just didn't forensically match up. Arntfield also determined that Lynda's arm had not been removed by animals, as investigators at the time were wont to believe. He believes it was removed purposefully and disposed of elsewhere or kept as a souvenir.

My source at the OPP told me that, based on her autopsy report, they think she had been disposed of there shortly after she was murdered.

At the time, without modern forensics, the investigators simply informed the family that they had found Lynda. They could offer no answers as to where or how she had died and didn't see how they ever could.

Where was Lynda during those five years? When and how did she die?

Just a month before her body was recovered, Lynda's clothing had been found about twenty-six miles west of the body in Bayham Township near Vienna, together with part of a surveyor's range pole. Police tracked down her roommate Ann Hall to identify the clothes, which were not the clothes Lynda had worn to write her exam but were definitely hers. They were presumably the ones she had changed into before heading out on the town that November night — or clothes taken by the killer when he returned to the house, undetected, and stuffed the others under the bed.

Her jewellery and other personal items were never found.

Neighbours had reported a bad smell in the area in the month of June 1972. This date and time of year matches the physical evidence of body decomposition, according to Dr. Arntfield. It's also the same time period of David Bodemer's trial and when City Council in London rescinded the award for information regarding London's unsolved killings.

Another important detail found by Dr. Arntfield was that the area had been under construction by the Canadian National Railway in 1967. During this time, workers from the province had spent a great deal of time in this isolated area. Was one of the

Detective Dennis Alsop just before he moved to Toronto.

workers responsible for the crime? David Bodemer worked for the CNR during this period, but his detailed employment record is unavailable.

In the summer of 1973, Detective Alsop was heavily involved in the Lynda White investigation, meeting with his colleagues and interviewing for potential leads. However, it was the last homicide he worked on in the London area; Alsop then moved to Toronto for his new job as a superintendent.

MAY 26, 1974. Four years after she went missing, Soraya O'Connell's skeletal remains were found in Gore of Downie Township near Stratford on the grounds of a former dump. She was discovered by Mr. and Mrs. Lloyd Wilson, who were scouting for bottles. She was skeletal, lying on her back, partially covered by branches. Underneath her pelvis was some material similar to that used in the manufacture of pantie girdles — a final attempt to suck in her plump waist at the dance. No hard parts of clothing such as buttons or clasps were found, indicating that the rest of her clothing had not disintegrated around her. Next to her body were her earrings, neatly placed side by side, invoking memories of Jackie English. She was identified by dental records.

The cause of death was not established. Pathologist Dr. John Hilsdon-Smith said that it appeared she had been dead for nine to eighteen months, but it was possible she had been there since her disappearance. He seemed to think it was unlikely.

Where was Soraya between the time she was picked up and the time she died?

Right next to where she was discovered, a team of workers had cut down a large dead elm tree in December 1971. None of them had seen her body at that time.

Downie Township is located almost exactly along the CNR line between London and Stratford.

JULY 25, 1974. A report from the Criminal Investigation Bureau (CIB) of the Ontario Provincial Police tried to connect the unsolved murders in London, Ontario. The victims listed included Jacqueline Dunleavy, Jackie English, Lynda White, and Soraya O'Connell. Other murder victims were presumably excluded from the list because they didn't fit the same victimology: teenaged and female. As mentioned earlier, the assumption that serial killers are consistent in their choice of victims has been debunked.

Taking this into account, names that the CIB did not include on this list could be considered victims of the same killer: Frankie Jensen, Scott Leishman, Helga Beer, and Bruce Stapylton. Looking outside the city would add even more names to the potential roster, like Ljubica Topic, who was killed in Windsor in 1971.

There were other unsolved homicides in the Forest City during the 1970s, such as that of Suzanne Miller in 1974[84] or Priscilla Merle in 1972,[85] but none that demonstrated the same pattern apparent in the killings that took place in London between 1968 and 1972. The later serial sexual homicides of the 1970s were ascribed to the "Big Three": Russell Johnson, Christian Magee, and Gerald Thomas Archer. When it came to the Forest City Killer, after 1972, it seemed as if he had moved away or become otherwise immobilized from continuing his chosen field of work.

---

84 Miller lived in the apartment above my parents when she was murdered.

85 Law enforcement believe they know who killed both Miller and Merle, but were unable to make an arrest.

In 1982,[86] David Bodemer was released from prison after serving only ten years of his life sentence at the Kingston Penitentiary.

---

86 Privacy laws prevent me from getting an exact date of his release, or any record of his time in jail. In Canada, convicts receive exceptional privileges in that regard, contrasting with those in the United States, making it much harder for civilian researchers like me to access important information about crime or track their whereabouts upon release.

CHAPTER THIRTY-ONE

THE MURDER OF DONNA AWCOCK

"We never close the book on a murder case."

— DETECTIVE LEONARD HAMILTON

I took the 2 Dundas bus out to the east end to meet up with Tammy Dennett. Her sister's thirty-five-year-old murder case is unsolved. I wanted to find out if Donna Awcock could have been a victim of the Forest City Killer.

Tammy and Wally Dennett live in a modest red-brick house near Argyle Mall. As I knocked on the door, I noticed a bumper sticker on their mailbox that read, "I'm Donna Awcock, do you know who killed me?" There's a colour photograph of Donna, with her blonde hair and green eyes, taken three days before she died. I've seen this green bumper sticker before in the form of a Facebook banner online. Tammy runs the Justice for Donna Jean Awcock Facebook page, what she calls "Donna's wall," where she shares memories about her sister's case, as well as current missing and murdered persons news stories and tips, and connects with the public. She's been running the page since 2010.

Inside her house are more pictures of petite Donna — only five-foot-two and 105 pounds — overlooking the comfortable working-class home that reminds me of the Conners' house on

Donna Awcock.

Courtesy of Tammy Dennett.

Roseanne. Tammy's a woman with a big heart, and this is a space that is welcoming for kids and grown-ups, anyone who's ready to be genuine and friendly. I felt at home immediately.

We sat down at the dining-room table. I could tell that Tammy was the kind of person I could really get along with next to a campfire, but she knew why I was there and she was ready to get down to business. She's used to talking to reporters and journalists and being on camera. She's a no-nonsense lady when it comes to Donna's murder, and she was ready to — once again — go over the most horrible thing that ever happened to her.

The Awcocks were, and have remained, a very close family. In 1983, Donna's parents, Carolyn and Donald Awcock, had been renting an apartment at 88 Cheyenne in London for about two years. They'd been married for twenty-three years.

Everyone called Donald "Bud." It was a nickname he got from his mother, who called him her "little rosebud." Bud was working as a local route truck driver for Great Lakes Brick and Stone. He'd previously been a gardener at the London Psychiatric Hospital for about twenty years, a job he got from his dad, who had also been a long-term employee. Donald had some great horror stories to tell about the psych hospital and loved thrilling his kids with a good yarn.

Donna's mom, Carolyn, worked odd jobs around town, as a

crossing guard or cook. For a while she returned lost airline luggage, which was a job she loved because people were always happy to see her. However, with her three children, a son-in-law, and two small grandkids running around her modest two-bedroom apartment, she was probably too busy to work in the fall of 1983.

Their teenaged daughters, Laura and Donna, shared one of the bedrooms. Their older daughter, Colleen, had an apartment upstairs in the same building. Tammy lived across the hall from Colleen, with her boyfriend, Wally Dennett, and their two kids. The whole family was living in the same building at 88 Cheyenne, making it easy for them to get together for their weekly Sunday roast beef dinner at Mom and Dad's. The only sibling missing from those dinners was Bill, because he'd moved up north. That summer, on June 10, Tammy married Wally, and they were expecting their third child. He was due on October 23 and they knew their apartment was just not going to be big enough. They applied for housing so they could get a bigger place and put all their stuff in storage. Carolyn and Bud let the young family take up their living room on the first floor of 88 Cheyenne, sleeping on the pull-out couch. When Donna disappeared, their home was full to the brim, loud and in constant motion.

———

"Sadly, I don't remember a lot. I don't know if I blocked it out." Tammy's memory can be spotty at times, much like Anne English's. This is a common trait for trauma survivors. I asked her if she could remember any particularly happy times before Donna was taken.

"It was all usually happy times. We were all very close . . .

"I have so many people that come up to me and say 'I went to school with Donna at Montcalm.' Donna didn't go to Montcalm,"[87]

———

87 Montcalm Secondary School is the closest high school to 88 Cheyenne.

says Tammy. "Donna was kind of a slow learner, quiet, kept to herself." Donna had dropped out of her enrolment at Thames Secondary School, a high school that specialized in vocational studies. "Donna didn't have a lot of friends, but the friends she did have, she kept close to her."

Donna was a slender seventeen-year-old blonde tomboy who spent a lot of time outside. She played baseball. Neighbourhood youngsters would meet at schoolyards in the summer to use the baseball diamonds for casual games. Donna ran around in the field outside her apartment with the kids from the apartment complex, most of them younger than her. She didn't hang out with kids her own age. Much like Wayne Hebblethwaite, Donna found that younger children gave her the joy of being looked up to and spent time with her without judgement. She could reveal a side that was otherwise only seen by her family — the wacky, playful, funny side. With grown-ups or other seventeen-year-olds, she was quiet and reserved. Uncomfortable. Perhaps years of remedial schooling had taught her that she wasn't good enough, and this made her even more reclusive than most. Everyone loved Donna. Her older sister Colleen was what Tammy calls a "kitchen sitter," but that wasn't Donna's cup of tea. She stayed out of gossip and didn't visit as much with the neighbours. Tammy says this is a quality she shared with her sister. They were loners and kept to themselves. In October 1983, Donna was particularly focused on playing with Tammy's two babies.

In the next building over lived the Maynards, Michelle and Michael. They were siblings and had separate apartments. Michelle was in her early twenties and had two kids. Her involvement in Donna's disappearance may have tainted Tammy's perspective, but still, she says that Michelle didn't make a good impression on the Awcock family from the get-go. She dated men much older than herself and partied quite a bit. She seemed like trouble.

OCTOBER 13, 1983. Michelle Maynard asked Donna to babysit her kids. Donna agreed and headed over to her apartment. After Michelle headed out, Donna's family could see Donna from their place, which faced Michelle's. They waved to each other across the balcony. Michael Maynard was partying with some friends nearby. Someone later told Tammy that they heard him say to Donna, "I'm gonna have my way with you tonight, one way or another."

Meanwhile, Michelle had gone to the Town and Country bar on Dundas Street in the East Village. This bar closed years later and has since reopened under a new name, thereby shedding most of its terrible reputation. However, in its day, the Town and Country, or T and C as locals called it, had a very bad rap. I know someone who became a quadriplegic after being hit by a drunk driver who'd been hanging out there. I also — and this is going to sound weird — did my laundry there for a while when I lived on Ontario Street in my twenties. Back then, the Old East Village was not the burgeoning boho district it is now. There were needles on the sidewalks, and prostitutes arguing with their pimps. Their shouts could be heard over morning coffee. The closest laundromat was in the Town and Country bar. My roommate and I would lug our laundry over in rolling carts and then have a beer while we waited for our underwear to dry. It smelled like stale cigarette smoke and spilled drinks during the day. It wasn't a place you admitted to hanging around in, except for a few hipsters who partied there ironically.

In 1983, the bar was filled with bikers and working-class single men. There were active pool tables and women who were on the hunt for fellows who wouldn't mind their baggage. More than a few drug deals were made in the bathroom. This is where Michelle went to drink. These were her people.

Michelle sat at a table with a group, including a man she didn't know and a woman named Joanne, who would later explain on the show *To Catch a Killer* that she had helped police put together a composite sketch of him. He was described as being in his late twenties or thirties, with a slim build and average-to-tall height, with bushy eyebrows, a clean-shaven face, and sideburns. He may have been driving a light-coloured Ford Torino. He was reported to be wearing cowboy boots, faded blue jeans, and a long-sleeved blue shirt. He'd been seen at a couple of local bars, and some regulars at the T and C helped to create the composite along with Joanne. She recently put together a new composite that she believes could help find the mystery man.

Joanne also said that Michelle was really drunk that night, but Joanne had been drinking as well.

ABOVE LEFT: Composite image of the mystery man who drove Michelle Maynard home the night Donna Awcock was murdered.

ABOVE RIGHT: A revised composite of the man seen at the Town & Country bar the night Donna Awcock was murdered, drawn by Joanne.

This strange guy, whose name no one remembers, offered Michelle a ride home. They stopped and got pizza at a place called Originals at 1165 Oxford Street East. This pizzeria, managed by Mike Firth, is no longer around. They drove towards Michelle's apartment, eating pizza in the car. By the time they got back to the Cheyenne apartments, Michelle recalled that there were about four pieces left.[88]

As they pulled into the apartment complex, they would have turned in off Huron Street. They pulled into the unlit shared parking lot at the back of 88 Cheyenne. She told the stranger to wait in his car while she went upstairs and got rid of the babysitter. Presumably, she told him the apartment number. She may have told him to watch for the young blonde woman exiting the building, so he would know that it was safe to come upstairs.

Michelle was extremely drunk. She took the remaining pizza with her and stumbled up the stairs to her end unit apartment. Donna was awake inside. It was about 2:30 a.m. Michelle's story, which has changed over the years, tells us that they shared the last four slices of pizza. At some point, the stranger from the car came upstairs and knocked. Michelle said he wanted some more pizza. Michelle didn't let him in but told him to wait for her in his car. Then she gave Donna some money and asked her to go buy some cigarettes at the corner store, less than 100 metres away from the apartment. Donna left the building.

When Donna didn't come back with her smokes, Michelle ended up walking to the store herself to get some. However, she did not seem to remember what happened next.

The clerk later said that before Michelle came in for her own cigarettes, Donna had shown up looking red in the face and might have been upset. Donna asked to use the phone, and the clerk refused her.

---

88 Source: *To Catch a Killer*

OCTOBER 14, 1983. "Mom had got up and looked in the bedroom and Donna wasn't there," remembers Tammy. "You know what the oddest thing is, and I have no idea why, but I had woken up and a feeling came over me, like 'Oh, my God, Donna's not home yet,' and I didn't even know that. I didn't even know, but just that feeling, right? It was weird. Weird. I dunno. It was just weird that I had that feeling, and I have no idea why."

Carolyn Awcock assumed that her daughter had simply fallen asleep at Michelle's house. "She sent Laura across the field and she said, 'Go ask Michelle to send Donna home.'"

When Laura got there and knocked, Michelle wouldn't open the door. Through the door, she told Laura that Donna had gone home the night before.

Laura came back with the terrible news that Donna was nowhere to be found. The family immediately began to search for her. This was not Donna's normal behaviour. First, they called other people that Donna babysat for. They called her friends. Soon, they were knocking on doors. If you were in the Cheyenne apartment complex on the morning of October 14, 1983, you knew that something was going on.

Carolyn called the police and was told that she had to wait twenty-four hours before reporting her daughter missing. Donna had probably just run away.

Knowing that they weren't going to receive any help from law enforcement, the Awcocks and their neighbours started to search for Donna on their own. Tammy remembers a crowd of

Donna Awcock at the time of her disappearance.

London Free Press Collection of Photographic Negatives, Archives and Special Collections, Western Libraries, Western University.

about 200 people who started to look for Donna as early as 10 a.m. that morning. Being nine months pregnant, Tammy stayed home and watched the apartment in case Donna returned or called. Most of the search parties were gone for two to three hours. They came back one by one around lunch time. No one had seen Donna.

Only two of the searchers hadn't come back yet: Thomas Kearns and Todd Ireland. Todd was Donna's ex-boyfriend. He'd heard Carolyn Awcock's repeated prescient statements about her daughter, "She's up at Fanshawe, she's up at Fanshawe," referring to the nearby conservation area. It was as if Carolyn was making a psychic prediction. Todd got his roommate's dog and set out with Tom to see if they could find Donna.

They walked up Clarke Side Road heading north, a stretch of road surrounded by green empty fields and industry. They made their way up to the back entry to the Fanshawe Conservation Area. This is the spot where you can sneak into the park for free, as my family sometimes did on our bikes to go see the fireworks in the 1980s. The breach in the perimeter is at the end of Kilally Road, a winding country lane that is really the end of a concession stretching east and west. There are a couple of houses you pass as you head east towards the dam, and as you pass the last house, you are left with a dirt walking path along the top of the ravine. Misstep and you'll go tumbling down towards the Thames River. In October, even after the corn had been cut, there were still no windows on the side of the old farmhouse that would let you see what was happening along that pathway. It was totally isolated. Thomas Kearns and Todd Ireland knew the spot. The kids called it Pecker's Peak. They went there to party and have sex.

It was the perfect place to hide in the bushes and watch teenagers get it on. A veteran homicide investigator told me that voyeurs who do this often have a religious background. They feel shame about their sexual impulses, and that's why they are more comfortable hiding in the shadows, watching others.

The scene where Donna Awcock was found.

London Free Press Collection of Photographic Negatives, [1983-10-15], Archives and Special Collections, Western Libraries, Western University.

In the bright sun of daylight, however, Todd was following his roommate's dog and hoping to find something. He wanted to find Donna alive and well. Maybe she was injured. Maybe she was lost.

Maybe she was dead.

The dog started to whine and pull on the leash. It dragged them towards a sharp drop-off towards the Thames. Looking down, they saw Donna about fifty feet below the crest of the ravine. She was face down in the brush. Her pants and shoes were removed, leaving her lower body bare except for her socks. It looked like someone had rolled her down the hill towards the river, discarded like something used and broken.

———————

Back at the Cheyenne apartments, Tammy and Wally wondered why the boys hadn't yet returned. Through a gut feeling or just natural worry, Tammy said, "Well, let's take a walk." They headed out the door towards Fanshawe, but they didn't even get out of the complex before they saw Thomas and Todd coming towards them. The boys had already dropped off the dog and called the police.

"They pulled Wally to the side, and I knew," says Tammy. Then she watched helplessly as Wally's anger overcame him. In grief, he lashed out at the teenagers. Tammy says he started to beat the shit out of both of them.

All she could do was hold on to her belly and yell for him to stop.

———

Although Todd Ireland called the police about Donna's body around 6 p.m., it took officers two hours to secure the scene. First, London Police and Ontario Provincial Police had to fight about jurisdiction. The OPP lost the battle and were stuck with the murder case. The delays, however, meant that Bud and Carolyn Awcock waited until after 2 a.m. on October 15 to get confirmation that the body found there belonged to their precious daughter. Officials asked the Awcocks to come to the hospital and identify Donna, so the exhausted couple mournfully got in their car and drove to the morgue.

At first, Carolyn said she would make the identification, but when they got there, she broke down in tears. Bud stepped in. He sat his wife down in the hallway and went through the doors to the exam room, where he was confronted with the battered, beaten, and raped body of his dear seventeen-year-old daughter Donna lying on a metal slab. "I don't think he even expected to see what he was gonna see," says Tammy. They had done nothing to clean Donna up for him. Most horrifyingly, the killer had stuffed an orange plastic bag in her mouth that was still protruding from her extended jaw.

Bud had nightmares for the rest of his life. "My dad stopped living," says Tammy.

Donna had been strangled. She had been beaten about the head and raped. Her shirt had been pulled up, exposing her breasts. Her blue running shoes, Bullitt brand, were missing, as were the house keys she wore around her neck on a lanyard and her new pack of cigarettes. The plastic bag stuffed in her throat sported a partial fingerprint that could not be run through the national database, since it wasn't complete. It has not since been re-examined with new fingerprint technology and has never been run through the system to see if there's a match.

Victims' families of the Forest City Killer had consistently received strange phone calls after the death of their loved ones. While the Awcocks may have received such calls, Tammy thinks her parents could have kept that from the kids, to save them from the emotional turmoil the harassment caused.

I asked Anne English if her mother had been harassed by phone calls. She said no. They couldn't have. They didn't have a phone in their apartment on Kent Street. I'm not sure if the Dunleavy family got any calls, but the Jensens and O'Connells certainly did, as did Georgia Jackson's family in the days after she went missing. If the killer had wanted to harass Lynda White's family, he would have had to ask the operator for their number in Burlington and that might have made it easier for police to track him. Perhaps he had to settle for going back to her house and stashing her clothes under the bed instead. At any rate, the Forest City Killer sure did enjoy toying with the loved ones of his victims.

Tammy did remember that a strange man had come to the door once asking if Donna was there after her much publicized murder. Could that have been him?

After the funeral, doctors told the Awcocks to keep a close eye on their daughter Tammy. The emotional trauma during her pregnancy would make her susceptible to all kinds of things, both physical and mental.

"I couldn't cry, and I don't know why. I don't know if I just remained strong for the family because my mom was so broken," she remembers.

Tammy was nothing but resilient. Her strength kept her baby tucked inside her where she knew he would be safe, and by November 7, Tammy still had not gone into labour. She had to be induced. She gave birth to a healthy baby boy. Afterwards, the lady in the next hospital bed asked her where she lived.

"In the east end," said Tammy. "The Cheyenne apartments."

"Oh!" said the other young mom. "What do you think of that murder over there?"

Tammy felt her stomach drop. "That was my sister."

"It's hard, living with a murder in the family."

The effects of the murder have never left the Awcocks. Their continued mourning is palpable, and I have to say that speaking to Tammy was the most heart-rending interview I conducted for this project. She cried many times while we spoke and reflected on life in the thirty-five years since her sister died.

"Everything changed," she says. "I became a crazy mom. I wanted to hide my kids in the closet. It was horrible. My daughter kept saying, 'Mom, you can't do this to me.' I said, 'I have to.' She didn't understand. Now she does. She's got two boys. Thank God she didn't have a girl. Thank God. They all know now, they all understand now. They weren't allowed to do anything. You played in the house. You played on the porch. If you're out of my sight, you've gone too far . . . I need to know, everywhere they went, everywhere."

In retrospect, she is grateful that her baby boy missed his due date and that no one in the family has an October birthday. "You would not believe the feelings I get in October. I wish I could sleep the month away. I remember that night, it was cold and windy, and a chill comes over me the entire month of October.

"I'm constantly looking behind me. Thirty-five years later and I'm afraid to go out by myself at night. He just didn't kill Donna. He killed us too."

Michelle Maynard spoke to police on October 14, 1983. Then she disappeared for about a week and was not interviewed again until she returned. No one knows where she went or why. This is reminiscent of Joe Clarke's behaviour after Jacqueline Dunleavy was murdered.

For his television show, *To Catch a Killer*, Michael Arntfield hired expert Don O'Connor to give Michelle a polygraph test. They wanted to see if she was lying or hiding anything about Donna's murder. She passed the test. However, the Awcock family is still very suspicious of her, and particularly her brother.

After Donna's death, Michelle went on to have more children, although some of them were taken away from her by authorities. She died of cancer on March 22, 2016. She was buried in Peterborough.

Her brother Michael is also deceased. He died July 27, 2001, after being beaten to death while living in British Columbia. What makes Michael suspicious is his friendship with the guy he was partying with the night Donna was killed, Joe Tripp. It turns out, in 1978, Joe Tripp had escaped with two other inmates from the Bradley County Jail in Tennessee, where he was serving time for killing Cathy Clowers, age fourteen, and Roxanne Woodson, age fifteen, both from Monroe County. His real name was Joe Shepherd. He had come to London where his sister was renting an apartment in the same building as the Maynards. He spent a lot of time at the Cheyenne apartments and probably knew Donna.

In 1988, the Joe Shepherd case was featured on the first ever episode of *Unsolved Mysteries*. A London resident saw the show, recognized Joe, and alerted authorities. He was caught and shipped back to Tennessee, where he was incarcerated. Until the day he died, he maintained that he was innocent. He was sentenced to life in prison. His DNA was tested in relation to Donna's case in 1995 and they cleared him as a suspect. He died in prison in 2010 at the age of fifty-seven.

The boys who found Donna's body were also ruled out as suspects. Her ex-boyfriend Todd Ireland voluntarily provided his DNA, which was tested against evidence found at the crime scene. He was cleared of all suspicion and is friends with Tammy Dennett on Facebook.

Since her sister died, Tammy has raised money to hire a private investigator. She pushed the OPP to double their reward for information regarding her sister's death, and she also pushed them for years until they returned one of her sister's possessions: her purse. At first the OPP were just going to give the family scans of the purse's contents, but it was successfully returned to them in November 2016.

"I cried for hours after I got it. The pictures that were in it, I had no clue those were even in there . . . I don't understand why they wanted it. Why? She didn't have it with her [the night she died]. And to have it that long . . . I kept fighting for it. I said, why do you need it? It had nothing to do with her murder. Nothing . . . I kept bugging them and bugging them."

The officer who brought it back to Tammy was very kind with her. He told her to wait until he was gone to open it, and to do it when she had some time alone, because, "There's a lot of memories in there," he said. The black leather bag was packed with family photographs, as well as some of her personal belongings. The pictures show how right Tammy was when she told me that Donna's face lit up when she smiled. The portrait of her that usually accompanies her story in the press doesn't do her justice.

In 2010, Tammy started a group called Donna's Angels, to remember her sister and bring something positive out of her murder. Each year, she picks a family of five to help out over the holidays. She raises money to buy presents for all the kids based on a wish list they provide and gives something to the parents too. Then they buy the family all the fixings for a Christmas dinner. Finally, they include a $50 gift card for No Frills, so the family can buy groceries in the New Year.

One of the volunteers for Donna's Angels was Sharla Smith, the same woman who helped me track down Janet, the host of the sleepover Marilyn Hird attended on October 3, 1969. Sharla is always at Jackie's Walk on October 4 and is an avid member of the Unsolved Canada community. In 2016, her family had fallen on hard times. Tammy decided that Donna's Angels would surreptitiously choose the Smith family to receive their special Christmas present. When she spoke to the press about the gift, Sharla said, "I firmly believe Donna and other young victims work in mysterious ways, and I believe she's guided this all on her own. I can't explain how."

Christmas is a particularly important holiday for the Awcock family. They used to get together at Bud and Carolyn's house, but after Bud died in 2004, they moved the gathering to Tammy and Wally's place.

"My oldest grandson," says Tammy. "He's the biggest kid, he's twenty-two, and he'll call me at four in the morning and say, 'Can I come over now, Gram?'

"My husband is the one who hands out the gifts. When I put them under the tree, I try to sort them so it's not always one person . . . one for Aidan, one for Jackson, one for Austin, one for Trevor . . . and for the adults, they all get pushed to the back."

The entire family sits down to supper together. "I got two tables that I put together right here, and it takes up the whole . . ."

Tammy stretches out her arms to demonstrate. "Everyone sits at the table and eats."

Christmas has the same importance as their old Sunday dinners. "Every Sunday. My brother, his wife, their three kids, me, Wally, my three kids, my sister [and] Mike and their two kids, quite the bunch. We'd make a nice roast beef . . . every Sunday." Even after Donna died. "There was always a seat at the table that was missing and it was always hers. We would light candles . . . that would have their name on it. Donna, then my dad, and then my mom. There are too many candles. I don't want any more."

Bud Awcock died in 2004. Carolyn lived on her own until 2012, when she moved in with Wally and Tammy, who took care of her for six years. When I went to visit Tammy, her mom had recently died on May 10, 2018. She'd woken up on Tammy's birthday, May 7, in a terrific mood. She opened the curtains and said, "Oh the sun's shining for your birthday. Happy birthday, sweetheart." Those are the last words Tammy ever heard from her mother. Carolyn suffered a stroke. She died three days later and is buried with her husband and daughter in Mount Pleasant Cemetery.

Tammy believes her parents and sister are together now, but she still works every day to bring peace to her family. Her husband, Wally, told her it was taking over her life.

"I can't let it go," she explains.

Having Donna's picture around her comforts her. "I just want the person caught and held accountable for what he's done. I want him to look me in my fucking eye while I tell him the hell my family has gone through."

EPILOGUE

It's only been four years for me. For the surviving families of the many victims, and their supporters, these unsolved cases have resonated throughout their lives for decades. My experience holds no comparison to theirs, but it still has had a profound effect on me. I'm up late at night, scrolling and scrolling through files, my eyes watering. I know I should go to bed. For a while, even sleep was a problem because I had constant nightmares. I don't know why I kept at it, but there was something about this story, this horror show in my hometown, that I couldn't turn away from. The deeper I got, the more determined I was to solve the puzzle.

As a result, my head is host to a constant parade of theories. Sometimes I'm sure all of these unsolved cases must be related to the Forest City Killer. Other times, I'm not so sure. Sometimes I think FCK is just one person and other times I think it's a pair of like-minded murderers, driving around looking for prey, like the two men seen with Georgia Jackson, or the two men seen in the car that picked up Jackie English, or the two men who attacked Betty Harrison. Perhaps it was even a subversive group, like the kind Alsop consulted the FBI about. I imagine them gathering in the basement of Stanley Variety to swap smut mags and watch pornographic movies on an old projector. Almost every day I think of something new or find myself drawn to the former home of a suspect, a victim, their work-place, or the site of an abduction. I visit the places the bodies were found. Until the cases are solved, I'm not sure this feeling will ever leave me. My brother sighs in exasperation as we drive to a family dinner and I point out an FCK landmark. I ask Jason if we can take a detour and pull the car over to the side of the highway so I can explore an idea, driving up laneways and dirt roads, getting weird looks from the locals as I tromp through the brush. I call librarians in surrounding counties, asking them to help me track down obscure information, addresses, lots, and concession numbers, and make the archivists pull out boxes of records from deep in storage. I read books about psychopaths and serial killers, hoping that a new insight will click something over in my brain and suddenly I'll be able to put it all together. I troll the internet until the wee hours, checking forums for new leads and reading articles on cases in other regions that might be connected to the ones in the Forest City. When things get too muddled, I look for commonalities. I go over them time and time again.

All of the murders involved a vehicle. The cars of main interest in the Jackie English case are Ford brand, particularly with square tail lights. They range from dark maroon to light blue in colour. Remember the man in the green jacket, loitering around the Metropolitan before Jackie disappeared, who drove a clean maroon car? There were several other dark-coloured car sightings around the time Jackie English disappeared. Betty Harrison said she was attacked by someone in a dark-coloured Ford Falcon. But then, there are also several eyewitness accounts of light-coloured or white vehicles, Pontiac or Chrysler, in the abductions of Jacqueline Dunleavy, Frankie Jensen, and Scott Leishman.

Cars were a special hobby to the possible suspects I have explored most in this book, Glen Fryer and David Bodemer. They both owned a lot of cars. Bodemer owned the Peugeot that had a fold-down couchette in the backseat, a brand that was uncommon enough in Canada in the 1960s that it's possible it could have been mistaken for another make and model by eyewitnesses who couldn't identify it as anything recognizable. On the other hand, rarity could have made the car even more distinctive. Peugeot was later bought by Citroen, and Glen Fryer was the president of the Canadian Citroen Autoclub, which is probably a coincidence, but a weird one.

A car was needed to transport each victim from the abduction to the scene of the murder and then to the body disposal site. The body disposal sites were all outdoors. The only exception was Helga Beer, who was found in her car in a public parking lot. That's still "outdoors" to me. It's certainly not inside a building of any kind.

The victims were all found lying on their backs, except for Frankie Jensen, who could have been turned over in the tumultuous spring current of the Thames River. The partially clothed victims had their genitals exposed, except for Scott Leishman, who had been redressed. The naked victims were found in a skeletal state. Soraya was naked except for her girdle, and there were no clothes found around Lynda White. Instead, Lynda White's clothes were scattered relatively near her body disposal site — just as were the clothes of so many others.

The victims were all killed by blunt-force trauma to the head or strangulation. Jacqueline Dunleavy, Frankie Jensen, and Donna Awcock all had items stuffed in their mouths.

There was sexual assault or necrophilia involved in all of the murders. All of the victims had their clothing removed at some point during the attack. There was genital penetration in some of the cases, but also a fair amount of semen ejaculation found outside of the bodies, on clothes and skin. Type-O semen was found at the crime scenes of Georgia Jackson, Jacqueline Dunleavy, and Jackie English. A second sample of unknown type was found in Jackie English's panties. No typing was made of the semen found inside Helga Beer or on her clothes, and the samples from that crime scene were incorrectly stored and can no longer be tested. The other crime scenes had been exposed to natural elements that degraded or washed away the DNA evidence, as far as I know.

The geography of the crimes seem to point to some kind of

pattern. Jacqueline Dunleavy was found close to where Frankie Jensen was abducted. Frankie Jensen was found close to where Scott Leishman was abducted. Scott Leishman was found in the same body of water where Jackie English would later be found, and in the same general region as the discoveries of Jackie English and Lynda White. Donna Awcock was found next to the Thames River many years later, the same body of water where they had found Frankie Jensen. Donna's body was also found off a road that leads from London to Thorndale.

Frankie Jensen was found close to Thorndale in the Thames River near Valleyview Road, only a mile from the Leishman house on the same byway. Valleyview Road is en route between London and Stratford. If you take the scenic drive from London to Stratford or vice versa, avoiding the main highways, you essentially have to drive through Thorndale. Both of the main possible suspects, David Bodemer and Glen Fryer, grew up in Stratford. For Stratford residents, a drive to London is a regular trip where you can access the amenities of a larger city. People who live there still do this today, all the time.

Soraya O'Connell was found directly between London and Stratford.

Most of the body disposal sites were adjacent to "lover's lanes," areas where youth were known to gather for activities such as sex and drinking. As mentioned by the veteran homicide detective I spoke with, these types of locations attract voyeurs, many who have a religious background and internalized feelings of shame in regards to their deviant sexual desires. Both of the main possible suspects, David Bodemer and Glen Fryer, had unique, deeply religious backgrounds. David Bodemer had been arrested in regards to deviant sexual behaviour.

Most of the victims were either taken from or found adjacent to CNR railway tracks. David Bodemer grew up next to a CNR rail yard and worked for CNR in the 1960s. Glen Fryer's father, grandfather, and uncles all worked for CNR in Stratford.

The families of Georgia Jackson, Frankie Jensen, and Soraya O'Connell all received harassing phone calls while they were missing, much like the calls Betty Harrison said she got after she went to the police. I myself received a mysterious phone call, the first strange perverted crank phone call I've ever received in my life, that happened to come three weeks to the day after I interviewed Glen Fryer.

Cigarette butts found in the Harrison vehicle came from a non-secretor, so no blood type was determined, but whoever attacked Betty Harrison was a smoker. Cigarette butts were also found at the scene of Jackie English's body disposal. The man in the green jacket seen around the Metropolitan before she disappeared was seen conspicuously smoking in the children's department of the store. A man with a green jacket was also seen in the fields behind Frankie Jensen's school in the weeks before he was taken.

Composite images and descriptions in the cases of Jackie English and Donna Awcock describe a man with thick eyebrows.

The killer took trophies from the victims — items they had when they went missing that were never accounted for. Soraya's earrings were left with her body, just as Jackie's were. A biological trophy was taken from Georgia Jackson (her ear) and Lynda White (her arm).

It sometimes appeared as if the bodies could have been stored between death and disposal. Georgia Jackson was not seen by Bob Heffren when he was in the maple bush just a few days before she was found, so her body may have been kept in another location and then put in the sugar bush right before she was discovered. The same might be said of Jackie English, as her body appeared in varying reports not to have been in the water the entire time since her abduction. Likewise, according to forensic tests, there is no way that Lynda White's or Soraya O'Connell's bodies could have been where they were found for the entire periods they were missing.

David Bodemer's garage in Avon, Ontario, was torn down prior to the spring of 1972, and the refuse disposed of at Roy

Ferguson's farm in Dorchester. Michael Arntfield suggests in his book *Murder City* that Bodemer had electricity in his Avon garage that could have powered a refrigerating unit. I asked a friend of mine, who is a funeral director, about storing bodies for necrophilic use. He said it would be possible to use a chest freezer, kept at a higher temperature than normal, to maintain a pliable condition in a body and resist decomposition for quite a long period of time.

There was a smell of decomposition around Lynda's disposal site in the spring of 1972, when David Bodemer was in custody.

While Detective Alsop found Georgia Jackson's glove in the garage debris in the spring of 1972, the grounds of the Ferguson farm have never been searched for items that might belong to other victims that could have been stored in the same demolished building. Likewise, there is an old well at the back of the property in Avon where Bodemer rented the garage. It's been in disuse for years and has never been searched for other possibly incriminating evidence.

Glen Fryer and David Bodemer were prime possible suspects for Detective Alsop. He kept an eye on Bodemer for years. He found it suspicious that, unlike the other people living on his street, Bodemer would never put his garbage out the night before the trucks were due. He would wait for the garbage collectors to be on his block in the morning and then he would take it out. This made it impossible for Alsop to acquire a discarded blood or DNA sample from his refuse. At some point, an officer — perhaps Alsop himself — found a way around these obstacles. A source has informed me that the OPP did finally acquire a sample of David Bodemer's DNA, but that it has never been tested against samples left by the Forest City Killer.

Bodemer has lived a full life over his past thirty-six years of freedom. He's had a variety of jobs similar to those he had before he served his truncated life sentence, meaning manual labour and unskilled trade work. He has been married twice more, had a bunch of kids, and currently lives in Brampton. He enjoys going to Blue Jays games and spending time at the trailer. According to posts on Facebook, on the fiftieth anniversary of Georgia Jackson's murder, Bodemer had a serious medical incident and ended up in hospital for an extended period of time.

He is currently alive and well.

Ruth Fryer died in 2012. A lengthy obituary on the Citroen Autoclub website shed some light on what the Fryers' lives looked like once they moved to Toronto and put the disaster of London, Ontario, behind them. Ruth and Glen retreated into religious life, participating heavily in their Christian community. They had seven grandchildren and four great-grandchildren. She worked as a nurse in Toronto, while Glen worked in special education. As he told me, he worked with the most challenging kids in a field with the highest burnout rate. It was the only job he could get after what happened in London, but he found it to be a field in which he thrived. They travelled, and sent all their grandchildren to faith-based Camp Mini-Yo-We, which I only mention because all of my cousins went there too.

Glen spoke to me in glowing terms about his wife. He wanted me to know that he had loved her intensely, that they'd been happy, and they'd had a marriage based on Godly principles. He told me he did not remember Dr. Harvey Murphy or his wife, Dorothea — or, by extension, their affair. He also did not mention the violent fights and suicide attempts that had patterned his marriage for many years. Then again, these are things too unpleasant to talk about.

––––––––––

Abigail, the woman who claims Fryer tried to abduct her in the early 1960s, went on to live a happy life. That horrible episode was long behind her when renewed interest in London's unsolved murders made her remember Fryer in his station wagon. She remembered his eyes focusing on her as he drove past the police cruiser on High Street. She remembered the fear of thinking he would come back and take her away from her life forever.

Wondering what had happened to Fryer, she searched online and discovered the Unsolved Canada website, where she read that Fryer had been teaching for decades, had been around countless children, and had never been found guilty of any crime whatsoever. Her sense of injustice in this regard motivated her to call law enforcement. A detective came her house, where she sat down with him and recounted her story, which he recorded. He told her that he could find no police record of the attempted abduction. There was no report, no paperwork, nothing to indicate at all that in the early 1960s, Fryer had been thrashed by London Police after trying to pick up a little girl. She figured perhaps they didn't want to keep it on record that they had beaten someone up. I had to wonder how many times London Police dealt with deviant behaviour in this way, and how many stories are lost that, if they were compiled, might demonstrate repeated and escalating incidents with potential sexual predators in the Forest City.

Her cousin, the police officer, now has dementia. Her mother is deceased. There is no one to back up — or dispute — Abigail's story but her — and Glen Fryer.

———

Dennis Alsop moved to Toronto after Bodemer's conviction and became an OPP superintendent. It wasn't his kind of work. Previously, his notebooks were filled with details of cases he was working on, names of persons of interest, the daily grunt work of a detective on the streets. They looked a lot like the scrapbooks he'd kept as a teenager. Now, he wrote mostly about his family. He chronicled the development of his children and grandchildren and wrote down all of their visits. "The police work became secondary. The family became important. And I guess that's why families are important, because they're always the fallback," says Dennis Jr.

After he retired, Detective Dennis Alsop discovered that he was not a man of leisure. He kept himself busy working as a volunteer for the Cancer Society, and he distinguished himself even there, winning the Volunteer Order of Ontario for his efforts. While work had taken him to Toronto, and he and Emelia continued to live there in his later years, he loved seeing his grandkids when they came to visit from out of town. He was not a lonely old man. He was just as busy as ever.

A fall in 2012 left ninety-two-year-old Dennis Alsop unconscious and in hospital. His children felt that he could hear them, and so they sat with him and chatted, telling him about their daily goings-on. Once he was moved into palliative care, they expected him to pass on quickly, but he kept going for another two weeks. His son recalls, "For a ninety-two-year-old guy, there were a lot of people at his funeral, and I didn't know any of them, and there were only two cops. He was buried in his dress uniform."

When Emelia saw him laid out, she commented that his uniform reminded her of her grandfather's. She was gripped by the knowledge that her husband had been a good man, a respectable man, and she expressed regret for all the times she'd been less than kind to him. That uniform signified respect and success. She tearfully said to Dennis Jr., "He must have done all right."

"I know he did great," he replied.

———

Emelia Alsop was on her own for several years after her husband's death, in perfect health. Her ending came about quite differently from Alsop's. In 2016, she announced to her eldest son, "I'm going now." The two of them sat down and made a plan. When she was in palliative care, Dennis Jr. had his last conversation with his mom.

"I trust Dad is helping you through this," he said.

"He is," she assured him.

"Well, ask him to do something about this Jackie English case," he replied. "It's driving me nuts."

"Who is that?"

"That little girl."

"Oh, I know that little girl," she said. "I remember that little girl."

Those were the last words she ever said to him.

The Saturday after his mother's funeral, Dennis Jr. returned to London, Ontario, and got a phone call from Anne English. He hadn't heard from her in almost a year. She told him, "I met this girl, and she's writing a book about my sister."

He told me that the news brought him to tears. He felt as though his father was speaking to him.

"You can never be un-Catholic, but am I practising? No. This is . . . just because I'm not a practising Catholic doesn't mean that I don't believe there's an afterlife. I definitely believe there is, and I think my father's controlling a lot of this stuff. And I think my father wants this to be closed," says Dennis.

"Guide me somewhere . . . go and get other people."

APPENDIX

DAVID BODEMER'S
FIRST CONFESSION

Picked up Georgia Jackson, Friday, February 18th, 1966 when she finished working. Picked her up in front of Spicer's Bakery and drove around block by the theater [sic] and then drove to her home. Stopped in front and talked about Dennis and Linda Sullivan. David did not know where they lived, so Georgia said she would show David where they live. Drove over to Dennis & Linda's home on Caverly Road and turned around went to South St. and parked by Freeman Electric.

Stopped the car and Georgia Jackson asked why? David said he wanted to talk to her. David then said he put his arm around her and she fought back and struggled. David then hit her with a pop bottle that was on the back seat on the back of her head. They were sitting in the front seat. She was stunned and struggling. She asked David to stop this as her mother and father were expecting her at home. She screamed before David hit her and after too — just before she fainted.

Then David drove out of town with Georgia Jackson lying on his shoulders still unconscious. Went out of town south on

Highway number 73 to a side road left to a secluded area and stopped again. Georgia Jackson was then coming too [sic]. At this time David Bodemer noticed he had blood on the sleeve of his coat and the shoulder too. Georgia Jackson then started to scream again and David put his hand over her mouth and struggled with her. David said he hated to see anyone cry. Kept his hand over her mouth while struggling, covering her nose too. Held hand over mouth and nose hoping she would pass out but held hand firmly too long and Georgia Jackson smothered to death. All the while David admitted he was trying to attack and rape her and succeeded. Noticed her face was puffed up and she was lifeless after attack and rape was finished. Become scared and frightened as David admitted than he knew she was dead. Knew to he had to get rid of her.

Drove to Springfield Road by bush looking for place to dispose of Georgia Jackson. Put it into the bush where found. Carried her part of the way and dragged her the rest of the way to where left, behind your tree, correction, behind heavy shrubs.

Came back to the car and noticed that Georgia Jackson's coat was still in car. So drove around next road towards town, stopped and put coat behind a tree. Does not remember about scarfe [sic].

Then David Bodemer went to work with his father-in-law, Bert Crooker, who was cleaning the Bank of Montreal corner of Talbot and John Sts. Worked with father-in-law for 2 hours. Arrived at bank about 7:30 p.m. to work.

In meantime looking out window noticed, Dennis Sullivan walking around looking for whereabouts of Georgia Jackson. Dennis Sullivan came to the bank and asked if David had seen Georgia. David said No. Dennis Sullivan came back to bank again to tell Bert Crooker about Georgia Jackson missing. So Bert Crooker and David Bodemer stopped work and went with him (Dennis Sullivan)[89] to look for Georgia. Then all went to the

---

89 This clarification in parentheses was added to the letter by Detective Alsop.

police station and they had been notified by this time about her disappearance.

David Bodemer then went home to Avon. He planned to join search again next day, Saturday. Then David Bodemer hid his coat and her glove between south wall, stuffing it down at bottom of wall near foundation. Wiped seat off with snow and rag. Blood was on the seat. The house was being rented from DeGroot.

Next day, Saturday, David Bodemer joined search party to look for Georgia Jackson.

Kept this to himself until questioned further on Friday, January 21st, 1972, by Arthur Powley and Charles Ross. When questioned did not confess at that time. Wanted to tell wife first. Sunday night at 8:00 p.m. told wife about the rape and murder of Georgia Jackson. Phoned home of Herb Katzmier, then phoned father-in-law, Bert Crooker talking to him at 12:00 p.m. told him to arrange meeting with Arthur Powley again as David has something important to confess.

Meeting arranged for Monday morning, January 24th, 1972 at the home of Daivid [sic] Bodemer, when he confessed the above.

I, David Bodemer, testify that the above is my true confession related to Arthur Polly [sic], Charles Ross and Albert Crooker. That the above is the truthful account of my rape and death of Georgia Jackson. And that I volunteered without any duress the above confession.

SELECTED SOURCES

BOOKS AND FILES

Addington, Charles. *A History of the London Police Force: 125 Years of Police Service*. London: Phelps Publishing, 1980.

Alsop, Dennis. Jackie English File: Interviews, Reports and Notebooks. 1969–1978.

Alsop, Dennis. Georgia Jackson File: Interviews, Reports and Notebooks. 1966–1978.

Arntfield, Michael. *Murder City: The Untold Story of Canada's Serial Killer Capital, 1959–1984*. Victoria: Friesen Press, 2015.

City of London Council Meeting Minutes. November 3, 1969; June 7, 12, 13, 14, 1972.

Cowie, John. Assorted Research Notes. [Undated].

Elgin County Branch of the Ontario Genealogical Society. *Places of Worship*. 2006.

English, Anne. Assorted Notes and Files. [Undated].

English, Fred. *Justice for Jackie*. Unpublished.

English, Jackie. Personal Diary. 1969.

Hare, Robert. *Without Conscience: The Disturbing World of Psychopaths Among Us*. New York: Guilford Press, 1993.

Jones, Frank. *Trail of Blood: A Canadian Murder Odyssey*. Toronto: McClelland & Stewart-Bantam, 1984.

Keith, Rod. Assorted Research Notes. [Undated].

Kessler, Robert K.. Ann W. Burgess, John E. Douglas, *Sexual Homicide: Patterns and Motives*. Free Press, 1988.

LeBourdais, Isabel. *The Trial of Steven Truscott*. Toronto: McClelland & Stewart, 1966.

Leyton, Elliott. *Hunting Humans*. New York: Pocket Books, 1988.

Leyton, Elliott. *Men of Blood*. Toronto: McClelland & Stewart, 1995.

Perth County Branch, Ontario Genealogical Society. *Places of Worship Inventory - Stratford - Perth County*. Perth County Branch, Ontario Genealogical Society: Stratford, 2009.

Regina V. Bodemer. Supreme Court of Canada. Appeal Book. March 9, 1973. Library & Archives Canada.

Richardson, Mark. *On the Beat: 150 Years of Policing in London, Ontario.* London: Aylmer Express, 2005.

Ruhl, Barry. *A Viable Suspect: The Story of Multiple Murders and How a Police Force's Reach Proved Too Short for Canada's Most Notorious Cold Case.* Vancouver: Friesen Press, 2014.

Sher, Julian. *"Until You Are Dead": Steven Truscott's Long Ride Into History.* Toronto: Knopf Canada, 2001.

Trent, Bill. *The Steven Truscott Story.* Toronto: Simon & Schuster, 1971.

—. *Who Killed Lynne Harper?* Montreal, Toronto: Optimum, 1979.

West Nissouri Historical Society. *West Nissouri Township: 1818–2000.* Thorndale, Ontario: West Nissouri Historical Society, 2004.

SELECTED INTERVIEWS

Alsop, Dennis Jr. Recorded Interview. June 27, 2017.

Dennett, Tammy. Recorded Interview. September 4, 2018.

English, Anne. Recorded Interview. April 20, 2016.

Fryer, Glen. Telephone Interview. September 9, 2018.

DIRECTORIES

Stratford 1921–1961

London 1959–1972, 1983

Aylmer 1959–1972

YEARBOOKS

Banting High School, Alliston: 1961.

Clarke Road Secondary School, London: 1968.

Oakridge Secondary School, London: 1968.

South Secondary High School, London: 1968.

WEBSITES

Aylmer – A History of a Town. http://www.elgincounty.ca

CBC Windsor. "London woman helps needy families in honour of her murdered sister." December 21, 2016.

Elgin County Archives. http://www.elgincounty.ca/archives

Elgin County Branch of the Ontario Genealogical Society. https://sites.google.com/site/elginbranchogs/

Elgin County Branch of the Ontario Genealogical Society. Places of Worship Inventory Project. https://elgin.ogs.on.ca/home/ancestor-indexes/places-of-worship/malahide-aylmer-churches/

Facebook Groups:
  Justice for Jackie English
  Justice for Donna Jean Awcock
  Ontario Family and Friends of Unsolved Murder Victims
  If You Grew Up In London, Ontario, You Will Remember When . . .
  Vintage London
  London Ontario Blast from the Past
Find a Grave. http://www.findagrave.com
London Police. https://www.londonpolice.ca/en/about/Unsolved-
  Murders.aspx
McCulloch, John. Citroen Club Canada. "Special Anniversary Profile: Glen
  Fryer - Founding President of Citroen Autoclub Canada." Fall 2003.
OPP. https://www.opp.ca
Toronto Police:
  https://www.torontopolice.on.ca/homicide/coldcases.php
  https://www.torontopolice.on.ca/homicide/search.php
The True Crime Files. https://thetruecrimefiles.com/jacqueline-dunleavy-
  murder/
UnsolvedCanada.ca
  Donna Jean Awcock - 17 - Murdered - October 13, 1983 - London, ON
  Helga Beer - London, ON - Murdered - 1968
  Susan Cadieux - January 7, 1956 - Age 5 - Murdered - London
  Karen Caughlin (14) - Murder - Sarnia, ON - March 16, 1974
  Jacqueline Dunleavy, 16 - London, ON - Murdered - 1968
  Jacqueline English - London, ON - Murdered - 1969
  Sylvia Fink, 7 years old, murdered Nov. 13th, 1961, London, ON
  Lynne Harper - 1959 - Murdered - Clinton
  Georgia Jackson - 18 - Murdered - February, 1966 - Aylmer, ON
  Frankie Jensen - London, ON - Murdered - 1968
  Christine Jessop - October 3, 1984 - Age 9 - Murdered
  Scott Leishman - Thorndale, ON - Murdered - 1968
  Mistie Murray - May 31, 1995 - Age 16 - Missing - Goderich, ON
  Soraya O'Connell - London, ON - Murdered - 1970
  Project Angel January 1997 to June 2000 - Unsolved Murders
  Margaret Sheeler - London, ON - Murdered - 1963
  Robert Bruce Stapylton, 11, - London, ON - Murdered - 1969
  Ljubica Topic, 6, UNSOLVED MURDER May 14, 1971 (Windsor, ON)
  Lynda White - Burlington, ON - Murdered - 1968
Unsolved Mysteries Wiki. http://unsolvedmysteries.wikia.com

Websleuths. http://www.websleuths.com
  Canada - Donna Awcock, 17, London, Ont, 13 Oct 1983
  Canada - Helga Beer, 31, London, Ontario, 6 August 1968
  Canada - Jacqueline Dunleavy, 16, London, On, Jan 9 1968
  Canada - Unsolved murders of young people in London, Ont, 1960s–70s
  Canada - Lynda White, 19, Campus of Western Ontario, London, Ontario,
    1963 [sic]
Willmon, Rene. "Behind the Scenes of TCAK: Forensic Face Analysis." March
  24, 2014. https://reneewillmon.wordpress.com/2014/03/24/behind-the-
  scenes-of-tcak-forensic-facial-analysis/#more-187

PODCASTS

Murder Was the Case
1995
My Favourite Murder
Dark Poutine
Canadian True Crime
The Murder in My Family

TELEVISION, FILM, RADIO

The Fifth Estate. *Steven Truscott — His Word Against History*. CBC, March
  29, 2000.
Arntfield, Michael. *To Catch a Killer*. OWN Canada, Ocean Entertainment,
  2014.
  Cold Case #83-125: Donna Awcock (March 1, 2014)
  Cold Case #69-52: Jacqueline English (March 22, 2014)
  Cold Case #68-160533: Lynda White (April 19, 2014)
"Purse from unsolved London, Ont. murder returned 33 years later."
  November 14, 2016. CBC.
Sherren, Reg. *The Secrets of Oak Ridge*. CBC's The National, March 1,
  2016.
"London woman helps needy families in honour of her murdered sister."
  December 21, 2016. CBC.
"Purse from unsolved murder of Donna Awcock returned to family."
  January 11, 2017. CTV London.
"Police appeal for information in 34-year-old cold case murder investiga-
  tion." November 10, 2017. Global News.
Grant, Chloe. "Jackie English: one of London's most troubling cold cases."
  January 31, 2018. 106.9 The Ex FM. Fanshawe College Radio.

Gerster, Jane. "Who killed Helga Beer? Time is running out to find her murderer." August 6, 2018. Global News.

LONDON FREE PRESS ARTICLES (CHRONOLOGICAL)

Ratcliffe, John; Campbell, Fred. "3 Men Find Body Hanging by Belt In Old Store Attic." November 14, 1961.

"Order Mental Test For Boy in Slaying." November 28, 1961.

Finch, Eric. "Sent to School at Bowmanville as Delinquent." January 12, 1962.

"Charge 17-Year-Old In Slaying." November 28, 1963.

"City Slaying Suspect Sent To Hospital." December 19, 1963.

["The nude body of a 20-year-old woman . . ."]. January 24, 1964.

"Met Death in Field." January 25, 1964.

"Sheeler Death Laid to Fracture." February 6, 1964.

Stotts, Ron. "Of London's 14 Slayings in Decade, 3 Still Unsolved." August 14, 1964.

"Theories on Disappearance of Aylmer Girl, 20, Differ." February 21, 1966.

"300 Jehovah's Witnesses Scour Two Counties For Aylmer Girl, 20." February 21, 1966.

"Police Doubt Girl Abducted 'Think She'll Turn Up Ok.'" February 22, 1966.

"Red-Stained Coat Of Missing Girl Found by Boys." March 1, 1966.

Massecar, Bob. "Bloodstained Coat Believed Planted; 'Copter in Search." March 2, 1966.

Massecar, Bob. "Wants Full OPP Help in Missing Girl Case." March 3, 1966.

"Rule Out Stains in Barn As Clue to Missing Girl." March 3, 1966.

"Girl 'Vanished into Thin Air' Claims OPP Leader of Hunt." March 4, 1966.

Henderson, Jim. "Did Georgia Run Away?" March 4, 1966.

"Police Check Reports Missing Girl in Orillia." March 4, 1966.

Morris, Neil. "Police Deny Religious Prejudice." March 5, 1966.

"Truscott Trial Review Demanded by Liberal." March 8, 1966.

"Aylmer Authorizes Reward of $500 In Hunt for Girl." March 8, 1966.

"'Stained' Scarf Latest Discovery In Hunt for Girl." March 9, 1966.

"Area Where Scarf Found Yields No Clues to Girl." March 10, 1966.

"Police Check of Blood-Stains On Girl's Clothing Not Completed." March 16, 1966.

McClelland, Joe. "Book Claims Truscott Not Given Fair Trial in 1959." March 16, 1966.

Morris, Neil. "'We'll Never Know' If Police Did Enough, Says Anguished Father." March 17, 1966.

"Press Search for Slayer of Georgia." March 17, 1966.

Caney, Graham. "Faith in Daughter Vindicated." March 17, 1966.

Ibsen, Norm. "Ontario to Probe Police Action In Slaying of Aylmer Girl." March 18, 1966.

Hutchison, George. "'It's Kinda Scary': Sex Slaying of Georgia Jackson Jolts Aylmer, Keeps Women Off Streets, On Guard." March 19, 1966.

Caney, Graham. "Claim Chief Lax in Search, Seek Ouster." March 19, 1966.

"Where Georgia Jackson Lived and Died." March 19, 1966.

"Truscott Case Going to Cabinet." March 19, 1966.

"Author 'Able to Take My Time' In Assessing Truscott Case." March 21, 1966.

"Students Seek Truscott Inquiry." March 21, 1966.

"Knifed boy, 5, listed serious, youth arrested." June 28, 1966.

Sanderson, Gordon. "Sound Off." February 1967.

Massecar, Bob. "City nurse attacked, knifed." February 4, 1967.

McGuire, Bill and Jones, Bob. [Untitled]. January 10, 1968.

"Autopsy confirms strangling cause of Dunleavy girl's death." January 12, 1968.

"Mayor scolds Menzies in hassle over detained youths." January 26, 1968.

"Death of city woman still puzzles police." February 4, 1969.

McGuire, Bill. "Hundreds hunt for London boy, 9." February 10, 1968.

"Hope dim after 1,000 fail to find boy." February 12, 1968.

McGuire, Bill. "Her son is gone and 'the waiting is almost too much.'" February 12, 1968.

"Father says 9-year-old no runaway." February 13, 1968.

"Report Jensen boy sighted proves false." February 15, 1968.

"101 paddle for crippled children." April 8, 1966.

Thompson, Ralph. "Jensen boy's body found at Thorndale." April 13, 1968.

"Frankie found dead police hunt killer." April 13, 1968.

Dennett, Chris. "Hunt sex-killer but deny murders in London linked." April 15, 1968.

Thompson, Ralph. "Arrest believed imminent: Jensen, Dunleavy murders linked." April 15, 1968.

McDougall, Warren. "They Never Stopped Hoping." April 15, 1968.

"Divers seek murder clues in Thames." April 16, 1966.

"Public asked to search yards for Frankie's missing clothing." April 16, 1968.

"Seek site where body entered river." April 18, 1966.

"Police report new lead in Jensen case." April 20, 1968.

McGuire, Bill. "Nearly nude, badly beaten, woman found dead in car." August 6, 1968.

"May be area's 6th unsolved slaying." August 6, 1968.

"Police confirm man sought in Beer death." August 13, 1968.

"Co-ed reported missing." November 15, 1968.

McGuire, Bill and Hayashi, Julian. "'Bubbly' co-ed vanishes family, friends worry." November 16, 1968.

"Police still baffled by Lynda White case." December 30, 1968.

"5 school areas get 'block parents.'" March 4, 1969.

"Fate of co-ed still a mystery." July 30, 1969.

McGuire, Bill. "Decomposed body believed boy, 11." September 24, 1969.

Jones, Bob. "Dead Boy, Shack Link Studied." September 25, 1969.

"$5,000 reward offered for aid in locating missing Lynda White." September 27, 1969.

Hayashi, Julian. "The two faces of Lynda White." October 1,1969.

"Girl, 15, reported missing." October 6, 1969.

McGuire, Bill. "Grade 3 pupil, class pray for return of missing baby-sitter Jackie English.". October 7, 1969.

McGuire, Bill; Jones, Bob. "Girl's body found battered, nude." October 10, 1969.

Wallace, Helen. "Friends sure Jackie English must have been forced into car." October 10, 1969.

Ross, Helen. "Store's policy to only hire girls with rides." October 10, 1969.

Jones, Bob. "Nude body of London girl found in creek at Otterville." October 10, 1969.

"Pills put mother in hospital." October 11, 1969.

"All of us share the blame." October 11, 1969.

"Police hunt clues in slaying of girl with plane, dog." October 11, 1969.

"Police 'extend' investigation of girl's slaying." c. October 12, 1969.

McGuire, Bill. "Jackie's clothing found near creek." October 14, 1969.

"Jackie English accepted ride in dark car." c. October 14, 1969.

Eluchon, Bill. "Jackie English buried, police check mourners." October 15, 1969.

McGuire, Bill; Echulon, Bill. "Study parts of burned car in Jackie English slaying." October 15, 1969.

Brown, G. S. "Police shake-up overdue." October 15, 1969.

Armstrong, S. "Only so much a parent today can do." October 15, 1969.

"Body of boy positively identified." October 15, 1969.

"Open line caller requested to help slaying investigation." October 17, 1969.

"The murderer in our midst." October 18, 1969.

"Sex Killer in London area." October 18, 1969.

McGuire, Bill. "Police picture man who talked to Jackie." October 20, 1969.

"Hundreds call regarding police sketch." October 21, 1969.

Bulani, Brent. "Must become 'involved' to end killings." October 21, 1969.

"A first break in the English case." c. October 21, 1969.

Gartley, Mrs. D. E. "Police-citizen co-operation vital now." October 22, 1969.

Peters, J. H. "Reward might be useful in detection of criminal." October 22, 1969.

Wright, Russ. "Reduction of punishment increases crime." October 22, 1969.

McLagan, Harvey. "Put public weal first." October 22, 1969.

"Tip gives OPP 'fighting chance' to solve murder of Jackie." October 22, 1969.

"New lead gives police chance to solve English slaying." October 22, 1969.

English, Doris. "Mrs. English asks: Please help find him." October 23, 1969.

Jones, Bob. "Shoes found in farm pond may belong to murdered girl." October 23, 1969.

"'Hidden witness' reward offered." October 25, 1969.

"$10,000 city reward sought in murders." October 28, 1969.

"New clue found in English murder, 'Hidden Witness' draws eight tips." October 28, 1969.

"Proposes city offer $10,000 for lead to Jackie's murderer." October 29, 1969.

Hutchison, George. "Students to oppose hitch-hiking ban." c. October 29, 1969.

"Some items found from Jackie's purse." October 29, 1969.

"Pencils, perfume from murdered girl's purse found on street." October 30, 1969.

"Councillors OK reward of $10,000 in slayings." October 30, 1969.

"Quick decision essential." October 30, 1969.

"London council OKs offer of $10,000 for murder leads." October 31, 1969.

"15,000 students to get 'hidden witness' plan." October 31, 1969.

"Rewards in murders limited to $11,000." October 1969.

"Teen-agers set up reward for killer." November 1, 1969.

"Dozen police still seeking killer of Jackie English." November 1969.

Etherington, Jim. "$10,000 reward approved by council." November 3, 1969.

"Mayor criticizes police in English and other murders." November 7, 1969.

Feeman, C.M. "Public needs to be informed, aroused on murders." November 7, 1969.

"English murder case rewards up to $21,000." November 8, 1969.

"Assault suspect pleads innocent." November 29, 1969.

McGuire, Bill. "London woman victim of savage knife attack." December 12, 1969.

"Victim of knife attack under guard in hospital." c. December 12, 1969.

Williams, Tom. "Not beautiful, but brave." c. December 12, 1969.

"Investigators hoping passerby may offer tip leading to slasher." December 1969.

Taylor, Jim. "Law can't help, woman's attacker 'put away.'" December 13, 1969.

"Police canvas area of attack on woman." December 15, 1969.

"Investigation continues in stabbing." December 1969.

"Knife victim satisfactory, still guarded." December 17, 1969.

"A stalemate in the courts." December 22, 1969.

McGuire, Bill. "Elusive killer haunts sleuths during holiday break." December 24, 1969.

"Unsolved death toll now stands at six." December 24, 1969.

"Hunt man who assaulted 2 teen-aged city girls." December 29, 1969.

"Nurse's assailant described like man in earlier case." February 2, 1970.

"Principal charged in woman attack." April 27, 1970.

Jones, Bob. "Police hold suspect in attack on woman." April 1970.

"Fryer remanded on $5,000 bail in stabbing." April 1970.

Taylor, Jim; Etherington, Jim. "Cricket MacIvor dies in fire." August 7, 1970.

"80 pay last respects to 'Cricket.'" August 8, 1970.

"Police, firemen reconstruct girl's apartment blaze death." August 8, 1970.

"London girl, 15, missing four days." August 18, 1970.

"Fears rise for safety of girl." August 19, 1970.

"Soraya's father offers $1,000 for lead to missing girl." August 19. 1970.

"Police team presses search for Soraya." August 20, 1970.

"No trace found of Soraya." August 20, 1970.

"The fears that won't subside." August 21, 1970.

"Police comb fields in search for missing Soraya O'Connell." August 21, 1970.

"Soraya O'Connell case chronology." August 21, 1970.

"Police comb fields, brush for missing teen-aged girl." August 25, 1970.

"McBride joins search for Soraya." August 26, 1970.

"Baffled by Soraya case, police plead for help." August 28, 1970.

"Handbag felt major clue." August 29, 1970.

"Police seek aid from citizens." August 29, 1970.

Hutchison, George. "Missing Person: Most teen-aged girls come home, but Soraya's been gone 2 weeks." September 1, 1970.

Hayashi, Julian. "Soraya's parents report crank calls." September 1, 1970.

"Hunt for girl spreads to coast." September 9, 1970.

"Interpol checks Europe for friend of Soraya." September 16, 1970.

"Fryer trial to start Nov. 23." October 16, 1970.

Greer, Harold. "Law's logic inadequate for illogical crimes." November 1970.

Sallaway, Paul; Hutchison, George. "Defence: 'Nothing connects Fryer with the events.'" November 1970.

"Threats on Fryer's life probed." November 1970.

Schroeder, Bob. "Defence questions Fryer trial witness." November 25, 1970.

Schroeder, Bob. "Constable tells of wounds woman suffered." November 28, 1970.

Schroeder, Bob. "Victim tells of beating, struggle with man." November 29, 1970.

Schroeder, Bob. "Doctor says Glen Fryer 'two people.'" December 1, 1970.

Schroeder, Bob. "Fryer's boots 'similar' to prints at crime scene." December 2, 1970.

Schroeder, Bob. "'The charge isn't right,' wounding suspect told officer." December 3, 1970.

Schroeder, Bob. "'I never met the woman,' Fryer quoted in attack denial." December 4, 1970.

Schroeder, Bob. "Character witness testifies as Fryer trial ends 2nd week." December 5, 1970.

"Nurse's attacker awaiting sentence." December 5, 1970.

"Can't say Fryer wrote notes." December 8, 1970.

Schroeder, Bob. "Court told Fryer wore bandage soon after woman attacked." December 9, 1970. Schroeder, Bob. "Fryer testifies in own defence, denies wounding Mrs. Harrison." December 10, 1970.

"Prosecution seeks reopening Fryer case for new evidence." December 11, 1970.

"Crown to reopen case in Fryer wounding trial." December 12, 1970.

"Man jailed 3 years." December 12, 1970.

"Wounding trial enters fourth week." December 14, 1970.

Schroeder, Bob. "Glen Fryer again placed at Met." December 16, 1970.

Schroeder, Bob. "Fryer tells court he wasn't in store." December 16, 1970.

Schroeder, Bob. "Fryer case argument scheduled for Friday." December 17, 1970.

Schroeder, Bob. "Judge rejects Fryer case bid." December 18, 1970.

Schroeder, Bob. "Fryer wounding trial decision due Tuesday." December 19, 1970.

Schroeder, Bob. "Closing Arguments." December 20, 1970.

Schroeder, Bob. "Fryer acquitted: Only you know the truth, says judge." December 22, 1970.

Hutchison, George; Turner, Isaac. "Greatest suspicion is not sufficient to convict." December 23, 1970.

Collins, Kit. "Fryer's faith restored." December 24, 1970.

Sallaway, Paul. "New leads scarce in cases of missing girls." April 29, 1971.

Sallaway, Paul. "Lynda Whites's wallet found at Burlington." June 29, 1971.

Hayashi, Julian. "Diggers probing for body of girl." June 30, 1971.

Hayashi, Julian. "Diggers abandon search for Lynda." July 1, 1971.

"Believe wallet left in different area." July 8, 1971.

"Ex-friends of Lynda White to be interviewed by police." July 9, 1971.

McGuire, Bill. "Father of five charged in 1966 slaying of girl." January 25, 1972.

Jones, Bob; Thompson, Ralph. "Man, 26, charged in Jackson murder." January 25, 1972.

"Reward in murders may be withdrawn." June 8, 1972.

Sallaway, Paul. "Slaying trial plagued by fading memories." June 20, 1972.

Sallaway, Paul. "Bodemer murder trial jury dismissed for voir dire." June 21, 1972.

Sallaway, Paul. "Murder trial still stalled on legalities." June 22, 1972.

Sallaway, Paul. "Bodemer statement admits rape, murder." June 23, 1972.

Sallaway, Paul. "Bodemer 'can't remember everything': Second rape-murder confession read." June 24, 1972.

Sallaway, Paul. "Bodemer case goes to St. Thomas jury." June 27, 1972.

Sallaway, Paul. "Defence alleges 'Bible-thumping': Confession truth argued." June 27, 1972.

Sallaway, Paul. "Bodemer sentences to life in prison." June 28, 1972.

"Police urgently need assistance." October 16, 1972.

"Refuses to jump, mother dies with 3 children in blaze." November 17, 1972.

Thompson, Ralph; Jones, Bob. "Mother, 3 children perish in blaze." November 17, 1972.

"Wortley pupils start drive to help fire-hit families." November 18, 1972.

"Three of four fire victims within steps of escape." November 19, 1972.

"Alsop promoted to inspector." December 30, 1970.

Jones, Bob. "Couple, son and family dog die as London home swept by fire." January 9, 1973.

"Coroner says inquest probably in fire deaths of Harrisons." January 9, 1973.

"Harrison's, dog suffocated in house fire." January 10, 1973.

"Police intensify probe of London fire deaths." Undated.

"Harrison fire deaths ruled accidental." Undated.

"Jury finds Harrisons died in accidental fire." Undated.

Jones, Bob. "Skeleton identified as missing Lynda White. Team of experts probing death of co-ed." May 30, 1973.

Taylor, Jim. "Telephone call dashes hope of girl's family." May 30, 1973.

McKegney, Tom; Floryck, Gene. "Battered body of girl found near Petrolia." March 18, 1974

Floryck, Gene. "Teen-aged girl's beaten body found in ditch near Petrolia." March 18, 1974.

"Police divulge nothing in search for girl's killer." March 19, 1974.

Jones, Bob. "Skeleton identified as missing city girl." June 4, 1974.

Obituary for Soraya O'Connell. June 14, 1974.

Floryck, Gene. "Dozen area deaths unsolved." July 6, 1974.

Jones, Bob. "Few clues, facts leaves police mystified over slaying of girl." July 6, 1974.

Hill, Jane. "London, B. C. sex slayings not connected, OPP report." August 20, 1974.

Funston, Mike. "Free ride sometimes fatal for females." August 23, 1975.

"Police think body may be missing teen." October 15, 1983.

"Police think body of girl may be missing baby-sitter." October 15, 1983.

"Police appeal for help in slaying probes." October 15, 1983.

"Friends helping slain girl's family." October 15, 1983.

McGuire, Bill; Rose, Sid. "Slayings of teen, woman, 70, probed." October 16, 1983.

Obituary for Donna Awcock, October 17, 1983.

McGuire, Bill. "Slayings of teen, woman, 70, probed." October 17, 1983.

"Police seek public's help in probes of two slayings." October 18, 1983.

Lindsay, Bill. "Friends, neighbours chipping in to assist strangled girl's family." October 19, 1983.

Hamilton, John. "Kin, neighbours, friends say goodbye." October 19, 1983.

Dray, Roger. "Awcock murder stirs some painful memories." October 23, 1983.

"Mystery man sought in Awcock slaying." November 9, 1983.

"Interest resparked in teen's slaying." November 10, 1983.

"Reward offered in girl's murder." February 18, 1984.

"31 respond to reward for killer of teenager." February 21, 1984.

Hamilton, John. "Mother of slain girl pours out agony in her heart." August 17, 1985.

Hamilton, John. "Murder victim's mom denied compensation." September 7, 1985.

McKenzie, Rob; Sanderson, Gordon. "Just good neighbour Joe: Fugitive always willing to help out." November 22, 1988.

"Reward for clues to killer of teenager still unclaimed." November 26, 1988.

Pugliese, David; Kehoe, Mary. "Investigators never close their files of brutal murders in district." January 3, 1989.

Sims, Jane. "Boy vanished on his way to school." January 10, 1990.

Sims, Jane. "London teen's body found in Tillsonburg creek area." January 13, 1990.

Massecar, Bob. "Clues still sought in teen girl's death." November 16, 1990.

Bass, Alan. "One in every six murders goes unsolved in Canada." January 10, 1991.

"Shepherd co-operates." December 9, 1995.

Sims, Jane. "High-tech offers hope." February 5, 1998.

Beaubien, Roxanne; Herbert, John. "Bill offers fresh hope." October 7, 1998.

Herbert, John. "Mother may find peace at last." February 16, 2004.

Sims, Jane. "Sister hopes social media will put the heat on the case." December 21, 2010.

Sims, Jane. "'I didn't bury them. . . I didn't kill them.'" January 3, 2011.

"London police publish list of 10 unsolved murders." May 21, 2013.

Carrothers, Dale. "The long hunt for a killer." May 30, 2011.

Richmond, Randy. "In grief, paths suddenly cross." October 28, 2011.

O'Brien, Jennifer. "London woman hopes $50K reward will lead to arrest of sister Donna Awcock's killer." July 31, 2013.

Bender, Eric. "Jensen built niche in Scandinavian furniture." March 11, 2014

Sims, Jane. "Boxing in a serial killer." March 21, 2014.

Sims, Jane. "Box of clues found in late cop's home may help solve cold cases." March 22, 2014.

Sims, Jane. "'We deserve some answers.'" March 23, 2014.

Sims, Jane. "London cold-case slaying thrust under new spotlight." April 18, 2014.

Sims, Jane. "Ex-cop criminologist's new book calls London 'Canada's serial killer capital' of the 1960s, '70s and '80s." June 22, 2015.

Sims, Jane. "Son battles OPP to get back late cop's diaries which may hold clues to unsolved murders." August 31, 2016.

Sims, Jane. "Dennis Alsop Jr.: Move to keep late cop's documents shows force brass don't know limits of power, academic says." August 31, 2016.

Sher, Jonathan. "Investigators say Sarnia teen killed in 1974 when she was hit by a vehicle while walking." December 15, 2017.

Patterson, Troy. "Lois Hanna: 30th anniversary nears in Kindcardine woman's mysterious disappearance." February 2, 2018.

Carruthers, Dale. "Police renew push for tips on anniversary of teen Karen Caughlin's 1974 death." March 16, 2018.
"The enduring Mistie Murray mystery." July 14, 2018.

ST. THOMAS TIMES JOURNAL (CHRONOLOGICAL)

"Autopsy This Afternoon To Find Cause of Death." March 17, 1966.
"Pledges Aid of Sect to Find Girl's Killer." March 17, 1966.
"'It's All Over Now,' Says Mrs. Jackson." March 17, 1966.
"Georgia Jackson Funeral Held Today While Police Search for Murderer." March 19, 1966.
"Under Fire." March 19, 1966.
"Where Georgia Worked." March 19, 1966.
"Fear Grows Maniac Slew Aylmer Girl." March 19, 1966.
"Police Keep Watch at Jackson Funeral." March 21, 1966.
"Jackson Case on Aylmer Council Agenda Tonight." March 21, 1966.
"Aylmer Man Reports Seeing Miss Jackson on Main Street." March 22, 1966.
"Council Offers $1,000 Reward For Information On Murderer." March 22, 1966.
"Former Avon resident charged in 1966 murder of Georgina Jackson." January 25, 1972.
"Remand Bodemer until February 3 on murder charge." January 26, 1972.
"Bodemer to undergo psychiatric examination." February 3, 1972.
"Man, 26, charged with sex-slaying remanded to mental health centre; car traced to Kitchener junkyard." February 11, 1972.
"Non-capital murder preliminary date set for Kitchener man, 26." March 10, 1972.
"Bodemer remanded to March 24." March 17, 1972.
"Remanded on murder." April 1, 1972.
"Man remanded." April 8, 1972.
"Bodemer again remanded." April 15, 1972.
"Decision expected today in non-capital murder preliminary hearing." April 28, 1972.
"Man committed for trial charged with murder." May 3, 1972.
"Town Topics. . . Trial date set." June 10, 1972.
"Bodemer pleads not guilty to murder of Aylmer girl." June 20, 1972.
"Father-in-law says Bodemer with him when girl vanished." June 21, 1972.
"Legal arguments continue in Elgin murder trial." June 22, 1972.
"Bodemer trial development." June 22, 1972.

"Truth Questioned by defence: Confession by Bodemer to Jackson murder."
June 23, 1972.

"Second confession by David Bodemer." June 23, 1972.

"Second Bodemer confession is read." June 24, 1972.

"Defence lawyer contends Bodemer lied when confessing to 1966 rape-murder." June 26, 1972.

"Rape-murder trial summations concluded. Contends Bodemer 'bible-thumped.'" June 27, 1972.

"Guilty of non-capital murder. Life in prison for Bodemer." June 28, 1972.

Morrison, Harold. "A girl, a town and a murder." August 19, 1966.

"Bodemer appeal dismissed." March 24, 1973.

OTHER PRINT MEDIA

"Awcock family tries to find closure." *The Londoner*. November 17, 2010.

"Blood Marks on Girl's Coat." *Aylmer Express*. March 2, 1966.

"Blood-Stained Coat Sparks Area Search for Georgia Jackson." *Aylmer Express*. March 2, 1966.

Legall, Paul. "1968 murder still haunts friend: Slaying made teen grow up fast." *Hamilton Spectator*. February 7, 1998.

Morrison, Harold. "A girl, a town and a murder." *Toronto Star*. August 19, 1966.

"Offer Reward Jackson Case." *Aylmer Express*. March 23, 1966.

Pron, Nicholas; Donaldson, John. "Elusive killers leave cold trail for police." *Toronto Star*. April 2, 1992.

Pron, Nicholas; Donaldson, John. "Police test computer to investigate murders." *Toronto Star*. March 31, 1992.

Pron, Nicholas; Donaldson, John. "Unsolved murders: Are they linked?" *Toronto Star*. March 30, 1992.

Sgambati, Sue. "Who killed Cindy Halliday?" *Barrie Today*. April 19, 2017.

Wolff, Joseph E. "Ontario city tense after 8 mystery killings." *Detroit News*. October 26, 1969.

ACKNOWLEDGEMENTS

Thank you to Anne English, Jackie's sister and champion; Dennis Alsop Jr., a messenger for otherworldly spirits; Tammy Dennett and the Awcock family; Michael Arntfield; all of the folks from Unsolved Canada who never gave up; Carol and Agnes Murray; Sharla Smith; my faithful and talented writing group partners Natalie Hebert and Karen Hendry; truth-seeker Lorimer Shenher; Elizabeth Spicer, who I've never met but whose handwriting I can now decipher; the keepers of local lore, archivists Arthur McClelland, Jeff Causier, Barb Scott, Patrick Lewis, Mark Richardson, Chris Harrington, Ellen Thomas, Jennifer Gibson, Liz Mayville, Barry Arnott, Jean Hung, and Theresa Regnier; title searcher Helen Kantzos; Vaughn Thurman at the Alliston Library; Joe O'Neil; forensic biologist Cecilia Hageman; Andrea Halwa, Rebecca Morrison-Wize, and the London Arts Council; the one who was there first and shared it all with me, Rod Keith; London Police history expert John Lisowksi; Murray Faulkner; my anonymous source, you know who you are and I know what you take in your Tim's; discriminating reader Kailee Wakeman and her one-eyed cat Jack; my fellow murderinos Alison Arn and Ashlie Hawkins; Karen and Georgia, who have no idea how important they are to the rest of us; my parents and stepparents, who give me an absurd level of never-ending support; my brother Sean and his Photoshop skills; Herman Goodden, whose late-night oil I saw also burning across the street; accordion champion Jen; my Aunt Kate, a kindred spirit, who died before she could read this book; and finally my first reader, my partner, and the only person whose opinion really matters, Jason Dickson. SSDGM — VB